The Sex Role Sys

D0876670

The Sex Role System

Psychological and
sociological perspectives

EDITED BY

JANE CHETWYND

and

OONAGH HARTNETT

ROUTLEDGE & KEGAN PAUL
London, Henley and Boston

First published in 1978
by Routledge & Kegan Paul Ltd
39 Store Street,
London WC1E 7DD,
Broadway House,
Newtown Road,
Henley-on-Thames,
Oxon RG9 1EN and
9 Park Street,
Boston, Mass. 02108, USA
Printed in Great Britain by
Redwood Burn Ltd
Trowbridge and Esher
© Routledge & Kegan Paul 1977

British Library Cataloguing in Publication Data

The sex-role system.
  1. Sex role
  I. Chetwynd, Jane II. Hartnett, Oonagh
  301.41   BF692.2   77-30324

ISBN 0-7100-8722-5

Contents

Acknowledgments

The Editors wish to thank many people for their support and constructive criticism. We are particularly grateful to Sonia Davies and Gill Boden of the Women's Rights Committee for Wales and the Cardiff Women's Action Group and to Sue Hamilton and the Women and Alcohol Group of the Institute of Psychiatry, London, SE5, also to colleagues in the Department of Applied Psychology UWIST, Cardiff, together with numerous friends, male as well as female.

Notes on Contributors

JOHN ARCHER is a lecturer in psychology at Preston Polytechnic. He has a BSc in Zoology (Wales, 1965), and a PhD in Psychology (Bristol, 1969). He worked as a research fellow at Sussex University, on sex hormones and behaviour in animals, from 1969 to 1975.

JANE CHETWYND convened the 1975 British Psychological Society Symposium on Sex-Role Stereotyping and Psychology - the symposium from which this book has evolved. Formerly of St George's Hospital Medical School, London, she is now Director of the Institute for Advanced Study in Applied Psychology in Christchurch, New Zealand.

MARY FULLER is an active member of BSA Women's Caucus. She is currently involved in research into community care of the mentally handicapped and the perceptions of male and female roles of white British, Asian and Caribbean adolescents. She has done previous research on occupational sociology and race relations, and is a graduate in sociology from the University of Bath.

OONAGH HARTNETT convenes a Women's Studies course in Cardiff and lectures in Psychology at UWIST. She belongs to the Women's Movement; is a member of the British Psychological Society's Working Party on sex discrimination; co-edited 'Women's Studies in the UK'; and initiated the discussion of these topics within the BPS.

HILARY LAND is a lecturer in Social Administration at Bristol University. Her research interests include the development of social policies and in particular their impact on the family and she is currently engaged in a study of the family, the State and the labour market. She is a graduate in maths and psychology from the University of Bristol and holds a Diploma in Social Administration from LSE.

SUSAN LIPSHITZ at present is training at the Tavistock
    Clinic as a psychotherapist.   Her particular interests
    are theories of the cultural construction of feminine
    psychology and psychoanalytic theory.   She studied
    psychology at the University of Sussex and has worked
    as a university tutor and researcher.   She has been
    in the Women's Movement since 1970.
GLORIA K. LITMAN is a Clinical Research Psychologist at
    the Addiction Research Unit of the Institute of Psy-
    chiatry in London.   She is also an Honorary Psycholo-
    gist at the Maudsley Hospital and lecturer, University
    of London.   Both her research and clinical interests
    are in alcoholism and depression, particularly in
    women, and she has published widely in academic jour-
    nals and the popular press on these subjects and on
    therapies designed specifically for women.
GLENYS LOBBAN is currently a doctoral student in Clinical
    Psychology at the City University of New York.   She
    has previously taught in primary schools in London and
    lectured in Psychology at Chiswick Polytechnic.   For
    her MA in Psychology she investigated the influence of
    sex-roles on self-concept, and has published papers on
    various aspects of sexism in education.   She has been
    involved in the Women's Movement since 1970.
JOHN and ELIZABETH NEWSON jointly direct the Child Devel-
    opment Research Unit at the University of Nottingham,
    where they are engaged in long-term research on mother-
    baby interaction, child-rearing in social context, and
    parent support in the remediation of their children's
    handicaps.
RHONA RAPOPORT is a co-founder and co-director of the In-
    stitute of Family and Environmental Research, London.
    She has done research into a number of fields, includ-
    ing the study of therapeutic communities, changing
    roles of men and women, mid-career development and
    parents' needs and family influences on young school
    leavers.   She has co-authored many publications on
    the results of her studies.
DIANE RICHARDSON trained in child psychology at Notting-
    ham.   Her research interests are in sex-roles and
    gender identity, and she also writes plays and poetry.
JOYCE SCAIFE trained in child psychology at Nottingham
    and has worked on the Newsons' study of child rearing.
    She is currently involved in the assessment of children
    with behavioural difficulties.
HELEN WEINREICH is a lecturer in Psychology at the Univer-
    sity of Bath, and describes herself as a developmental
    social psychologist.   In addition to her interest in
    aspects of sex-role, she has done research on the dev-

elopment of moral and social ideology in adolescents.
She has also worked on fear of success in British
undergraduates, and on sex-role stereotypes.

1 Introduction

The 'Sex-Role System' encompasses the network of attitudes, feelings and behaviours which result from the per-
vasiveness of sex-role stereotyping within our culture.
The term has evolved with our increasing awareness of the
complexity of the phenomena and with our recognition of
the need continually to keep in mind the context of the
total network. In this book we attempt to use psychological and sociological perspectives to examine some of
the manifestations and workings of the sex-role system in
our society. The sex-role system by definition is a
multi-faceted phenomenon but three factors can be isolated as being of major importance to its operation:

1 The assignment, on the basis of sex, of one of two
   different series of personality traits, the masculine
   and feminine stereotypes: these stereotypes are
   thought of as forming opposite ends of a single con-
   tinuum, i.e. as being mutually exclusive. The traits
   associated with each stereotype vary from culture to
   culture and from time to time. In our culture, dominance, aggression and objectivity have been associated
   with the Male while passivity, tenderness and subjec-
   tivity have been associated with the Female. However, the view that this opposition and dissociation
   can be destructive appears to be gaining currency.
2 The allocation, on the basis of sex, of different categories of those activities considered to be necessary
   or useful for the sustenance and improvement of
   living: the division of labour, like the division of
   traits, varies also across cultures and between times.
   The division current in our culture tends to make sex
   itself, rather than the work to be done, the major
   criterion for deciding who does what. However, our
   culture appears to be changing so that we are now
   beginning to look at the requirements of the work
   itself.

1

3 The investing of the male with a higher value than the
   female: this is a universally displayed phenomenon
   whereby those characteristics, traits, activities,
   etc., associated with the male are deemed to have more
   importance and to have greater value than those associated with the female.   The activities, characteristics, etc., may differ widely across societies so that
   it seems that it is the male or female association
   which accounts for value rather than the activity or
   trait itself.   This means that maleness and attributes considered to be masculine are highly valued
   whereas femaleness and attributes labelled feminine
   are comparatively less valued.

Each of these three components of the sex-role system
interacts and, within the historical setting of our culture, this has given rise to what is coming to be known as
'Sexism', that is prejudice based on sex with unfair discrimination as its end-product.

In this book we attempt to combine an empirical approach to the analysis of the sex-role system with a discussion of the ethical issues involved.   Each of the
chapters delineates and describes a particular aspect of
the system.   The second chapter discusses the conceptual,
social and semantic issues associated with biological explanations of sex-role stereotypes.   It warns against the
ready acceptance of biological arguments as justifications
of the 'natural order'.   The next three chapters, taken
together, outline some of the problems involved in trying
to understand the interaction between sex-role stereotyping and the socialisation process.   They give examples of
its functioning at home and at school.   Chapters 6 and 7
are concerned to develop a number of themes about problems
associated with carrying out the dual role of parent and
worker.   The discussion covers sex-role stereotyping in
studies of marriage and the family and at the place of
work.   In effect both chapters reach the same conclusion,
namely, that provision should be made for more flexible
and varied life styles.   Chapters 8 and 9 examine psychiatry and its possible power for good or ill.   It is suggested that psychological theory should include a consideration of 'social and historical conditions' and should
distinguish these from 'the myths and stereotypes of our
gender ideals'.   Depression and alcoholism in women are
two of the topics discussed.   Chapter 10 picks out the
element of sex-role stereotyping in the social security
and income tax systems.   It attacks the myth of the male
being the only or even chief breadwinner.   The last chapter makes a plea for social scientists to develop conceptual models which will avoid sex-role stereotyping.   The

notion that women are 'naturally' politically immature is
questioned.   The implication is that women, as well as
being parents and workers, are also citizens and that this
should be recognised and encouraged.

No introduction to a book about sex-role stereotyping
would be complete without some reflection upon language.
We must be on our guard against the ways in which language
itself may structure our perceptions so that they conform
to the sex-role system.   As authors we have made a conscious effort to eliminate sexism from our language, yet
we have no doubt but that it will have crept in somewhere
and it behoves us therefore to urge readers to be vigi-
lant.

A European Commission Report on a recent survey of
people's attitudes to a number of problems in our society
concluded that 'The improvement of women's social status
and social change are doubtless one and the same thing'
(Commission of the European Communities, 1975b).   Such a
conclusion supports the notion that the sex-role system is
at the core of our cultural norms.   It follows that the
study of this system and its effects is a prerequisite for
the understanding of ourselves, other people and society
in general.

2 Biological Explanations of Sex-Role Stereotypes

Conceptual, Social and
Semantic Issues

John Archer

GENERAL INTRODUCTION: PSYCHOLOGY AND THE NATURE-NURTURE
ISSUE

The question of whether individual differences can be
accounted for in terms of heredity or in terms of environmental conditions forms the essence of the nature-nurture
controversy.   It is one which has recurred in academic
debates throughout the history of psychology.   Theories
relying heavily on one or other source of influence have,
at different times and in different places, alternated
with the opposing viewpoint in being the most influential
type of explanation.   In many instances, the prevailing
view can be linked to the social and political climate of
opinion.   Scientific theories, particularly those from
the social sciences, have often been used to support
either conservative or radical policies, and in turn the
political climate can influence the type of theory which
becomes accepted.   For example, in Nazi Germany, a type
of social Darwinism was used to support racialist doc-
trines, which in turn provided a political atmosphere in
which theories emphasising the importance of heredity
(e.g. those of Konrad Lorenz) could develop (Crook, 1970).
    At about the same time, behaviourism was dominating
American psychological thought.   Crook (1970) has suggested that the focus on individual enterprise within an
ethnically diverse population in North America encouraged
this emphasis on the environment in the study of behaviour.   More recently, criticisms from a variety of
sources have been levelled at the shortcomings and narrow-
ness of the behaviourist approach to psychology.   Included in these criticisms are attacks on the behaviourists'
one-sided emphasis on environmental determinants of behaviour.   Although this is generally a valid criticism,
one unfortunate result has been the reassertion of rather

4

crude nativist explanations in some areas of the behavioural sciences.   Thus the German school of ethologists, following the earlier writings of Konrad Lorenz, have extended concepts such as 'instinct' and 'fixed action patterns' to human behaviour (Eibl-Eibesfeldt, 1970), and a number of popular but misleading works have sought to explain wide areas of complex human behaviour using simple concepts derived from observational studies of animals (e.g. Morris, 1967; Ardrey, 1967).   The race and IQ debate provides another area in which simple-minded views of the application of genetics to behaviour have flourished (Richardson et al., 1972).   Similarly, some of the theories attempting to explain psychological sex differences are of this type.

However, many of the current generation of ethologists and developmental psychologists have emphasised the necessity to consider the interaction of nature and nurture in formulating an adequate explanation of human behaviour (Blurton-Jones, 1972;   Richards, 1974;   Archer and Lloyd, 1975).

Despite the existence of this interactionist approach, which is clearly more realistic than emphasising only environment or heredity, the question of deciding which source of influence is foremost in determining a particular aspect of behaviour, is often regarded as being of practical importance in debates about appropriate social policy.   For example, if one takes the view that criminals are such because of their genetic make-up (Eysenck, 1975), the implication is that money spent on improving social conditions as a way of eradicating crime will be largely wasted.   However, if one takes the view that some identifiable environmental conditions are the important factors, one can then suggest social remedies to prevent crime.

In making inferences affecting social policy from nativist or environmental theories, it is therefore implied that an environmentally influenced characteristic is readily modifiable whereas an hereditary character is largely unchangeable.   This implication is the result of some misconceptions.   The first of these, pointed out by Blurton-Jones (1972) and Hinde (1974) is the artificial nature of dividing influences on development into innate and acquired: no characteristic can be produced by *either* heredity *or* the environment, since it must require both sources of influence from the beginning of its development.   The genetic material in the chromosomes provides a flexible plan for the sequence of development, but this is by no means a rigid blueprint: it provides the developing organism with ways of acting on the environment, rather

than specifying the outcome of these actions (Richards,
1974).   The outcome depends on the result of each successive interaction between the organism and the environment.   A common fault of writers on the subject of 'genetic' or 'innate' influences on behaviour is to ignore the
complexities of this interaction and to discuss genetic
and environmental influences as if they had a simple addi-
tive relationship (Archer and Lloyd, 1975).   An interactionist approach to development thus renders the nature-
nurture controversy obsolete.

SEX ROLES, NATURE AND NURTURE

In the early part of this century, North American psychologists characteristically explained the existence of
measurable sex differences in abilities and temperament in
terms of differential learning associated with the establishment of sex-role behaviour (Kagan and Moss, 1962;
Mischel, 1967).   During the last ten years, as part of a
general reaction against these wholly environmental
theories, there has been a reversion to attempts at ex-
plaining psychological sex differences in terms of biological characteristics (e.g. sex hormones, brain development).   These arguments have also been extended to include evolution, with the suggestion that present-day sex
roles are adaptive features resulting from natural selection during hominid evolution.   Such ideas are often used
to imply a relatively fixed biological basis for the sex
roles, claiming either that they cannot be changed (Goldberg, 1973;   Tiger, 1970) or that they cannot be changed
without risks for the 'well-being' of those concerned
(Hutt, 1972a, 1972b).   To derive such inferences from the
existence of a biological influence in development is, as
discussed in the first section, unwarranted.   But it is
this particular aspect of biological explanations which
has made them attractive to defendants of traditional sex
roles at a time when they are being challenged by the
Women's Movement (e.g. Stassinopoulos, 1972).   It is this
social use of biological theories of sex roles which will
be next discussed.

SOCIAL USE OF BIOLOGICAL THEORIES

If we consider the way in which biological and related
arguments have been used in other societies, it is apparent that a wide variety of such explanations - many of
which we would dismiss in terms of factual content - have

been used at one time or another to justify prevailing
attitudes to sex roles.   By taking such a view, the content of the argument can be separated from the use which
is made of it.

In one of the New Guinea tribes referred to in Margaret
Mead's famous study (Mead, 1950), sex roles were described
as being largely the reverse of those found in modern western societies, with the women being the dominant partner
and manager of business.   The men were described as more
dependent than, and submissive to, the women, and more
responsive to the feelings of the children than were the
women.   What is particularly interesting for the present
discussion is that the members of this tribe regarded
these sex roles as 'biologically natural'.   Many societies have ideas of this type to justify their particular
sex-role arrangements.   Whether the ideas are religious
or scientific, and whether we would accept or dismiss
their factual content, they all serve the same purpose -
to justify the status quo;   in other words, to equate
'what is' with 'what ought to be' (Lloyd, 1976).

The general argument that men and women not only have
clearly defined respective roles in society, but that they
are each *designed* for a particular role, is used in almost
exactly the same manner by those arguing from religious
sources and by those using evidence from biology.   For
example, a Jehovah's Witness writer has attacked the ideas
of Women's Liberation on the grounds that each sex is
'designed for a role' ('Guardian', 1972).   A report of a
scouting manual involved a more specific argument, stating
that a girl's hormones cause her to possess a 'more adaptive and subtle nature' which fits her for being the one
who will make the home ('Ink', 1972).

Since the time of Charles Darwin, the notion of an evolutionary plan has gradually come to eclipse that of a
divine plan as an argument used to justify the preservation of traditional arrangements in society.   In the
nineteenth century, Darwin's ideas were used as a basis
for arguments linking brain size with the supposedly lower
intelligence of women (Burnstyn, 1971).   Even Darwin himself viewed the evolution of mental and physical differences between the sexes in a way that was strongly influenced by the ideas of Victorian society.   He remarked
that, intellectually, men attain higher excellence in
whatever they take up, whether this requires deep thought,
reason, imagination or skill with the hands (Darwin,
1871).   Darwin viewed the evolutionary origins of this
intellectual superiority in terms of men always having had
to provide for and defend their womenfolk.   Modern anthropological studies of surviving hunter-gatherers (e.g.

Draper, 1975) indicate that this is an unrealistic view of
the economic role of women in prehistoric societies (see
also Slocum, 1975).

This last example in particular illustrates the dependence of particular biological explanations of sex roles
on the wider attitudes of the society from which they
arose, and the preceding discussion showed how such explanations may be used to justify conservative views of
sex roles, in a manner almost identical to the use of
religious arguments.   Crook (1970) made the general point
that biological explanations may provide a substitute for
the ethical code, lost when religious beliefs are no
longer followed, and he suggested that this is particularly likely to be the case in a society (such as our own)
where there are many conflicting standards and norms of
social behaviour.   It is therefore reassuring for many
people to believe that their own particular norm, although
perhaps considered old-fashioned by some members of society, is nevertheless the one which is consistent with the
'natural order'.

Crook (1970) also offered other reasons why biological
explanations of social behaviour seem to be readily accepted.   One is that they are relatively easy to understand;
thus a doctrine of the instinctive nature of aggression
(e.g. Lorenz, 1966) is easily understood, whereas a more
realistic multifactorial analysis (Archer, 1976b) is more
difficult to grasp.   Archer and Lloyd (1975) made a similar point in relation to the 'interactionist' approach to
sex differences: because this involves a relatively complex model of the processes involved, it may fail to produce an easily comprehensible explanation, so that even
writers who begin by recognising its value often revert to
an approach based largely on either biological or environmental factors.

A third reason for the ready acceptance of biological
explanations concerns the notion of 'reductionism' in science.   Reductionist philosophy involves the arrangement
of sciences in a hierarchical order, from 'higher level'
disciplines such as sociology and anthropology, through to
psychology, biology, chemistry and physics at the base,
and claims that higher level sciences can be explained in
terms of lower level ones (Rose and Rose, 1973).   This
general approach is certainly apparent in the way that
much research in psychology is carried out, and one consequence is that explanations for psychological phenomena
are often sought at a 'lower' (i.e. biological) level.
Archer and Lloyd (1975) have also suggested that the
appearance of more material reality in the variables measured by biologists may impress those working in the social

sciences and cause them to be attracted by explanations
involving biological terminology.

There are, therefore, at least three reasons why biological explanations of a behavioural feature such as our
sex roles have proved attractive despite any intellectual
faults they may have. These are first their use in arguments on social policy to imply the existence of simple
natural order, second their ease of understanding, and
third that they follow directly from a reductionist philosophy. Having discussed in some detail the reasons for
the widespread acceptance of biological explanations, I
shall now consider the stereotypes to which these biological explanations have been applied.

PSYCHOLOGICAL SEX DIFFERENCES AND SEX-ROLE STEREOTYPES

In the previous section, I discussed how biological theories have been used to imply that traditional sex roles
are the 'natural ones'. It is also apparent that widespread notions of sex-role stereotypes have influenced the
theories themselves. The stereotypes entail a far wider
range of attributes than those on which psychologists have
actually found sex differences (Maccoby and Jacklin,
1974a). There is *some* overlap between the perceived
stereotypes and the measured attributes (e.g. in aggression), but a recent survey of the psychological literature
by Maccoby and Jacklin (1974a) revealed that there was no
evidence for differences in a number of other characteristics on which men and women were supposed to differ;
e.g. there was no evidence that women are more 'social'
than men or that they were more suggestible, or lacking in
achievement motivation, all of which are commonly held
stereotypes about masculinity and feminity in western society (e.g. Bem, 1975).

The review of psychological sex differences by Maccoby
and Jacklin is very useful in that it enables us to assess
those psychological abilities and attributes for which
there is good evidence for the existence of sex differences. It also concentrates on the test measures themselves and does not make unwarranted generalisations.
Other reviews of similar research areas, particularly by
those authors offering biological explanations, tend to
conclude that there is a wider range of attributes on
which men and women differ, and that these can be described by a number of general psychological characteristics.
These accounts are, however, inconsistent in their identification of the characteristics. Broverman et al.
(1968) referred to 'activation' and 'inhibition' as the

important concepts for considering psychological sex differences on a variety of test measures.   Garai and
Scheinfeld (1968) suggested a number of differences including male 'orientation to the environment' contrasting
with female 'response orientation', male interest in nov-
elty and complexity, contrasting with female affiliative
needs.   Hutt (1972a, 1972b) proposed the characteristics
of conformity, consistency and nurturance as female ones,
and she described men as more exploratory, vigorous and
group-orientated.   More specific abilities and attributes
have also been mentioned: these include the widely recognised differences in aggression, verbal, spatial and
mathematical abilities (Maccoby and Jacklin, 1974a; Buffery and Gray, 1972; Gray, 1971; Hutt, 1972a, 1972b),
but also a number of others, such as clerical abilities
(Garai and Scheinfeld, 1968), rote memory, and creativity
or divergent thinking (Hutt, 1972a) which have not been
identified in Maccoby and Jacklin's review.

There are also examples of specific test measures being
related to a more generalised characteristic, thus making
the sex difference appear more wide ranging than the measures justify.   Hutt (1972a) generalised from measures of
'aggression' to include also sex differences in 'ambition'
and 'drive'.   Witkin et al. (1962) generalised from tests
involving visual-spatial tasks to more general sex differences in 'cognitive style' or approach to the environment.

In the ways described above, the extent of psychological differences between the sexes is made to appear greater than a careful examination of the evidence would justify.   Hence the supposed sex differences are often regarded as conforming more closely to widely held stereotypes than the evidence would warrant.   There are two
general issues raised by this wide range of, and wide
variety of, names given to psychological characteristics
on which men and women are supposed to differ.   One is
that by giving two different aspects of behaviour the same
label, a relationship is implied between them.   The
second is that such labels are, in the behavioural sciences, seldom value-free.   Thus a name can not only imply
relationships to general phenomena but also a value-
judgment.

Considering the first of these points, many terms used
in the behavioural sciences are imprecise and therefore
lend themselves to different usages.   It is thus not surprising to find that words which have been used to describe psychological sex differences often refer to a
heterogeneous class of characteristics whose sole justification for being placed together is convenience for the
author's theoretical viewpoint.   One extreme example of

this is in the theory of Broverman et al. (1968), referred
to in the next section.   Speed of colour naming, clerical
aptitude tests, speech and reading abilities, manual dexterity, speed of eyeblink conditioning, and sensory thres-
holds were all referred to as tests of 'rapid repetitive
responding' and it was claimed that the same characteristic was measured in rats by tests of wheel-running activity, distance travelled in a novel arena and speed of
learning a conditioned avoidance response.   Similarly,
Gray's (1971) theory of sex differences in fear and aggression referred to a variety of measures not necessarily
related to one another (Archer, 1971, 1975, 1976a).
   The second issue is that of implied value-judgments in-
fluencing descriptive terms.   When studying sex differences, it appears to be difficult for research workers not
to be influenced by attitudes about sex-role stereotypes.
This influence affects both description and interpretation.
   Even the supposedly 'value-free' descriptions of the
biological sciences may show influences of this type.
Thus, in naming the steroid hormones secreted by the sex
organs ('sex hormones'), what are referred to as 'male
hormones' (androgens) are secreted in relatively large
quantities by the testes of the male, in lesser quantities
by the adrenal cortex of both sexes, and by the ovary of
the female.   The difference in concentrations of androgens between the sexes is, therefore, a statistical one,
and not an absolute one as is implied by the name 'male
hormone'.   This is not merely a pedantic point, since
androgens have been found to have physiological influences
in women, such as facilitating growth of pubic and axilla
hair (Glucksmann, 1974) and increasing sexual interest
(Money and Ehrhardt, 1972).
   Descriptive labels attached to findings from studies of
hormones and behaviour can also be misleading.   Hutt
(1972a) used the term 'male brain' to describe the physiological changes produced by the administration of androgens to newborn female rats.   This very general term implies a much wider ranging and clearer cut type of neural
differentiation between the sexes than is the case: androgens administered at this time act on certain parts of
the brain which control the adult pattern of sex hormone
secretion, and also sexual and aggressive behaviour, thus
the term 'male brain' is a deduction from later behavioural differences between animals treated with androgen and
those not, rather than a direct description of anatomical
or physiological changes in the brain during infancy.
Describing these behavioural differences as resulting from
a 'male brain' implies that they can be related to defi-

nite structural (and permanent) changes in the developing
brain.   It can also lead to some misleading ideas if the
term is used in general discussions of human sex differences, since it implies that there are widespread anatomical differences in the brain between the sexes.   It is
then but a short step to arguments that these differences
are responsible for psychological sex differences.

A third example of how the choice of terminology can
reflect wider beliefs comes from the studies of Witkin and
his colleagues (e.g. Witkin et al., 1962; Witkin, 1967).
They have carried out a series of studies involving two
tests of whether a particular visual stimulus is perceived
as separate from the surrounding field or as part of it
(embedded figure and rod and frame tests).   In many of
these studies, men are found to separate the stimulus from
the background to a greater extent than women (Maccoby and
Jacklin, 1974a).   Although it appears unlikely that anything more than visual-spatial differences underlie these
findings (Maccoby and Jacklin, 1974; Sherman, 1967),
Witkin has interpreted the differences as indicating different 'cognitive styles' between the sexes.   He described the typically male characteristics of separating the
visual stimulus from its background as 'field independence' and the typically female characteristic of per-
ceiving the stimulus as part of the background as 'field
dependence'.   This terminology reflects and reinforces
society's stereotypes of the passive dependent female and
active independent male (McGuinness, 1976).   This is particularly so in view of Witkin's claim that the tests
measure a general personality dimension or approach to the
environment, rather than being specifically related to
visual-spatial analysis.   Hartnett (personal communication) suggests that renaming 'field dependence' as 'context awareness' would eliminate the negative connotations
of being passive and dependent.

These three examples show the importance of choosing
appropriate terminology when dealing with a research area
which has controversial social and political implications.

BIOLOGICAL THEORIES OF PSYCHOLOGICAL SEX DIFFERENCES

In this section, I shall outline the main types of biologically based theories which, on the one hand, have been
used to justify sex-role stereotypes, and on the other
reflect in their formulation popular notions about sex
differences.   I have already discussed a number of general criticisms of this type of explanation, notably the
simplification of the nature-nurture issue, and the use

of general concepts to describe more restricted test measures. In this section I shall also mention a number of additional problems associated with each type of explanation.

Hormone theories

These include several suggestions that sex hormones, either early in development (Dawson, 1972) or later in life (Broverman et al., 1968; Andrew, 1972) affect cognitive abilities. Detailed arguments have been presented against each of these, e.g. that Dawson misinterpreted research on sex hormones in development (Archer, 1976a), that Broverman et al. selected the evidence to fit their basic premise concerning the nature of the sex differences involved (Parlee, 1972; Archer, 1976a), and that Andrew's theory cannot explain the direction of sex differences in visual-spatial tests (Archer, 1976a).

Various writers have implicated the high levels of androgens in the male as an explanation for male aggression (e.g. Hutt, 1972a; Gray, 1971; Maccoby and Jacklin, 1974a; Goldberg, 1971). Although this is the one behavioural characteristic for which there is some direct experimental evidence on the possible involvement of sex hormones in the human male, there are nevertheless serious flaws in these particular arguments. First, they derive nearly all their evidence from experiments on rodents. There is now increasing evidence that hormonal influences on behaviour are different in rodents and primates (e.g. Herbert, 1970; Money and Ehrhardt, 1972). Second, the recently available data from studies investigating the relationship between hormone levels and measures of aggression in adult men have produced largely negative results (e.g. Kreuz and Rose, 1972; Doering et al., 1974). Inferences derived only or largely from rodent experiments are not adequate bases for deciding the relationship between androgens and aggression in humans. The eagerness of some writers (e.g. Goldberg, 1971; Gray, 1971) to find evidence for a relationship between the two measures has led to their making premature conclusions based on very limited evidence. A more thorough examination of a wider range of animals reveals a more complex picture, both in relation to sex differences and in relation to hormonal influences on aggression (Archer, 1976b).

Another point to consider in relation to research on hormones and sex differences in aggression is the extent to which our ideas about appropriate sex-role behaviour have influenced research in animal behaviour. Doty

(1974) has referred to a male bias in the study of courtship and copulation in rodents.   If one examines studies
of aggression in rodents, it becomes apparent that a similar bias exists there.   Research has concentrated on male
aggression, of the type that occurs when male strangers
encounter one another.   Maternal aggression, aggression
by females during late pregnancy and lactation, also
occurs in many mammals, but has been little studied.
Rather less obvious than maternal aggression are forms of
female aggression which are not concerned with protection
of young.   This has been almost completely ignored (except in recent studies of hamsters, e.g. Payne and Swanson, 1972).   It has long been claimed, for example, that
female mice seldom fight, but recently two (women) research workers have examined female aggression in wild
mice and found that 25 per cent would fight following a
period of isolation (Ebert and Hyde, 1976).
    Other theories involving hormones include that of Gray
(1971) on sex differences in fear, which is again based on
generalisations from experiments on rodents.   I have
argued (Archer, 1971, 1975) that the rodent sex differences are not as clear-cut as Gray has suggested, that his
choice of tests sampled only a proportion of the measures
related to fear, and that the measures involve a wide
range of characteristics besides fear.   Similarly, Gray's
inferences from human studies also involved a wider range
of characteristics than could adequately be described by
the term 'fearfulness'.

Brain development

Although theories involving sex hormones are the most
common form of biological theory of psychological sex differences, a different line of argument has implicated lateralisation of the brain.   It has been shown that the
two halves of the cerebral cortex control different types
of skills, the left or dominant hemisphere being concerned
with verbal abilities and the right being concerned with
spatial abilities.   Buffery and Gray (1972) suggested
that, owing to the more advanced development of the brain
of the female at the time of language acquisition, verbal
skills become more completely localised in the dominant
hemisphere of young girls.   They then suggested that male
superiority in spatial skills is an indirect consequence
of the greater lateralisation of language ability in the
female, so that spatial ability becomes localised more bi-
laterally in males, giving better three-dimensional representation.

McGuiness (1976) has criticised the lateralisation
hypothesis on the grounds that many skills on which there
is no male superiority are also located in the non-domi-
nant hemisphere (e.g. singing ability).   Maccoby and
Jacklin (1974a) also point out that many functions controlled by the dominant hemisphere do not show female
superiority.

Evolutionary theories

A third type of biological theory concerns evolutionary
origins.   In many ways these explanations illustrate
better than any the general points made in previous sections about the social influences on, and the uses made
of, biological theories.   Arguments such as those of
Hutt (1972a), Tiger (1970) and Gray and Buffery (1971)
claim that the psychological make-up of men and women
clearly reflect evolutionary adaptations for different sex
roles.   Their choice of characteristics on which the
sexes differ include male ability to form bonds with other
men, male ability to dominate political life (Tiger,
1970), and female conformity and nurturance (Hutt, 1972b);
this choice is very much influenced by our present notions
of stereotyped sex roles, and contains many unwarranted
generalisations and assumptions (see previous sections,
and Archer, 1976a).   They also involve some dubious arguments from human evolution, notably their emphasis (and
dependence) on the importance of male co-operative hunting
as the major economic force in the lives of developing
hominids (see Draper, 1975; Slocum, 1975, for arguments
against this view).

Theories suggesting evolutionary adaptation for different sex roles have also been used to justify the continuation of these roles nowadays.   The most extreme
variant of this argument is that men and women possess
psychological characteristics which have adapted them for
different sex roles, men for hunting in groups (or some
modern substitute) and women for a domestic and child-
rearing role; consequently they are genetically program-
med to pursue such activities in modern societies.   I
have already discussed at some length the fallacy of arguments which use the term genetic in the sense of fixed and
unmodifiable.   There is also a more subtle variation of
the argument (e.g. Hutt, 1972a) - not that we cannot
change our sex roles, but that it is not desirable to do
so.   This argument claims that there are disadvantages in
adopting sex roles different from those for which we are
assumed to have been adapted in the course of evolution.

Such disadvantages might involve personal unhappiness or
long-term deleterious consequences for the species as a
whole.   It is uncertain what sex roles evolving humans
adopted, but evidence from surviving hunter-gatherer
groups (Martin and Voorhies, 1975; Draper, 1975) indicates that they were probably very different from what we
today regard as 'traditional' sex roles; thus, the
assumptions made about evolutionary adaptations by Tiger,
Hutt and others are very likely to be incorrect, and to
portray an unjustified sedentary role for women.   They
are also illogical in that, on the one hand, they argue
against changing the role of women, and on the other,
accept that the present-day role of men is very different
from their original one of hunting large game.   In fact,
many aspects of our contemporary lives bear little relation to the lives and activities of evolving human beings.
Thus, to start examining sex roles against a hypothetical
criterion of 'naturalness', we should not only find no
evidence to justify existing stereotypes but we should
also have to question many other major areas of contemporary life.

CONCLUSIONS

In this article I have discussed issues relating to biological theories of sex differences in human behaviour.   My
main conclusion is the importance of viewing such theories
in their wider social context rather than as the totally
objective statements of 'experts', from which there follow certain clear implications for social policy.
Social context is used in a broad sense to indicate influences within the biological and social sciences, and from
the prevailing political and social climate of opinion.
Some of the main influences within the academic disciplines themselves include the ready acceptance of biological explanations into the reductionist framework of psychological research, and the ready acceptance of nativist
arguments as a reaction against extreme environmentalist
viewpoints.   Wider influences include the easily under-
standable nature of simple biological arguments, and
their ready acceptance as justifications of the 'natural
order' in place of a religious justification.

ACKNOWLEDGMENTS

Many of the ideas and points made in this chapter have
arisen from discussions with colleagues, in particular

with Barbara Lloyd in the preparation of 'Exploring Sex
Differences' (1975), and with Oonagh Hartnett, Jane
Chetwynd and others concerned with the 1975 BPS symposium
on psychology and female stereotypes.

3 Sex-Role Socialisation

Helen Weinreich

> All women become like their mothers, that's their
> tragedy; no man ever does, that's his. (Oscar Wilde)

Socialisation is the transmission of behaviour, roles,
attitudes and beliefs to the next generation. By direct
prescription, by example and by implicit expectation, a
variety of people in a variety of relationships influence
the growing individual. Gradually the child *internalises*
what s/he has been taught. Becoming a person, capable of
functioning adequately in the society in which one lives,
is the desired end product of development. In principle,
children of both sexes are brought up as *people*; in practice, gender is a highly significant factor in their up-
bringing and there are differences in the socialisation of
boys and girls. Socialising agents hold stereotypical
beliefs about sex-appropriate characteristics. Sex-
role socialisation reflects expectations based upon these
beliefs.

These expectations are important in a number of ways.
Undoubtedly there are sex differences which have a biological base, but many aspects of sex roles do not derive
directly from such differences. Rather, sex roles and
their socialisation reflect people's often unfounded
beliefs about what sex differences are or should be.
Therefore when looking at socialisation it is necessary to
examine the evidence relating to both sex differences and
sex stereotypes. This is the first topic to be considered in this chapter. The second section will examine
some of the ways in which these stereotypical beliefs influence the content, processes and agents of socialisation. A third section will discuss the problems and conflicts which arise from current sex roles and their socialisation. Finally, possible alternatives to sex-role
stereotyping will be explored.

18

STEREOTYPES AND SEX DIFFERENCES

A recent review by Maccoby and Jacklin (1975) has questioned some long-standing beliefs about sex differences.
They find that there have been exaggerations, misinter-
pretations and even myths, and point out that both lay and
scientific assumptions about sex differences may be incorrect. Sometimes, apparently established sex differences have been based on a single, widely quoted study
which has not been replicated. The evidence does not
justify the stereotypical beliefs which exist in our society about major sex differences in ability and personality.

There are no reliable established differences in social
orientation, suggestibility, self-esteem, cognitive or
analytic ability. This is counter to a widespread
stereotypical assumption that women are more susceptible
to social influence and somehow less 'rational' than men.
Additionally, traditional assumptions about sex differences in anxiety, level of activity, competitiveness, dominance, compliance and nurturance are not substantiated.
The evidence for these remains ambiguous. The differences which do stand up to scrutiny are in measures of
aggression, and in verbal, spatial and mathematical test
scores. Girls tend to score higher on verbal tests, and
boys score higher on certain kinds of mathematical and
spatial tests. Boys were found to exhibit more aggressive behaviour. Even these differences were small.

In contrast with the findings which indicate few differences in ability, it is obvious when we look at the
adult world that there are large differences between the
sexes in what society regards as attainment. Comparatively few women hold positions of influence and authority. In any field where both sexes are represented,
women become proportionately fewer the higher up the
hierarchy one looks. Education is one example. Up to
GCE Ordinary Level, approximately as many girls as boys
are represented. The fall-off begins at Advanced Level,
where girls are under-represented and take fewer subjects
(HMSO Social Trends, 1975). At university level, one
third of undergraduates are female, but only 16 per cent
of graduate students and 9 per cent of university teaching
staff are female (Blackstone and Fulton, 1975). It is
still not uncommon for a class of predominantly female
Arts undergraduates to be taught almost entirely by male
lecturers. Terman and Oden (1959) reported a life-span
study of gifted individuals. By middle age, 86 per cent
of the men were in occupations defined as being in the two
highest professional categories. Only about 20 per cent

of the women were.   Fourteen per cent of the men, compared with 4 per cent of the women, held doctorates.
  These differences in attainment contrast sharply with
the few differences in ability found by Maccoby and Jacklin.   However, it is significant that they do mirror the
'sex differences' conventionally prescribed by stereotypical beliefs.   Broadly speaking, the male stereotype is
instrumental, active, skilled, technically competent,
directive and exploitative.   Men are expected to be successful, and to suppress overt emotion (Pleck and Sawyer,
1974).   The female stereotype is expressive, passive,
decorative, manipulative, non-combatant and non-competent
outside domestic and nurturing situations.   Salzman-Webb
(Garskof, 1971) expressed the theme as woman being 'secretary, sexpot, spender, sow, civic actor and sickie'.
  A number of studies show that women are perceived as
inferior and less competent than men.   This is particularly true in traditionally 'masculine' areas of activity,
but even in traditionally 'feminine' fields women are only
rated as being as good as men (Goldberg, 1968; O'Leary,
1974; Feldman-Summers and Kiesler, 1974).   When women do
well it is more likely to be attributed to luck or special
effort, rather than skill or ability.   Women are more
likely to be *perceived* as having failed.   Piacente et al.
(1974) set up a situation in which both sexes showed in-
competence, and found that females were more likely to be
labelled incompetent.   Failure was regarded as having
certain positive value for females, but not for males.
As Margaret Mead (1950) observed, success is unsexing to
a woman, failure is unsexing to a man.
  The evidence presented so far indicates that there are
stereotypical myths about sex differences, which despite
their inaccuracy, are reflected in behaviour.   These
myths influence beliefs about what sex roles should be,
and in particular they influence the agents, content and
processes of socialisation.

SOCIALISATION

Socialisation is the means by which culture, including
notions of appropriate sex roles, is transmitted.   The
agents of socialisation are primarily parents, teachers,
peer-group and the media.   There are four processes by
which socialisation occurs.   First, skills, habits and
some types of behaviour are learned as a consequence of
reward and punishment.   Second, parents and others provide models for roles and behaviour which children imitate.   Third, the child identifies with one or both

parents, a process which is more powerful than imitation,
through which the child incorporates and internalises the
roles and values of the parent or other significant adult.
Fourth, there is the part played by the growing individuals themselves.   They actively seek to structure the
world, to make sense and order of the environment.   The
categories available to the child for sorting out the environment play an important part in this process.   Gender
is obviously a primary category, so it is not surprising
that children pick up a great deal of information about
sex roles and stereotypes very quickly (Kohlberg, 1966).

Information reinforcing the stereotypical message is
constantly available to children and their parents from a
number of sources, including fiction and the media.   The
message is pervasive and unequivocal (Stemple and Tyler,
1974; Jacklin and Mischel, 1973; Pyke and Stewart,
1974).   It is that women are housebound and exclusively
preoccupied with domestic materialism and personal adorn-
ment.   They are presented as being passive and lacking in
initiative, and as being concerned with fantasy rather
than expertise or problem-solving.

In children's primary readers a similar image of little
girls is presented; girls appear less frequently than
boys and when they do appear, are shown as less active.
This image becomes stronger, the higher the age of the
children represented in the readers.   Cadogan and Craig
(1976) looked at a century of girls' fiction.   They found
that there was a tradition in which girls were autonomous,
independent, active and often overtly feminist.   However
these traits tended to be confined to adolescent schoolgirls.   When the heroines reached adulthood, or when
women apart from teachers were presented, there was a tendency for an earth-mother image to predominate.   The ex-
ceptions were women who obviously retained a determinedly
asexual adolescent style.   The same stereotype is manifested in the toyshop as well as in the bookshop.   Children can find Action Girl but not Action Woman; in contrast they can find Action Man rather than Action Boy.

In the visual media, women are presented as primarily
decorative, and dependent on males, often simply as
status-enhancing sex objects.   This stereotype is reinforced by the inclusion of anxiety-inducing pressures.
For example, marriage is generally regarded as a socially
desirable goal, and to some extent a symbol of personal
success, particularly for women.   A considerable amount
of advertising effort goes into persuading girls that the
happiest day of their life is their wedding day.   The
symbolic effect of marital failure is therefore considerable.   Manes and Melnyk (1974) analysed television film

and drama and found that working women were overwhelmingly portrayed as 'maritally unsuccessful' compared with only 5 per cent of housewives.   Occasionally women were shown combining a job with marriage.   Nevertheless they were portrayed as being dependent on their husbands, and as lacking commitment to their profession.   In the light of this evidence it is not surprising that Frueh and McGhee (1975) found that the more television children watched, the more likely they were to hold traditional sex-role attitudes.   The stereotypical message is thus being continually purveyed to children and their parents.

The message presented by the media and other sources is obvious and clear.   However, there is conflicting evidence about the extent to which parents overtly socialise their children into the images of the stereotypes, and certainly the way sex-role socialisation is carried out by parents is more subtle and complex than the media message would suggest.

An important aspect is that many of the behaviours which parents (especially mothers) regard as desirable are similar in both sexes.   These qualities include control of aggression, consideration for others, helpfulness and so forth.   Satisfactory performance at school is also required of both sexes.   In many ways, therefore, the desired end product of socialisation is not very different for the sexes.   Furthermore, Maccoby and Jacklin (1975) conclude that 'the evidence has not revealed any consistent process of "shaping" boys and girls toward a number of behaviours that are normally part of our sex stereotypes.'   By 'shaping', Maccoby and Jacklin mean acts of direct encouragement or discouragement.   Their conclusion is in contrast to some earlier conclusions.   For example in 1967, Biller and Borstelmann wrote; 'In line with cultural expectations, parents usually treat boys and girls quite differently.'   Not only have some studies suggested that parents do directly reinforce sex-appropriate behaviour and discourage sex-inappropriate behaviour, but studies have also found differences in parent-child interaction according to the sex of the child, from birth. Studies by Goldberg and Lewis (1969) and by Lewis (1972), among others, found that boy babies were more likely to be handled and encouraged in motor activity, whereas girl babies were likely to receive more verbal stimulation. However comparable studies have not consistently supported these findings.

Undisputed differences in socialisation between boys and girls seem to lie in the styles and degree of socialisation to which they are exposed.   'Boys receive more punishment, but probably also more praise and encourage-

ment.   Adults respond as if they find boys more interesting, and more attention-provoking, than girls' (Maccoby
and Jacklin, 1975).   Tolerance of sex-inappropriate behaviour, especially in the early years, is far greater for
girls than for boys.   Boys appear to be more actively de-
terred from cross-sex behaviour and traits, especially by
their fathers (Maccoby and Jacklin, 1975;   Hartley, 1959;
Biller and Borstlemann, 1967;   Feinman, 1974;   Fagot and
Litman, 1975).

One resolution of the apparent conflicts in the findings is to distinguish between direct socialisation or an
overt curriculum, and indirect socialisation, or a hidden
curriculum.   Most of the studies reviewed by Maccoby and
Jacklin concentrated on the overt curriculum.   Indirect
socialisation or the hidden curriculum operates through
expectations.   These expectations are influenced by the
beliefs that parents hold about sex differences.   For
example, expectations will tend to encourage the development of traits which are believed to be *naturally* characteristic of the sex to which the child belongs.   Baumrind
and Black (1967) argue that girls need to be actively
socialised to be assertive, because expectations tend to
operate against their developing assertiveness.

Direct and indirect socialisation therefore inculcate
both desirable behaviour *and* knowledge about what is sex-
appropriate.   Expectations are also conveyed through role
models, which are usually consistent with sex-role stereotypes.   The influence of role modelling may be deduced
from the evidence that the daughters of mothers who do not
work outside the home show less independence and more
traditional sex-role stereotyping than do the daughters of
working mothers (Miller, 1975).

The inconsistency of some of the evidence may be further explained by methodological factors.   Many of the
studies reviewed by Maccoby and Jacklin were observations
made in laboratories, where attention was paid to a com-
paritively narrow range of behaviour.   The observation of
behaviour and interaction under more naturalistic conditions, over a longer period of time tends to pick up a
wider range of data than do laboratory studies.   In an
account of observation in an Italian nursery school, Belotti (1975) describes the rigidity with which children
were assigned to their sex-specific roles in behaviour,
play and in their interaction with each other.   In the
USA, Serbin and O'Leary (1976) observed differences in the
kind of attention that boys and girls received from the
nursery school-teacher, particularly in the kinds of instruction given, and in the degree to which they were expected to be involved in problem-solving.   Glenys Lobban

elsewhere in this volume reports similar findings in
British schools.

PROBLEMS AND CONFLICTS

There are a number of conflicts and problems associated
with our current sex roles and their socialisation.
Three areas will be considered in detail.   First, there
are some important discontinuities for young people of
both sexes in the course of development.   For girls,
there is discontinuity around the time of puberty as a
consequence of the sharp reduction in the extent to which
tomboyish behaviour is tolerated.   For boys, the constraints on non-masculine or 'cissy' behaviour start much
earlier; for them, the main discontinuity comes when they
take on a family role.   Knox and Kupferer (1971) argue
that the requirements of the male family role are not
clearly defined in sex-role socialisation, and may be in
conflict with the traits and behaviour that a boy learns
are 'masculine'.   Tenderness, gentleness and nurturance
are examples of 'non-masculine' traits which the family
role requires.   In the case of girls the same reasoning
applies to conflicts concerned with her work role outside
the home - traits required for this role may be in conflict with traits and behaviour which a girl learns are
'feminine'.
     Second, Block, Von der Lippe and Block (1973) present
evidence of some of the problems arising from the interaction of sex-role socialisation and general socialisation.   General socialisation is defined as the inculca-
tion of desirable non-sex-specific qualities such as im-
pulse control and awareness of others.   For males, general socialisation counters the less attractive aspects of
sex-typing.   For females, general socialisation tends to
enhance rather than diminish the more limiting aspects of
the traditional female role, such as overcontrol, conservatism, conventionality and dependency.
     A third area of conflict is associated with motivation.
Conflicts occur between some learned motives as a result
of the demands of sex-role development.   Achievement
motivation is an area where, particularly for women, there
is conflict between the motive learned through the overt
curriculum and those learned through the hidden curriculum.   In a society which evaluates achievement highly,
both sexes are overtly socialised towards achievement orientation.   For males, both sex-role socialisation and
other aspects of socialisation emphasise achievement and
the importance of success.   However, for females there is

a conflict between achievement motivation and the feminine
stereotype.   Successful competition with men has negative
connotations.   The crisis seems to come to a head in the
college years.   Many women students show lack of confidence, and what has been termed 'fear of success'.

Horner originally identified fear of success among
women students at the University of Michigan in 1968.
She asked them to complete a story beginning with the cue,
'At the end of her first year at medical school, Anne
found herself at the top of her class.'   Male students
had the cue, 'John' instead of 'Anne'. Sixty-five per cent
of the women, compared with only 10 per cent of the men,
showed 'fear of success'.   This was defined as an emphasis on the negative consequences of success, concern about
the heroine's 'normality', or denial and distortion of the
story in order to avoid its implications.   Many responses
showed a very high degree of anxiety and defensiveness
about Anne's success.   She was described as grossly un-
attractive, was attacked physically by her classmates, or
was seen as doing the 'right thing' by dropping out or at
least lowering her standards.

Fear of success does not seem to be a fear of competence, of high performance per se, but to be connected
with competitive situations, particularly competition between the sexes.   Zuckerman and Wheeler (1975) and Mack
(1975) found that both sexes are more likely to co-oper-
ate than to compete in a cross-sex situation.   The most
stressful condition seems to occur when women compete successfully with men in traditionally male spheres.   In the
studies where Anne came top in traditionally female
spheres, such as nursing, less fear of success was elici-
ted.

Some very recent studies have not shown such large sex
differences (Tomlinson-Keasey, 1974; Tresemer, 1974) although both sexes are still more likely to react negatively to female rather than male success (Solomon, 1975;
Monahan, Kuhn and Shaver, 1974; Feather and Raphaelson,
1974; Feather, 1975).   A recent study found that British
students showed what might be regarded as realistic awareness of the problems associated with female success,
rather than the deep anxieties found in Horner's sample
(Weinreich and Chetwynd, 1976).

The orientation towards achievement motivation also
presents problems for males, but they are somewhat different from the costs experienced by females.   Hoffman
(1972) argues that male strivings for achievement may go
beyond a need to gain competence, and become instead a
neurotic fear of failure in competition.

These areas of conflict reflect some of the major prob-

lems of sex-role socialisation.   Problems arise from the
limitations of the traditional sex roles, and from the in-
consistencies and contradictions inherent in the socialisation process.   Sex-role socialisation for females is
inconsistent with other aspects of socialisation in a
number of ways.   A study by Rosenkrantz et al. (1968) and
a study by Broverman et al. (1970) have demonstrated that
those qualities which are considered 'desirable' and
'healthy' in an adult are much more likely to be qualities
associated with the male than the female stereotype.   On
the basis of the evidence, girls approaching adulthood are
placed 'in the conflictful position of having to decide
whether to exhibit those positive characteristics considered desirable for men and adults, and thus have their
"femininity" questioned, that is be deviant in terms of
being a woman, or to behave in the prescribed feminine
manner, accept second-class adult status and possibly live
a lie to boot' (Broverman et al., 1970).

ALTERNATIVES TO SEX-ROLE STEREOTYPING

Mischel (1974) and others have found that sex-role stereotypes are losing some of their force.   Two areas stand
out as being foci for change.   One is socialisation practices, the other is beliefs about the nature of sex differences and their relation to sex roles.
   Two groups of women have been researched in the quest
for alternative models for female socialisation.   One
group comprises feminists, that is, women who endorse the
basic principles and aims of the Women's Movement.   The
other group comprises professionally successful women.
Research on both groups provides a picture of the con-
stellation of attitudes, beliefs and family environment
associated with non-stereotyped development.
   Both feminists and professional women differ from traditional women in a number of ways.   Their attitudes and
outlook are more liberal.   They tend to be more intelligent and to perform better academically, and are more
likely to be career-orientated.   They tend to be more
independent, assertive and autonomous.   Consistently,
they have high self-esteem, a sense of control of their
own destiny, and have less need to define themselves in
terms of how others see them (Stoloff, 1973;   Arnott,
1973;   Pawlicki and Almquist, 1973;   Mahoney, 1975;
Stewart and Winter, 1974).   Rejection of a stereotypical
self-concept is associated with continuation of study
(Vogel et al., 1975) and with higher aspirations and orientation towards the future rather than the present

(Alper, 1973).   The single most consistent feature of the backgrounds of both groups of women is having a mother who worked or who was at least orientated to a life beyond the wife and mother role.   These mothers were on the whole pro-feminist, and encouraged positive independent attitudes in their daughters.   The encouragement of girls by fathers has also been found to be important in independence training, particularly in relation to achievement.

4 Perspectives in Sex-Role Stereotyping

Sex roles in adolescence
and pre-adolescence

John and Elizabeth Newson,
Diane Richardson and Joyce Scaife

INTRODUCTION

In considering sex roles, we are concerned with those behaviours, values and attitudes which are generally considered to be appropriate for males or for females.
Clearly such notions will vary from one culture to another
and within a single culture from one historical epoch to
the next.   This is not to say, however, that for any
given time and place these conceptions can be relegated to
the status of second-order factors, of only minor importance to the individuals within a culture.   On the contrary, we would argue that human beings are always constrained by the 'web of culture' and that socially defined
concepts can always be expected to influence our thoughts,
feelings and actions in very many profound ways.   Indeed
it often seems to be the case that our basic modes of
thinking are shot through with implicit meanings and expectations; and these keep us in thrall precisely to the
extent that we are unable to formulate them explicitly to
ourselves and to other people.
   Traditional psychological research into masculinity/
femininity seems, in retrospect, to offer few useful insights which are likely to be pertinent to the current
debate about changing roles of men and women in contemporary society.   The available tests are predicated upon a
static view of personality seen as a measurable set of
nomothetic traits largely uninfluenced by sociological and
situational factors.   They reflect the ethos of a time
when it seemed axiomatic that masculinity and femininity
could only be regarded as polar opposites on a single con-
tinuum easily definable by compiling a simple checklist
relating to conventional male and female interests and
attitudes.   To the extent that these basic assumptions
are now being questioned in society, the findings of

studies based wholly upon such an approach are today of
questionable relevance.

Our intention is to approach the subject of masculin-
ity/femininity from a somewhat different angle and with a
very different set of metatheoretical assumptions which
arise from a sociological or social psychological orientation. According to this view, the words *masculine* and
feminine do not refer in any simple way to fundamental
traits of personality, but to the learned styles of interpersonal interaction which are deemed to be socially
appropriate to specific social contexts, and which are
imposed upon, and sustain and extend, the sexual dichotomy. In the conduct of social life, our thoughts and
actions are continually influenced by social norms and by
the systems of customs, beliefs and values which make up
our culture. Thus we act towards other people in ways
which are not merely determined by our personal and idio-
syncratic whims; the whole of social life is so ordered
as to demand our conformity to appropriate social conven-
tions and cultural mores. Socialisation is the mechanism
by which we come to share a common set of assumptions,
beliefs and ways of looking at things, a common language
and an historical perspective which defines us as individuals negotiating the complex social network which is society as we know and experience it.

Whenever a woman enters a room full of strangers, her
role will be defined not merely by her superficial appearance and dress - her make-up, hairstyle and the way she
walks and talks, etc. - but by all her subsequent actions
towards and communication with the other persons with whom
she proceeds to interact, bearing in mind that they all
have their own conceptions about social propriety.   In
this sense, the roles she is called upon to play are not
merely elective, but must be regarded as a joint product
of both her own and other people's actions and expectations.   It is characteristic of social roles, in other
words, that they can never be simply put aside or aban-
doned unilaterally.   A woman may choose to adopt what is
perceived as a 'masculine' style of conduct; but if she
does so, outside certain very restricted social situations, she runs the risk of being described as 'butch'
rather than manly, and the stigma which attaches to the
former term provides an indication of what socialisation
and pressure towards social conformity are all about.

This approach need not, however, lead to the pessimis-
tic conviction that the role of women cannot be changed.
Rather we subscribe to the view that if we wish to change
it we must understand the subtleties and complexities of
the kinds of social forces which are always in operation.

We must raise our covert assumptions about masculinity and
femininity to a level of consciousness at which they can
become the subject of constructive dialogue and more
rational debate throughout society.

THE STUDIES

The illustrations and findings to be discussed come from
two related sources, (1) the first being a study for which
the fieldwork has been completed in which some 700 mothers
of eleven-year-olds were interviewed, in their own homes,
about a broad range of topics concerned with child-rearing. (2)   From this source we have selected just a few
questions which have a bearing on sex roles as seen
through the eyes of mothers at the pre-adolescent stage of
their children's development.   The second source is an
as-yet-uncompleted study in which proportion of the same
sample of children have themselves been interviewed on
reaching the age of sixteen.   We have also included some
data from an earlier study of the same children at seven.
No attempt is being made to give a comprehensive account
of the major findings of any of these studies.   They are
here being used in an admittedly illustrative and almost
anecdotal way.   Their strength for our present purposes
rests paradoxically on the fact that our questions were
asked in a context in which sex-role differences were
clearly not the prime focus of the investigation, so that
the views expressed were not contaminated by too specific
assumptions by our respondents about the fact that we
might be interested in sex roles.   Second, the questions
were addressed to a reasonably representative sample of
mothers and young persons in a not untypical urban community.   This means that the opinions of a large number of
people living in quite ordinary families have been can-
vassed.   Third, because we used a class-stratified sample
we were able both to form a balanced view of what is true,
on average, in a simple random sample and to gain some
appreciation of those sub-cultural differences which are
reliably associated with social class.

The eleven-year-old age stage

In contrast to our earlier studies of the children when
they were one and four-years-old, (Newson, 1965, 1968,
1976, 1977) it is already noticeable by seven years of
age - and still more by eleven - that the reported preoccupations and hobbies of the two sexes have drawn apart.

Indeed, they have polarised so sharply that a totally biological explanation is tempting, presumably also involving
a maturational hypothesis. We should keep in mind, however, that cultural factors are frequently responsible for
sharp discontinuities in the way people think and feel and
operate in prescribed social roles, and that sex roles are
not an exception to this just because they have also to
subsume biological maturational patterns.

At eleven years we found that approximately equal numbers of boys and girls (27 perccent in each case) were regarded by their mothers as being 'unusually good with
their hands'; but it was notable that girls practically
never seemed to get involved in carpentry or metal work,
and it was unusual for boys to be seriously interested in
sewing or needlecraft. Characteristically, when a boy
was reported as displaying this kind of interest, his
mother when talking about it would add that it was not an
activity which he would necessarily want all his friends
to know about.

'He loves knitting. It soothes him. It's like anybody smoking. He knits tea-cosies, you know, pan
handles, and little gonks and things.... Jane started
knitting, and he wanted to knit, you know. He must
know everything and he wanted to do it. He wouldn't
knit in front of the boys, I don't think - you know -
'cause he's here on his own you see.'

'Look at that embroidery he's done for school. He
drew it on a piece of material first and he started to
do it - Prince Rupert - and I told him I didn't think
it looked right. I said "I think if you fill it in,
Michael, all the way" ... and he filled every little
bit in but the face, and it was really - he had to
take it to the Headmaster when he'd finished it. I
said "Take it to the Boys' Brigade", because they have
Art there. "I'm not taking that", he said. Now that
was when he did think of anybody laughing at him. Because it was embroidery, not really a boy's....'

It is also of interest that a number of girls of this
age had gone on from hand sewing to becoming quite pro-
ficient in the use and adjustment of sewing machines:
but this skill was never cited as indicating their mechanical aptitude: which perhaps suggests that the whole
notion of 'mechanical skill' is popularly conceptualised
in a sex-loaded way. We do not wish to deny the possibility that innate sex-differentiating traits might swing
girls away from interest in mechanical things per se.

For instance, if, as Erikson suggests, girls are innately person-orientated and boys thing-orientated, girls might well see mechanical aids such as sewing machines simply *as* aids to a person-orientated goal (making something for someone), whereas boys might (and do seem to) enjoy the mechanical activity of taking things apart and putting them together again as a goal in its own right. Possibly mothers thus correctly reflect the child's focus vis-à-vis mechanical skill. When talking about their children's out-of-school activities, mothers appeared to be very conscious of the traditional sex-role stereotypes, comfortable if their children were conforming to them and somewhat self-conscious or defensive if they did not. Boys are supposed to be rough, outdoor types, often grubby and careless of their physical appearance, interested in building, carpentry or mechanical model-making or in pursuing technological hobbies like chemistry or electronics. A number were described as 'football-mad'. Girls are seen as more often following indoor pursuits, interested in making and exchanging gifts, writing stories and letters, buying or making clothes, keen on acting, dancing and so on.

If a boy deviates too far from the expected male sex-role stereotype, there may be social risks involved to which both parents and children are sensitive.

'Well he's got a piano accordion and he's learning to play the mouth organ. No lessons, but his Father taught himself the piano accordion and all our family have had musical instruments, so I think he might teach himself in the finish. I don't think he'd go off to lessons with a little musical case. He'd think that was "cissy"!'

For girls there is a corresponding risk that they may be labelled 'tomboys', but there is a subtle difference here. When a boy is described as a cissy, the implication is not that he is primarily interested in being *with* girls but that he likes engaging in 'girlish' activities. Furthermore, the term 'cissy' may be applied to older boys and even to fully grown men, and carries implications of inadequate sexuality, whereas the 'tomboy' syndrome seems to describe a transitional phase of female sexual development which some girls go through, perhaps partly because they are drawn to associating with men and boys.

'Since my son's been married - and as I say, we started about two years ago - they have the girls, like, while we go away for the week-end. And this year - we

always bring them a present back - well, we said "What
do you want this year?" - because she's been off toys
about two years.   "Oh, bring me a pair of football
boots."   Dad says "Football boots?"   Well, you know
she's football mad.   We had to buy her a pair of football boots.   My other two sons went with us like - the
other boy was at home then, the 20-year old - so they
ended up buying her the football gear.   She had football boots, socks, and you know....   They go off to
the Forest, and she puts them on underneath her slacks
till she gets up there.   Well, last year her teacher
turned round and took her to the, you know, the boys'
football team, the man who has the football team.   And
he turned round and said "You can play better than some
of our boys!"   Oh yes, she's really interested in
football.   I think if we were going out, and I'd say
"Are you coming?" and she was going footballing - she'd
go footballing.'

Note that in all these quotations the mother does in
fact defend the child's right as an individual to oppose
cultural norms.   She did teach him knitting or embroidery, encourage his music, buy the girl football boots.
In this she is carrying out what we have elsewhere (Newson, 1976) discussed as a distinctive aspect of the parental role: to protect the child's individuality from
the undiscriminating urgency of cultural demands, while
acting as long-term mediator of those demands.   In the
end, the mother has to be aware of the power of the culture - sometimes, as in the case of the three boys, because the peer group is less protective of the child's
individuality than she is.
   An important factor which seems to be bound up with
the conventional polarisation of interests and attitudes,
as a function of sex, is what we have elsewhere (Newson,
1976) considered under the term 'chaperonage'.   This reflects the desire of parents to protect girls, in particular, from contacts with strangers of the opposite sex.
It is generally accomplished by keeping girls more closely
to home and hearth, and giving them less opportunity than
boys to move around freely within the community at large,
except where reasonable adult supervision can be taken for
granted.   Typically, therefore, girls are only encouraged
to go out when they have somewhere 'sensible' to go to
such as a dancing class, swimming baths or a Brownie meeting, and where adequate 'chaperonage' can be more or less
guaranteed.   Whether or not it is openly discussed with
the child, the possibility of sexual assault is always at
the back of parents' minds as a real danger for the un-

accompanied girl, especially in a city environment.   At
seven, significantly more boys than girls are described
unequivocally as 'outdoor children', allowed to play or
roam around in the street, and said to be often unfindable
when wanted.   Significantly more girls than boys are subject to a firm rule that they should state their destina-
tion before going anywhere, and are escorted from school
by an adult.   Each of these differences is significant
at the 0.001 level.   These and other indications can be
summed up in an 'index of chaperonage' which again significantly differentiates boys' from girls' experience in
terms of the degree to which girls are kept under adult
surveillance.   The implications of these findings are not
merely that at seven girls are leading a more protected
and sheltered existence, but that this inevitably brings
them under consistently greater pressure towards conformity with adult standards and values (Newson, 1976).

Explicitly seen as a near-substitute for adult chaperonage for both boys and girls is peer companionship.   The
majority of children at age 11 have one 'best friend' (65
per cent in a random sample), and a further 8 per cent
have two equal best friends.   This leaves a minority of
just over one quarter (27 per cent) who had no specially
close friends.   Considering only those who did have one
single best friend, in 98 per cent this was a friend of
the same sex and in only 2 per cent was it a child of the
opposite sex.

How is this to be interpreted?   The theory that perhaps hangs together most convincingly is one which hypo-
thesizes, following Erikson, an initial difference in orientation (thing-orientated boys, person-orientated girls)
which is quickly built upon, sustained and perpetuated by
cultural forces.   It is suggested that the chain goes
thus: girls, orientating to persons, are rewarded by conversation and chat, (3) which moves them onto the escala-
tor of verbal precocity on which they will remain until
after puberty.   Their person-orientated games demand
verbal fluency to sustain them, and this they have, so
they continue to find such games satisfying and thus to
practise their verbal fluency.   Boys meanwhile, attracted
by things, confine their conversation more to information
exchange, and are less rewarded by chat for the sake of
it.   Their games are played out at the pre-school stage
in less close proximity to people, and greater physical
activity implies more fleeting social contact; verbal
fluency is depressed compared with that of the well-prac-
tised girls.   Since interests and the social skills
appropriate to them are mutually sustaining, boys and
girls are likely to become progressively less satisfying

playmates to each other.   This dichotomy is certainly
maintained by the development of peer-group norms of
mutual scorn (it is usual for what is seen as 'normal'
behaviour to acquire perceived value for the behaver).
Probably an additional cultural prop is an adult uneasi-
ness about opposite-sex friendships which might result in
pre-pubescent sexual experimentation: if adults feel more
comfortable with children's like-sex friendships, a more
hospitable environment is likely to be provided for their
growth.

Whatever the reason, it seems clear that, within the
child's peer group between seven and eleven, girls are
playing with girls and boys with boys.   When we come to
look at the interactions within the family at eleven, we
see a less striking same-sex pattern reflected in mother-
daughter/father-son relationships.   Girls are more likely
than boys to be spending time and sharing activities with
their mothers: 'She's an only girl and I'm inclined to be
the "girls together" type of thing.'   We found many
mothers describing what they saw as a 'sisterly' relationship: 'Yes, we're interested in the same things, yes,
make-up, pop music, and things like that.   She's like a
sister in that way, you know.'

We asked about special interests shared by one parent
with the child as a dyad.   Forty-three per cent of mothers shared such an interest with a male child compared
with 72 per cent of mothers with a female child.   Forty-
six per cent of fathers shared a special interest with a
daughter, compared with 65 per cent of fathers with a son.
These differences are significant at the 0.001 level, and
no significant social class differences are found here.
Thus there is a clear statistical tendency for the polarisation of interests by sex, so total in the choice of
friends, to be repeated in parent/child relationships,
though in a much less complete way.

Looking at the *kinds* of interests shared, again there
is a marked tendency for sex-typed activity.   Girls and
mothers together share shopping or 'going into town' as a
preferred activity, with sewing, baking and other domestic
occupations running a close second.   Boys' and fathers'
preferred joint activity is sport (participant or specta-
tor), with gardening, car-cleaning and other 'masculine'
home-maintenance jobs second.   Mothers' activities with
boys cover a wide range and cross sex-role boundaries:
shopping, table games, cooking, tennis, reading football
magazines, school subjects, making things, swimming and
needlework are all mentioned.   Fathers' activities with
girls, on the other hand, seem more limited in range and
to be more male-centred: gardening, car-cleaning, model
cars, swimming, serving in (father's) shop.

    There is a strong feeling of identification between
mothers and daughters, which extends from one activity to
another.   The chief interest, shopping in town, is one
which is likely to be focused on clothes, where there are
obvious opportunities for identification between females
to the exclusion of males.   Identifying with her mother,
the daughter is perhaps also likely to give more willing
help in the house;   she is anyway, as we have seen, more
likely than her brother to be in the house at all.
Shared activities naturally arise out of propinquity plus
identification.

    'We dance a lot together, we play tennis outside to-
    gether, sometimes we play rounders together, sometimes
    we torment Bill [her husband]. (4)   Sometimes we make
    the beds together, sometimes I wash the pots and she
    dries them.   Sometimes she'll get the duster and help
    me to dust.   We go shopping together.'

The data arrived at by focusing on shared interests is
substantiated by information, gained elsewhere in the
interview, on the household chores expected of the eleven-
year-old.   The following table breaks down these domestic
jobs into four categories as shown, and analyses mothers'
expectations of boys and of girls;   it will be seen that
sex differences are uniformly high in terms of *kind* of
chore expected, and nil in terms of *number* of chores.

TABLE 4.1   Eleven-year-olds' participation in household
duties

Duty	Boys	Girls	Both	Significance
	%	%	%	Boys vs girls
Washing up (washing pots)	40	63	51	p < .001
Indoor housework (tidy-ing, vacuum cleaning, dusting, bedmaking etc. but excluding tidying own room)	19	44	32	p < .001
Miscellaneous dirty/outside jobs (gardening, sweeping yard, cleaning car or windows, making or mending fires, peel-ing potatoes, shoeclean-ing, emptying bin, etc.)	36	8	22	p < .001
Going errands	39	21	30	p < .001

NUMBER OF CHORES LISTED
PER CHILD

None at all	11	9	10	n.s.
One only	39	37	38	n.s.
Two	33	40	37	n.s.
Three or more	17	14	15	n.s.

These figures are based upon reports from mothers about
things which children were expected to do, regardless of
how often they were expected to do them.   It might be
arguable therefore that some jobs, like washing up, recur
more frequently than others, such as emptying the dustbin
or cleaning the windows.   Also, in terms of the number of
chores undertaken there was a tendency to subsume girls'
jobs under the generic label of housework while listing
the boys' jobs individually, and this could account for
the absence of sex differences as a function of the numbers of different jobs which children were expected to do.
Leaving aside the question of whether boys in fact do less
than girls, it is clear that some tasks are thought more
appropriate for girls and others more appropriate for
boys, and that this division of labour runs broadly along
the indoor/outdoor dimensions.   It will be seen that
nearly half the children (48 per cent in a random sample)
are only expected to do one job or less;   and the manner
in which mothers answered our questions also supports the
conclusion that children are not exactly overburdened with
household duties at eleven, regardless of sex.
   It seems likely that tied up with the way chores are
apportioned is the mother's attitude to her child's
future;   how she sees her own role in preparing the child
for what she envisages will be his or her life-style.
In sharing her own daily routine with her daughter she is
in a sense performing a duty towards her child.   She is
preparing her for the day when she will have to play the
role of wife and mother, and for most mothers this is a
reality-based expectation about their daughters, inasmuch
as most girls do get married and have children, whatever
other roles might be wished for them.

   'If I say to Debbie, "Go and do the pots", and say
   she's not done them straight away, I say "Now you'll
   get a good hiding if you don't do it now.   Go and do
   what I say."   If I get angry, *he'll* run to the sink
   and do them.   He'll say "You go out, baby, I'll do
   them."   That is *wrong*: to me it is.   I know he's
   doing them for her, but she's got to understand the way
   of life in a home.   But she doesn't.   And what's her

husband going to say?   "Well", he'll say, *"you're* a
nice mother, why can't you do it?"'

Other mothers express themselves more indulgently, yet the
same feeling comes through: 'Well, she'll certainly have
to buck her ideas up a bit when she's got a house of her
own'; 'She'll make a good little mother, she's ever so
capable.' Boys' future roles as husbands place them on
the periphery of housekeeping, not as the central figure:
'He'll make someone a good husband, he's so thoughtful.'
The preparation of boys for the future includes a concern that they should have the 'proper' experience of
masculine activities. Fathers are seen as having a role
to play here, and their withdrawal from this duty is often
a source of discontent.

'It's funny, 'cause Michael loves football and my husband detests it. It's the one thing he doesn't compromise with, and he doesn't take him to the football
matches. *I've* had to take him to football matches ...
I should think three times. No, I wouldn't say often
- he'd *like* to go often of course - but I don't feel
it's really the place....'
(Would you take your daughter?)
'Oh no, it's no place for a girl - or a woman for that
matter.'

This pinpoints an important distinction between a person's
attitude and their behaviour. In thinking about sex
roles we must take care to look not just at what people
do, but also at how they feel about what they do, how they
perceive their actions. In such examples, it is important to the mothers that their sons be encouraged in pursuits appropriate to their masculinity; they do not regard active participation in this as a motherly role, yet
they do participate *as a substitute* for the father.
We have a pattern of relationships between seven and
eleven, then, in which a strong identification is shown
with the like-sex group, whether in peer-group or in
parent/child terms. Parents see themselves as explicitly
preparing their children for life; inasmuch as the roles
of men and women are distinct, children will be prepared
both explicitly and implicitly for the particular sex-role
appropriate to them. In this way the attitudes defining
masculinity and femininity are perpetuated in a very real
sense; in so far as individuals may become destructively
confined by these attitudes, we have to recognise them as
potentially inimical to the growth process.

THE SIXTEEN-YEAR-OLD AGE-STAGE

In Britain, as in contemporary Western society generally,
adolescents seem to occupy an intermediate position,
neither being treated as a child nor being conceded full
adult status.   This 'in-between' feeling is reflected in
some of the comments of our sixteen-year-olds.

Girl:
'I think honestly you're mixed up at the moment, 'cause
you're neither one type of thing....   You're not a
child any longer, yet there and again you're not a
grown up, and the different types of people....   Some
people treat you as though you're a little kid, which
gets me cross, and then somebody else, you know, treats
you as though you're ever so old, and you're not quite
sure you want to *be* old you know.   You are stuck in
the middle and you're not really one thing or the
other.'

Girl:
'At my age you go past the stage of wanting to play ...
but I don't think I'm into the stage where I want to
know what life is all about yet.'

Adolescence is also a protracted period of forced economic
and educational dependency, at a time when it is also evident that physical maturity has been achieved.   This con-
junction has suggested the hypothesis that adolescence is
a time of role insecurity as a result of which young
people tend to gravitate towards each other for emotional
support, seeking their values in a separate peer-group
sub-culture, and professing norms which are deviant from
those of the adult culture.   This is sometimes offered as
an explanation for both the delinquency and the idealism
or 'do-goodery' of particular groups of young people.   In
terms of sex roles, however, this is also a time when
young people have to learn how to interact in the knowledge that they now have sexual capabilities and feelings.
The adolescent search for a sense of identity is thus complicated by pressure to come to terms with a sex-role
identity which now includes the question of their desirability as a sexual partner.
   In our culture, with its special emphasis on individual
choice and romantic love, mate selection is obviously a
rather haphazard and capricious business;   and in the absence of any clear guidelines as to how it may be accomplished, we would expect young people initially to rely on
rather rigid and stereotyped conceptions concerning appropriate sex-role behaviour.

In forming a relationship with any unknown boy, a girl
will inevitably be influenced by ideas about how girls
are traditionally expected to behave when they go out
with boys, and of course, the same is true in reverse.
Notions of sex-appropriate behaviour are also hugely reinforced in our culture by all sorts of direct and indirect influences, as diverse as romantic fiction, nursery rhymes, television commercials, children's reading
books, films, plays and magazine advice columns, all of
which provide explicit models for sex-role-appropriate
behaviour.   The impact of these influences is to suggest
that a conventional and stereotyped mode of relating to
the opposite sex is the only method which will safely
guarantee success in the initial stages of mate selection.   Sex-role stereotypes prescribe that men need to
be aggressive and dominant in order to woo effectively,
and that women should be submissive, deferential and coy
in order to succeed with men.   If girls display characteristics considered appropriate to males, they are
likely to be described pejoratively as 'bossy' or 'unfeminine';   while boys who cannot sustain male dominance
encounters will be described as 'soft' or 'cissy', with
the implication that they may also be 'queer' (in itself
a word expressing a value judgment of *inappropriate* deviance).   For the majority of the population from which
our sample is drawn, in which manual workers predominate
by approximately three to one, our overall impression is
that these sorts of cultural pressures are deeply en-
trenched and immensely powerful, particularly at the age
we are now considering.

In this study, we deliberately chose *not* to ask our
adolescent respondents directly about whether or how often
they had themselves been involved in activities which
might be considered reprehensible or anti-social by adults
generally.   We were more interested in adolescent attitudes and values than in the estimation, on the unreliable
basis of self-confession, of the actual incidence of specific behaviours which our respondents knew or believed to
be illegal, immoral, or socially disapproved.   Consequently, any information which we have about the occur-
rence of such behaviour is the result of spontaneous comments by the respondents.   Frequently in such instances
there is an apparent discrepancy between the attitudes expressed and the incidents recounted.   It is one of the
advantages of the open-ended interviewing technique that
such apparent discrepancies can be probed more deeply to
provide a more complete picture of the respondent's views.

To explore the traditional concept of the aggressive
male, we asked our sixteen-year-olds about their attitudes

towards fighting and towards violence directed against
property. By this age, both boys and girls frequently
expressed the opinion that fighting was an inferior means
of dealing with disagreements or arguments, but girls were
the more likely to view fighting as thoroughly distasteful
and inappropriate, irrespective of circumstances. Boys,
on the other hand, were more likely to assert its effectiveness in certain situations, or as a last resort.
The following are fairly typical responses:

Boy:
'Well, not necessarily a *good* way [of dealing with disagreements or arguments] but sometimes it proves to be
the *only* way - because one side just won't listen to
the other, and he's, umm, set on getting his own way
... and the only way you can resist him is to fight
him - cut him down - get him back - and get him in a
position where you can tell him *your* side - make him
see what's....'

Girl:
'Well I don't really like it [fighting] anyway - be-
tween children or anything.   You can throw it right
out completely.'
(So there are no circumstances when it's all right?)
'No.'

During the course of the interview, however, a number of
girls did spontaneously talk about their own or their
friends' involvements in fights, both as aggressors and as
victims, and these same-sex fights were clearly serious
enough to dispel the notion that fighting between sixteen-
year-old girls is always restricted to verbal battles.
Thus, while it remains true that physical aggression is
generally regarded as an unfeminine method of resolving
conflicts, it is clearly by no means a uniquely male characteristic.

Girl:
'Well, I mean, my friend, she got involved in a fight,
and Vicky, I mean she'd never get involved.   She's
very placid really, you know, but at school ... she
got into this, you know.... It was sort of with this
girl in her class, and she nudged against her and Vicky
knocked a plant out of her hand that she was carrying
and she blamed it onto.... She said Vicky pushed her
deliberately and so then this got sort of involved a
bit.   Vicky says "Well, it wasn't me, it wasn't my
fault", and she stood by what she said but the girl

said "Oh, right, I'm going to get you then, now."   So
after school she said "You'd better wait for me or
else", you see; but Vicky was really scared.   She
didn't want to go, but if she didn't she knew that that
girl would get onto her for all her time at school and
always be digging at her because she didn't.   So she
went, and they had to have a fight, but the girl, she
went....   It was outside these shops and they were
fighting and the girl had changed into jeans and boots
and things - she was like a little skinhead - and like,
Vicky, she's only very small, that's why she picked on
her really; and this bloke came up and stopped it.
He said "What's this?   A lad fighting a girl?" -
'cause she looked like a boy, you see.   And he separated them and Vicky came home....   Her Mum was really
mad about it.   She says "Why were you fighting?   Why
didn't you just walk away, then?" and she says "Well, I
couldn't.   You get called a coward then."'

One of our questions to the sixteen-year-olds - 'Why do
boys fight more than girls?' - made the assumption that
the interviewer held this stereotyped viewpoint; but in
fact, a small proportion of both sexes challenged this.
Within this group boys were more likely than girls to deny
that boys fight more often, and frequently suggested that
fights between girls tended to be more vicious.   Occasionally this view was also expressed by girls.

Girl:
'Well girls, perhaps, can sort of get out of it by
crying or by having a big argument, but it seems wrong
for boys to stand there just crying or arguing -
bitchy sort of arguing - and then they can let out
their frustrations better by fighting.   And boys, at
least they fight fair; a bit better, because I mean
girls, they tend to fight, you know, *terribly*, pulling
hair and getting them down on the floor.   I mean, even
boys respect them, you know.   If they're on the floor
they'll wait for them to get up and fight them with
their hands, but girls don't.'

Girl:
'Do they?....   I think perhaps because girls think
that it's not ladylike to fight.   I know some girls
fight, fight worse than boys.   I think it's more manly
for boys to fight but it's not, you know ... girls
don't feel its ladylike to fight unless they get really
worked up.   Then I don't think they care.'

Several stereotypes of sex-appropriate behaviour are expressed in these quotations - 'Girls think it's unladylike to fight'.... 'It seems wrong for boys to stand there just crying' - but it appears that these may be overcome *if the provocation is sufficiently strong*. When girls do fight, therefore, we might expect the exchange to be more vicious on average, especially in view of the fact that there are few socially prescribed rules for physical combat and its resolution between girls as opposed to between boys. Such fighting, therefore, cannot be fully understood without reference to the cultural context in which it occurs.

There seems to be a general consensus, for example, that by the age of sixteen boys will have the edge over girls in trials of physical strength; but there will obviously be cultural sanctions against putting this to any direct test, since society as we know it is so organised as to prevent real physical fights *between* the sexes wherever possible. The sexual overtones of such an exchange would generate considerable emotional tension both in participants and onlookers. The whole concept that it is socially permissible for males, as opposed to females, to display certain forms of aggression is thus difficult to disentangle from the sanctions which govern public sexual behaviour.

On the whole it seems to be more culturally permissible for boys than for girls to admit openly to offences against property; though characteristically such events as were reported to us were safely in the past. Girls sometimes spontaneously admitted to such offences, but seemed more constrained to offer an excuse of response to special provocation. Their offences were more likely to be directed towards specific individuals, and personally motivated.

Girl:
(Why do people smash things up?)
'They've not had a proper education; they've not been brought up properly, that's the only reason I can see, because I've never smashed anything but that window next door.... Well, we used to stand outside when it was light, and a bit funny fella next door, they've got a kind of Mongolian child - she wets herself and running about the house, ever so funny, and they was all looking out that window, swearing at me, and that lot, and that's one thing I can't stand anybody doing when you've done nothing to them; so I just picked up a stone and lobbed it at the window.'

Male offences against property tended to be committed
in a group situation where the risk of being caught added
spice to the adventure.   Individual daring in such situations is socially rewarding and may be boasted about in
retrospect.   Our question on this topic was: 'Sometimes
people smash things up in the street because they're
angry, sometimes they do it just for fun or because
they're bored.   What do you think is the main reason?'

Boy:
'Boredom - or either to be *big* to other people.   You
go and smash them up and go to your mate and say "Oh, I
smashed this up last week", and it's just big-headed-
ness most of the time.'
(What do you feel about this sort of thing?)
'I don't know ... I've done it myself so.... (laughs).
Yeah, it's just big-headedness at the time.'

That violence against property is an expression of 'big-
ness', or 'lairiness' in Nottingham parlance, is the viewpoint most frequently expressed by both sexes.   Once more
it should be remembered here that, from a comparatively
early age, girls in the urban environment do not have the
same opportunities as boys for unsupervised group activities.
When our sixteen-year-olds leave school, what occupations do they aspire to?   Traditionally, of course, the
factors of occupation and employment have been seen as
central to role definition in the case of a man, but as of
only secondary importance in the case of a woman.   By
contrast, the central preoccupation of women has been,
traditionally, to marry, set up a home and bear children;
a role *qualitatively* different from that of men.   The
overwhelming impression from our interviews at sixteen is
that this basic qualitative difference in role definition
is still very much in evidence, except perhaps for a minority of predominantly middle-class girls with professional aspirations.   Even in such cases, girls are often
thinking in terms of a career which will complement their
role as a mother rather than replace it;   for instance,
teaching is frequently contemplated as a vocation which
allows them leisure hours corresponding to those of the
children they intend to bear.   Nursing is also very popular, perhaps because nurses are clearly in demand every-
where and the job is therefore compatible with breaks for
child-bearing of husbands' moves;   in addition it is compatible with the sex-role stereotype of compassionate nurturing.   Thus, despite apparently equal educational opportunities and more recent moves towards equal pay for

comparable work, those girls who are explicitly profes-
sion-orientated are still likely to select those specific
occupations which both reflect and make provision for the
'caring' role of the housewife and mother.   Girls who do
not have professional aspirations tend to hope for the
cleaner 'service' jobs: secretarial or clerical posts,
shop assistants' positions, hairdressing.   If they choose
a factory job, again it will tend to be something clean:
machining in the textile industry, cigarette packing.
Employment in factories is, however, rarely a *preferred*
choice for girls.   The majority of our sample who have
chosen such options would in fact prefer alternative employment, but their lack of qualifications, coupled with
economic and family pressures to find work, and the non-
availability of jobs in general, mean that they have
little alternative.

Boys, on the other hand, have available to them a much
wider range of apprenticeships in the engineering, building, printing or electrical trades or in mining, etc., and
traditionally have had easier access to professional
training.   They may be envisaging a few more years in
further education without necessarily taking a university
degree, and again the range of jobs considered in the scientific and technical, commercial or banking fields is
more extensive than that offered by the teacher/nurse/
secretarial complex.   Professional aspirations in law,
medicine, accountancy, architecture, science, etc., are
again broader in range than those of girls.

On the other hand, the preoccupation with nursing and
teaching for girls has interesting implications for girls
further down the social scale.   The very stereotypes
which seem confining for girls born into the professional
and managerial classes can be liberating for girls from
working-class homes, in that in social class terms the aspiration to teach, nurse or do secretarial work involves
an expectation of social mobility upwards into the middle
class, and, in the first two cases, into the professional
class.   This is not very characteristic of working-class
boys, who are tending to aim for skilled manual jobs.   It
is interesting that both the teaching/nursing stereotype,
and the enhanced class aspirations for girls compared with
boys that it implies, were already present for these children at the age of seven - both in the aspirations which
their mothers then had for them and in the ambitions (so
far as they were known to mothers) that they had for themselves.

Not one of the boys suggested that his major future
role might be that of husband and father.   This is not to
say, however, that they see the household chores and care

of the children as exclusively female preserves.   As husbands, the majority of the boys expect to be responsible for at least some of the chores, although the woman is generally seen as being primarily responsible for the day-to-day running of the home unless she engages in full-time employment elsewhere.   Nevertheless, there is a perceived division of chores along lines determined by traditional sex roles.   The 'heavier' chores such as gardening, cleaning the car and fetching coal are seen as the future responsibility of the boys, whereas ironing and baking are rarely mentioned as tasks they should be expected to undertake.   Between these extremes fall tasks such as washing-up and general household cleaning where no clear division of responsibility is apparent.   Boys generally expect to participate at least to some extent but, interestingly, it appears that the girls at this age expect somewhat less of them than they are prepared to give. There were frequent expressions by the girls denigrating men who took over the traditional feminine role:

Q: 'Should the household chores be shared between husband and wife?'

   Girl:
   'To a fair extent.   Well, after all, it is a woman's job I suppose, even though nowadays it is sort of equal rights, but it seems funny to see a man just going round with a duster.   It doesn't seem right for them, you know.   But my father, he's always tottering round with a vacuum cleaner because he thinks he *is* helping, but you're just watching an interesting programme and he's coming round with the vacuum cleaner.   He often does the washing up at night-time to help my mum, because she's had a hard day as well with the children all day, and my dad usually will do it anyway because he hasn't much else to do.'

   Girl:
   'Not so much the household, you know, as the outdoor, you know.   I think the husband should do all that, and leave the inside to the woman.'

The majority of our sample, both boys and girls, still see the running of the home as woman's work even when, as in the first quotation above, they are aware that sex roles are changing in our society, and have examples in their own families.   This stereotype emerged at every point of our interview when questions involved future roles. Except by some professionally orientated girls, woman's

role was viewed as that of housewife and mother, who might
be forced into the labour market by economic pressures,
but rarely by a wish for employment for the job's sake.
Work motivation in general is a complex issue; and we
must be careful not to assume to be a sexist attitude what
could be work attitudes held by the working-class group to
which most of our respondents belong.   Assuming that
middle-class people are likely to have a wider choice of
occupation available than their working-class counterparts, then we would expect work in general to have less
positive associations for those people who have had less
opportunity to choose jobs that they find intrinsically
interesting.   Perhaps many working-class men would choose
not to work outside the home if they were not convinced
that this is the necessary masculine role.

For our sixteen-year-olds, these are sex roles viewed
in anticipation and as such reflect the inexperience of
our respondents in an adult world.   It may well be that
the future lives of our sample will reflect their current
ideas; but the actuality of marriage, work, child-rearing
and running a home is not easy for young people to appre-
ciate until they directly experience it.   Clearly they
will mature in all sorts of ways as they engage in new
roles in an adult world.   Some boys and girls get hints
of changing states of married life by talking to and observing their elder siblings and other relatives, but perhaps it is not surprising that at this age their conceptions of how life will be for themselves as adults ten
years on in time are strictly limited, and do not encom-
pass any dramatic change in the way roles were determined
for their own parents.

CONCLUSIONS

The overall impression we are left with is that during
adolescence and pre-adolescence there are exceptionally
powerful cultural restraints operating on children and
young people to maintain conformity to sex-associated
attitudes and behaviour.   The implicit assumptions of
their parents and their peers tend overwhelmingly to reinforce traditional sex-role stereotypes.   Marriage and
parenthood are seen by both sexes as offering the main
route towards acceptability as a fully normal adult in
society, and those girls and boys who prematurely adopt
unconventional sex roles are seen as potentially 'at risk'
of not achieving this aim.   Experimentation with novel
sex-role relationships is, to begin with, likely to be
taken seriously only by a minority in the highly educated

middle class. Thence it may percolate slowly down the
social scale, provided that economic and legislative adaptations have produced a climate in which change is perceived as advantageous to both sexes. It may well be
that not only social class but age needs to be taken into
account as being associated with receptivity to new role
perceptions; beyond the elite minority of professionally
educated young men and women, sex-role questioning and
pressures for change may well be found among mature married women who are no longer preoccupied with the care of
young children of their own, but are seeking a new identity in the post-child-bearing period of early middle age.
Certainly pressure for radical innovation is not at all
evident within the mass of young people in the age groups
with which this chapter has been concerned; it has been
in their now middle-aged mothers that we have lately found
new capacities for the consideration of change in sex
roles and sex-linked expectations.

NOTES

1 John and Elizabeth Newson, P. Barnes and J. Scaife,
   both reports in preparation.
2 The respondents were all subjects in the Newsons'
   long-term follow-up study of 700 children living in
   Nottingham. The children comprised a stratified
   random sample using father's occupation as the basis
   for stratification, in accordance with the Registrar
   General's classification of occupations. A modification was however introduced to permit the wife's
   occupational classification to predominate over that
   of her husband if her's was higher in the Registrar
   General's scale. At any given age level the aim was
   to obtain a minimum of 100 children in each of 5
   groups. These can be defined as follows:

Non manual	I and II	Professional and managerial
	III wc	White collar: clerical and supervisory
	III	Skilled workers
Manual	IV	Semi-skilled workers
	V	Unskilled workers

   The terms 'middle class' and 'working class' as used
   later in this paper simply refer to the division between manual and non-manual occupations. Immigrant
   children were specifically excluded from this sample.
3 The word 'chat' like the word 'play' is perhaps deval-
   ued in popular currency. As developmental psychologists our own view of chat is that it has a unique

and almost irreplaceable role in effective language
development.

4   This sort of conspiracy between mothers and daughters
against males in general is paralleled by a similar
same-sex alliance between fathers and sons against
females, which however is less marked.

5 The Influence of the School on Sex-Role Stereotyping

Glenys Lobban

Various authors have argued that the school is an important agent of sex-role socialisation (Frazier and Sadker,
1973; Maccoby, 1966). They suggest that the different
patterns of achievement, aspiration and self-evaluation
that females and males show in school and elsewhere must
be to some extent due to the influence of the school.

In spite of the fact that the sexes are equal in overall measured intelligence in both the primary and secondary school, marked differences in favour of boys have
been shown in their actual level of academic achievement
in school as measured by pass rates and grades (Douglas,
1964; Maccoby, 1966; Maccoby and Jacklin, 1974a). In
British secondary schools the proportion of males taking
the academic 'O' and 'A' level exams exceeded the number
of females by 5 per cent and 32 per cent respectively in
1970. In addition, the mathematical ability (as measured
by tests) of British and American girls decreases in the
secondary school relative to their earlier scores while
that of boys increases (Maccoby, 1966; Ross and Simpson,
1971). In the higher levels of the primary school and in
the secondary school, girls make unrealistically low estimates of their ability whereas boys of equal ability do
not undervalue themselves (Sears and Feldman, 1966; Torrance, 1963; Wylie, 1963). Evidence of this kind suggests that some influence within the school operates to
depress girls' achievement and aspirations, and causes
them to have a lower estimate of their ability than boys
of equal ability. Secondary-school girls, like girls at
university, have been shown to exhibit 'fear of success'.
This motive was originally investigated by Horner (1970).
She argues that girls are in a conflict situation as regards achievement, they feel they are expected to do well
at school and at university, but that it is at the same
time unacceptable for them to 'beat' their male peers at

50

almost any task.   This conflict leads girls to want to
succeed, but not too much, and hence leads to the 'motive
to avoid success' (Horner, 1970).   This motive is measured by asking females and males to respond to a story
lead where someone of their sex is described as coming top
of her/his medical school class.   Horner (1970) found
that significantly more of the eighteen- and nineteen-
year-old females she tested described unpleasant events
and attributes when talking about a person of their own
sex than did the male subjects.   The successful woman was
described in negative terms by 65 per cent of the females,
while only 10 per cent of the males described the successful man in these terms.   Monohan et al. (1974) asked sixteen-year-olds to write stories about a successful female
medical student and about a successful male medical student using the same story lead as Horner (1970) for both
sexes.   They found that both sexes gave more negative
responses to the story about female success, and the male
subjects were even more negative than the females.   Both
sexes were equally positive about male success.   Maccoby
and Jacklin (1974a) report that a study of thirteen-year-
olds did not find a sex difference in fear of success, and
suggest that this motive may only develop after age thir-
teen.   It is unclear how much influence the school has on
the development of the fear of success motive.   The fact
that the motive seems to develop in high school and that
it is at this level that the most striking evidence of a
decrement in females' performance is found, suggests the
school may play a role.   Influences outside the school
also contribute to the development of the motive.

Different authors have different opinions on the question of whether it is the primary school or the secondary
school which is more important in sex typing.   British
research has tended to stress the sex differences in academic achievement found at secondary level.   It is therefore argued that the British secondary school is crucial
in shaping sex-typed behaviours (Davies and Meighan,
1975).   A great deal more research on the role of the
school in sex typing has been done in the USA than in
Britain.   Studies of American primary schools suggest
that they have a substantial influence on sex typing
(Frazier and Sadker, 1973).   In this chapter I will
review research on the messages about sex roles that are
communicated by primary and secondary schools.   I shall
look at what is learned in schools officially, as well as
what is communicated by the 'hidden' curriculum.   In my
conclusion I shall attempt to assess the impact that the
messages about sex roles have on the pupils' self concepts
and attitudes towards sex roles.

The official role of the school is to teach academic
skills to the pupils.   The official curriculum details
the skills the pupil is supposed to be learning, and the
avowed aims of the school and the education system of
which it is a part.   A number of authors have shown that
the pupil learns a variety of other things in addition to
mastering or failing at academic skills (Frazier and
Sadker, 1973;   Jackson, 1968).   The term 'hidden' curriculum is used to describe this learning.   Davies and
Meighan (1975, p. 171) define it thus:

> The hidden curriculum is a term used to refer to those
> aspects of learning in schools that are unofficial or
> unintentional, or undeclared consequences of the way in
> which teachers organize and execute teaching and learn-
> ing.

Jackson (1968) argues that the 'hidden' curriculum commu-
nicates similar messages to all children.   They all have
to learn to comply with three 'Rs': Rules, Routine and
Regulations, in order to cope with school.   Frazier and
Sadker (1973) argue that the 'hidden' curriculum is not
the same for all the children.   They argue that the
'hidden' curriculum in schools is sex differentiated and
that what is communicated to the pupils is what behaviours, attitudes and prestige are appropriate for each of
the sexes.   Because both explicit and 'hidden' curricula
exist in schools, one has to investigate both of these
levels for evidence of sex-role stereotyping.   The need
for investigations of the covert or informal structure has
long been recognised by organisational theorists as being
of at least as much, if not more, importance than the
study of the formal organisation.   It is possible as far
as official subjects are concerned that no sex differentiation may exist in a particular school, but that messages about what is 'correct' behaviour for the sexes are
being communicated none the less via the content of textbooks, the teachers' interactions and prohibitions, and
the pupils' observations of female and male teachers and
the staff hierarchy.   In the sections that follow I shall
review research on sex typing in both the official and
'hidden' curriculum.

1   THE OFFICIAL CURRICULUM

Various official pronouncements exist in Britain concerning what should be taught to pupils of different ages.
The Plowden report (1967) is the official document which
lays down guidelines for primary schools.   In this
report, it is presumed that boys and girls will do the

same subjects.   The only mention of sex differentiation
occurs in the section on games in the final year of
school, where it is suggested that girls will play netball
while boys play football.   The Plowden report favours co-
education and sees the aim of education as fostering individual development.   No mention is made of compensating
the sexes for experiences they may have lacked at the pre-
school level.   Reports on the practices in three London
primary schools show the official curriculum to be much
more sex typed than the Plowden report advises, however,
with girls doing cooking, sewing and netball while boys do
woodwork, metalwork and football (Lobban, 1975b; Loftus,
1974).   Further research on practices in British primary
schools is needed to see whether the suggestions made in
the Plowden report are frequently contravened in favour
of sex typing.

In primary schools, while curricula may in some cases
have been sex differentiated, social policy frowned on
this.   However, in secondary schools in Britain until the
advent of the Sex-Discrimination Act in late 1975 even
the official curriculum was sex differentiated.   Girls
and boys were channelled into different subjects with
girls doing languages, biology and homecrafts, while boys
did physics and chemistry and wood- and metalwork (Byrne,
1975; Davies and Meighan, 1975).   Byrne (1975) did a
survey of resource allocation (as measured by expenditure
per head and amount of teachers and equipment allocated)
to female and male pupils in 45 single-sex and 88 mixed
secondary schools in Britain over the period 1945-65.
She found that the female pupils were allocated fewer of
the resources.   In the single-sex schools the state spent
£75.3 per head on girls, while £87.8 was spent on boys.
In the mixed schools she found that the vast majority had
insufficient science laboratories to serve all the pupils.
In all but four cases, it was the male pupils who were
timetabled into the laboratory, while the girls were
taught biology in converted classrooms with minimal equipment.   In addition, Byrne found that the grants that the
schools got for subject development tended to go to the
male pupils, as they were very often given for subjects
that the male pupils took such as science and mechanics.
This means that, prior to the 1975 Sex Discrimination Act,
girls, at least those in the secondary schools, were re-
ceiving an education inferior to that of boys, which might
limit their life choices and chances, and both sexes were
being restricted in their subject choices.   It is argued
that this discriminatory attitude to girls is based on the
implicit assumption that girls will ultimately follow the
occupation of wife and mother to the exclusion of any

other (Byrne, 1975).   When the sex-discrimination legislation has been in operation in Britain for a sufficient
time to allow the effects to be monitored, it will be
interesting to see what research will reveal in the area
of official curriculum, and whether the primary and secondary school practices of assigning subjects and resources on the basis of sex will have been thoroughly
stamped out.

2   THE 'HIDDEN' CURRICULUM

The 'hidden' curriculum, because it is implicit and very
often implemented unconsciously, may be more resistant to
change than the official curriculum (Frazier and Sadker,
1973).   It is also argued that the 'hidden' curriculum
is more influential in shaping pupils' attitudes.   In
this section I will review research on four aspects of the
'hidden' curriculum; sex distribution in the staff hierarchy, curricula materials, teachers' attitudes to sex
roles and teachers' behaviour to each of the sexes in
teacher-pupil interactions in the classroom.   It must be
borne in mind that the research merely documents the content of the 'hidden' curriculum as it relates to sex
roles.
   In the *staff hierarchy* in British primary schools males
are more often found in prestigious and powerful positions.   The statistics on sex of headteacher demonstrate
this;   there are equal numbers of male and female head-
teachers in primary schools despite the preponderance of
female teachers at this level, and in secondary schools
the majority of heads are male (Byrne, 1975;   Plowden,
1967).   One of the frequent results of a merger of
schools when a comprehensive school is formed, is that it
is the male head of the boys school involved in the merger
who is given the headship.   This may mean that with the
national implementation of the comprehensive policy in
Britain the number of females who are heads of secondary
schools will further decrease.   The implicit message that
pupils may glean from observation of the male-dominated
staff hierarchy is that power and maleness are, and indeed
should be, associated, while femaleness is associated with
the subservient role.   Such a hierarchy provides the
female pupils with few powerful female role models.
   The type of *curricular material* whose sex-role content
has been most thoroughly investigated is the textbook.
In Britain the majority of the studies of primary school
materials have looked at reading books.   The sex-role
content of nine reading schemes that are widely used and

200 reading books has been analysed (Lobban, 1974 and
1975a; Moon, 1974; Northern Women's Education Study
Group, 1972). In each of the reading schemes and in the
set of 200 reading books, more male than female characters
were shown. The ratio of male to female characters
ranged from 2:1 (Lobban, 1974) to 4:1 (Moon, 1974). In
addition male central characters occurred five times as
often as female central characters (Lobban, 1975a). The
second finding of all these studies was that the child and
adult sex roles were rigidly and traditionally sex-differentiated. Boys and men were shown as active, aggressive
and courageous, while girls and women were shown as nurturant, passive and timid. In the two modern reading
schemes coded by Lobban (1975a), a total of 33 different
occupations were depicted for adult males and these were
both varied and realistic ways of earning a living. A
grand total of 8 occupations were shown for adult women,
and these were mum, granny, princess, queen, witch, handy-
woman about the house, teacher and shop assistant, so only
the latter two related to an achieved occupational status
outside the home. The final finding of all these studies
was that the male characters in the books were accorded
far more prestige than the female characters who were more
frequently shown as more uninteresting, stupid and evil,
and who appeared less and took fewer speaking parts in the
stories. The conclusion to be drawn from these findings
is clear; the content of reading schemes reinforces sex-
role stereotypes, and hence is unlikely to lead children
to question or change their attitudes (Lobban, 1975a).
Weitzman et al. (1972), who found a similar pattern in
American reading books, argue that primers have an important influence on children's attitudes as they are presented in a context of authority, the classroom, and inform
children about the 'real' world, and present them with
like-sex models to emulate.
    Secondary-school curricula materials used in Britain
have also been found to be sex biased. Nightingale
(1974) found a lack of adventure readers about girls.
The books for girls focused almost exclusively on dating
and romance. A pattern of neglect of women appears in
science and history books (Davies and Meighan, 1975).
Many books on sex education present the sexes as if they
belonged to different species. For example, Hoffman
(1975) quotes a book by Barnes (1958) in which he warns
young men that girls have an all-pervading weakness; 'the
tendency to let love, or what they think is love, swamp
all considerations of social outlook, politics, religion,
ethics, and indeed anything else'.
    In summary, most of the textbooks read by pupils in

schools endorse traditional sex-role stereotypes.   This
aspect of the 'hidden' curriculum, like the school hierarchy, presents a picture of the world in which males are
more prestigious and active than females.   Any learning
that the students glean from observing the staff hierarchy
or from reading their textbooks is unlikely to encourage
them to question these stereotypes.

Studies of *teachers' attitudes to the sexes and to sex-
roles* in the USA show that teachers endorse traditional
attitudes.   At the pre-school and primary levels,
teachers value female and male pupils equally but describe
their typical behaviour very differently (Maccoby and
Jacklin, 1974a).   Despite the fact that objective measures do not show any such difference, they see the typical girl as dependent and introverted and the typical boy
as aggressive and extroverted (Levitin and Chananie, 1972;
Feshbach, 1969).   Loo and Wenar (1971) asked pre-school
teachers to rate their girl and boy pupils in terms of how
active they were.   The teachers rated boys as more active
but an objective measure of activity showed no sex differences.   This suggests that teachers' stereotypes mediate
their perceptions of pupils.   Feshbach (1969) found that
junior school teachers preferred compliant pupils but the
sex of the child mediated their ratings with the independent girl getting the lowest ratings.

Studies at the secondary-school level suggest that
teachers of both sexes endorse traditional sex roles and
believe that boys make more interesting and challenging
pupils than girls.   Ricks and Pyke (1973) surveyed the
attitudes of thirty Canadian teachers of each sex.   The
majority of these teachers believed that male and female
pupils behaved differently;   that males are more aggressive while females are more passive.   The teachers said
that they 'preferred' teaching the boys.   This preference
seemed to come from the teachers' belief that male pupils
were more interesting and critical, and that their education was more important than that of the girls.   The
majority of the teachers believed that pupils of both
sexes preferred to be taught by a man rather than a woman.
Half of the teachers thought that girls and boys expected
different treatment.   They said that girls expected to be
treated in 'a more ladylike, genteel fashion, less sternly
with more consideration of their feelings' (Ricks and
Pyke, 1973, p. 29).   The boys on the other hand, were
described as expecting 'more sternness, setting of limits,
authority, having to be told how it is', and as rejecting
'mothering' (Ricks and Pyke, 1973, p. 29).   While 86 per
cent of the male teachers felt girls expected the 'feminine' treatment described above only 56 per cent of the

female teachers expressed a similar belief.   Ricks and
Pyke asked the teachers whether they saw any evidence in
their current pupils' behaviour as compared with the behaviour of past pupils to conclude that the male and
female roles were changing.   Sixty-three per cent of the
teachers said that girls' behaviour was changing and girls
were becoming more dominant, argumentative and interested
in careers.   Only one teacher mentioned male pupils; he
said that they had become less touchy about expressing
their feelings.   Despite these changes, the teachers did
not feel that they as teachers had a role to play in facilitating sex-role change.   Ricks and Pyke (1973, p. 32)
concluded that 'teacher perceptions and attitudes towards
sex-roles are traditional and presumably contribute towards maintaining sex-role prescriptions.'   Thomas and
Stewart (1971) asked American school guidance counsellors
to rate individual videotape recordings of schoolgirls.
The tapes were identical, but some counsellors were told
that the girl wanted to be an engineer, while others were
told that she wanted to be a home economist.   Counsellors
of both sexes scored the home economist goal as more appropriate, and rated the girls who chose the engineering
career as in need of further counselling.   The authors of
the study concluded that guidance counsellors' role was
that of urging the female client to conform to cultural
norms rather than fostering their uniqueness as individuals.

Teachers of both sexes thus appear to endorse sex-role
stereotypes.   They believe that extreme differences between males and females exist as early as age three.
They also appear to believe that it is appropriate to
behave differently to the sexes in accord with their
'natural' characteristics.   They seem to interpret behaviour according to stereotypes, they expect their female
pupils to be passive, dependent, compliant and on the way
to marriage as their only and life-consuming career, while
the males are expected to be active, independent, bright
and challenging and destined for a 'real' career.   Feshbach's (1969) research suggests that teachers may well
respond differently to the same behaviour depending on
whether it is a girl or a boy who is behaving.   However,
the effect that these beliefs about 'natural differences'
have on teachers' behaviour to females and males is not
clear.   For example, will they tend to ignore males'
aggression because they believe this to be 'natural' or
will this belief lead them to be more punitive in order to
tame males?   The next section on interaction between
teachers and pupils will consider some of these questions.

A number of observational studies of *teacher-pupil*

interaction have been carried out in American classrooms.
The pre-school and primary teachers studied interacted
more with the boys in class than with the girls and this
was true of both positive and negative contact (Brophy and
Good, 1970; Martin, 1972; Meyer and Thompson, 1956;
Sears and Feldman, 1966; Serbin et al., 1973; Spaulding,
1963).   Spaulding (1963) found that teachers accorded
boys' work and efforts in the class more approval than
they accorded to the girls' work.   Teachers spent more
time teaching and listening to the boys.   They also spent
more of their time reprimanding the misbehaviour of the
boys, while with the girls it was their lack of knowledge
and skill which incurred the teachers' disapproval.
Martin (1972) found that teachers gave boys significantly
more response opportunities, reading-recitation turns,
work contact, procedural contact and non-academic behavioural contact than they gave to girls.   When he analysed
his data further, Martin found that a particular group of
boys, those whom the teachers classified as behaviour
problems, accounted for the bulk of the teachers' contacts
with boys.   Girls whom the teachers classified as having
problems that were equally severe received significantly
less attention than the 'problem' boys.   Martin suggests
that it is the 'problem' boys rather than boys in general
who are favoured by the teacher because these boys express
their problems via acting-out behaviours, which are sal-
ient to the teacher because they disrupt the class.
Martin's data suggest that primary school girls with problems may be neglected by the teacher to an even greater
extent than the rest of the girls in the class.   Martin
did not distinguish between positive and negative teacher
responses to pupils whereas Good et al. (1973) in their
study of secondary classrooms did make such a distinction.
They found that teachers of both sexes interacted more
with male than female pupils and directed more of their
affect, both positive, to the boys.   When boys who were
high achievers were distinguished from boys who were low
achievers, an interesting pattern emerged.   The 'bright'
boys far surpassed all other pupils in the amount of positive contact they had with teachers, while the poorer
boys received more behaviour related reprimands than any
other group of pupils.   'Bright' girls received less encouragement than 'bright' boys, and the poor girls received as much teacher criticism for academic failure as
the poorer boys.   More research is needed at the primary
school level to see whether a similar pattern of discrimination against 'bright' girls exists there.
   The evidence on teacher-pupil interaction in American
schools shows that teachers tend to favour male pupils at

the primary and secondary levels.   There is some evidence
that teachers are unaware that their behaviour towards
boys and girls differs (Maccoby and Jacklin, 1974a).   It
is unclear why teachers behave in the way they do.   It
may be that pre-school and primary teachers start by per-
ceiving their female and male pupils in terms of the
stereotypes, and these perceptions go on to become a self-
fulfilling prophecy.   The primary boys increase in autonomy as they are reinforced for this, while the girls become more compliant and less academically adventurous as
they are criticised for their failures at one end of the
scale and ignored at the other.   High-school students
present what Good et al. (1973) describe as different
'presses' to their teachers, the boys demand the teacher's
attention more and answer questions more than the girls.
This behaviour may be the result of socialisation in the
primary school.   These pupil 'presses' probably interact
with the teachers' attitudes concerning the relative importance of boys' secondary education versus that of
girls' to produce the kinds of interaction patterns that
have been found.   Teachers are probably forced to pay
attention to boys who disrupt their classes.   Their preference for 'bright' boys may have to do with the fact that
they exhibit a degree of independence and confidence not
shown by the 'bright' girls whose socialisation at the
primary level was for compliance.

It is unclear whether British teachers neglect their
female pupils in the same way, or to the same extent as
has been found in the USA.   All the American studies reviewed were done in co-educational schools.   It is possible that different patterns would be found in British
schools generally, in British single-sex schools, or in
particular types of schools.   I am familiar with only one
British study of teacher-pupil interaction which looked at
the sex of the pupil (Garner and Bing, 1973).   These
authors found that teachers in the open-plan primary
schools they observed had sex-differentiated patterns of
interaction with their pupils but the particular pattern
varied from teacher to teacher.   It is unclear whether
this finding would be replicated with a larger sample, and
whether it can be generalised to secondary schools.   At
present, what can be concluded about teacher-pupil interaction is that the pupil's sex seems to be an important
variable determining teachers' behaviour in both countries, and that American teachers not only treat the sexes
differently, they treat males more favourably.   The implicit message inherent in these findings is that boys and
girls are different and merit different treatment, and
that it is boys whose difficulties or 'bright' answers

merit most attention.   In the concluding section I will
discuss the question of what impact such a message is
likely to have on the pupils.

CONCLUSIONS

The question that this paper attempted to investigate was
the role of the school in sex-role stereotyping.   We have
seen that both the official and 'hidden' curriculum adopts
traditional sex-role stereotyping and very often favours
males over females.   We have also seen that girls and
boys show different patterns of achievement, behaviour and
self-evaluations in school as well as in other situations.
Other chapters in this volume show that there are powerful
influences outside the school that affect sex-role attitudes.   Very few of the studies of the school's influence
on sex roles have separated out the role of the school per
se, or shown causal rather than correlational relations
between the messages contained in the curriculum and student's behaviour, achievement scores or self-evaluations.
   Certain studies have tried to evaluate the impact of
school climate on students' attitudes or behaviour.   Ross
et al. (1972) studied resource allocation in twelve British comprehensives.   They found that four of the schools
allocated fewer resources to girls than to boys, and in
these, but not the other schools, girls made less progress
than boys.   Byrne (1975) cites an example of the way in
which stereotypic attitudes can be ameliorated: one of the
schools surveyed by her had a deliberate policy of sending
intelligent girls to male-dominated industries on their
career-sampling course at fourteen-plus.   Proportionately
more girls from this school than from comparable neigh-
bouring schools went on to career-based or technical further education rather than unskilled jobs.   Minuchin
(1964) compared nine-year-olds in American traditional and
modern schools and found the pupils in the modern schools
were less sex typed in problem-solving and ability.
These studies suggest that policies and attitudes to the
sexes and sex roles may well influence the pupils.   The
work of Rosenthal and Jacobson (1968) shows that teacher's
expectations concerning pupils' ability affect the amount
of attention that they pay to particular students and
these pupils' attainment.   If these teacher expectations
have an impact on the students, then it is likely that
teachers' sex-role expectations are similarly influential.
   Other research also suggests that the school may have
an important role in sex-role socialisation.   Maccoby and
Jacklin (1974a) hypothesize that children are reinforced

for sex-type behaviour by 'relative strangers' more than
by their parents; this suggests that teachers who are
such 'relative strangers' may play an important role.
The cognitive theory of sex-role development (Kohlberg,
1966) stresses the child's active learning of sex roles.
Kohlberg shows that children attain gender identity, I am
a boy/girl, by about the age of three. They then actively seek out and process information about sex roles, and
what a person of their sex does, and feels, and this information-seeking goes on well past school age. Kohlberg
stresses that much of this information-seeking goes on
outside the home as the children seek to fill out their
picture of what a 'real' girl/woman and boy/man is. This
suggests that the example presented by the school, and
particularly by the primary school, may be very influential. Much of children's experience and learning occurs
at school and they presumably observe the books they read,
and their teachers' behaviour, status and expectations, in
order to fill out their picture of what a 'proper' girl or
boy is and will be. As we have seen, the bulk of the
material available in textbooks and in their interaction
with their teachers is unlikely to help the children to
come to a non-stereotyped conclusion about females and
males. Kohlberg argues that children will produce stereotypes about the sexes until such time as their experience offers them an alternative and they do not see only
males in positions of authority in society. Our review
of practices and curricular materials in schools suggests
that at present most children are being presented with a
set of experiences calculated to lead them to give stereotype content to their picture of each of the sexes.
     What we can conclude about the role of the school is
that the official and 'hidden' curriculum in British and
American schools is sex-role stereotyped. There are also
strong indications that pupils are influenced by the explicit and implicit messages this curriculum conveys.
Any influence that the majority of schools has on students
is likely to be in the direction of reinforcing sex-role
stereotypes and the negative female self-evaluations that
accompany these. If sex-role practices in schools were
changed and rendered non-sexist, the research of Byrne
(1975) and Minuchin (1964) suggests that pronounced
changes in behaviour and attitudes may follow. The education system at present is not encouraging individuals to
develop their unique potentials, it is fitting individuals
to restrictive stereotypes and thereby causing damage,
particularly to girls. It is time that educationalists
became aware that conscious and unconscious stereotyping
and discrimination occurs in the school in relation to sex
roles, and made some attempt to change these practices.

6 Sex-Role Stereotyping in Studies of Marriage and the Family

Rhona Rapoport

In the past few decades, the sex-role stereotyping in studies of marriage and the family has had a mainly male bias. In the past few years the bias has begun to be corrected (Bart, 1971b; Laws, 1971; Oakley, 1974a, 1974b). Some writers at present have a stereotyped approach to the marriage and family area, while a few - both men and women - are attempting to avoid sex-role stereotyping and to allow for the range of variation that can occur in people's lives (Bernard, 1972, 1975).

This paper will concentrate on the sex-role stereotyping that has been evident in studies made of marriage and the family until recently, and which continues in many. While only a few basic stereotypes will be considered, these form the origin of many others. They can be classified into three areas: husband-wife relationships; parent-child relationships; and the relations between the family and other social institutions.

Writing and research on the family has tended to describe 'what is' or those patterns which fit the ideal state of 'what is' as seen by the author. This approach is not orientated to change and is frequently backward orientated in the sense that it is assumed that the limits of human potential are reflected in what has been observed or thought to be observed and studied up to the present. Put another way, what has never been, can never be. Also, because of the practice of referring to social systems, cultural ideas, or statistical distributions the literature frequently leaves the 'people' out. Marriage has been treated primarily as a role relationship (Wells and Christie, 1970) in which duties, obligations, rights and perquisites have been assigned to the man-husband and woman-wife along structured lines. But men and women are people and normative definitions of marriage necessarily suppress the felt needs and interests of many.   This has

been more readily documented in recent years for women;
for example, many feel that with the existing set of
norms, their sexuality has been suppressed, that they have
been left with little power in the family as a result of
being the sole caretakers of the children and that there
have been powerful sanctions against the expression of
their talents and the assertion of their 'personhood in
the world outside the family, particularly as this takes
the form of paid work' (Laws, 1971).

One way to de-stereotype the images of sex roles used
in the study of families is to relate our formulation more
directly to people, their variability and their capacity
to change, adapt and invent.

When discussing the *husband-wife relationship*, sociologists have tended to emphasise patterns of activity and
structure: who does what, time regularly spent on different activities, accepted norms and expectations about how
each role incumbent (mother, father, husband, wife, child)
should behave. While some attention is given to how the
participants feel about the activities assigned to them
and their general patterns of behaviour, what satisfac-
tions they experience and what changes they themselves
might like in the balance of gratifications achieved, this
has been a relatively minor aspect in family sociology as
such, though it has been more evident in the literature
geared to the prediction of success or failure in marriage. It is seldom questioned, for example, whether a
woman likes children - it is assumed. These issues are
not only important in relation to social values (i.e. the
maintenance and development of a humanistic society), they
have scientific significance in relation to the study of
process. We are in a period of conspicuous change regarding sex roles. To ignore process in favour of concentrating on structure would be to disregard major aspects of the real world. Existing patterns, and patterns
which have been set up as 'normal' by professional 'experts' are being increasingly questioned by people placed
in family roles. The people are changing the role prescriptions. To the extent that social scientists continue to use older role concepts as though they are still
in force, their work suffers from lack of validity.

Up until now, the development of marriage and family
theory - the definition of key concepts, the way in which
the field is defined, the topics selected for empirical
research, the methods employed to do the research, and the
interpretation of research data - has tended to be biased
toward male-orientated values. This has been an unconscious or semiconscious product of the fact that most
sociologists are men, and that for the most part they des-

cribed what they 'saw'.   The emphasis on a mythical
value-free approach to social science research produced a
picture of what the perceivers saw as the status quo.
This has often lagged behind actual changes, and has been
taken to imply a sanction for retaining that status.
Thus, for example, when women work outside the home, the
phenomenon 'deviates' from the normative pattern which has
been described, and tends to be defined as a special problem for the families concerned - the husbands and the
children.   As male employment does not deviate from the
normative pattern, it is not problematic, and therefore
has not been an issue until recently.   The result has
been a great deal of empirical research that looks at the
effects of women's employment on the family but little research on the effects of men's employment on their wives
and other family members, or on themselves as husbands.

It could be argued that this is not male bias, but bias
due to using a static, structuralist conceptual approach.
Perhaps more centrally, another male bias is seen in
choice of research topics.   The study of how men's participation in the world of work is facilitated or impeded by
family concerns is an example.   These merely illustrate a
systematic bias seen in most topics of family sociology;
this results from a scientific paradigm (in Kuhn's terms),
a 'mental map' of sociologists which is now being re-
surveyed for new editions.

The orthodox model of the husband-wife relationship
used in the literature can be described in the following
way: the husband/father is normally expected to carry out
the economic provider role.   He is, in Parsons' terms
(Parsons and Bales, 1955) engaged in 'instrumental' activities, orientated to the external world and establishes
the social as well as the economic position of the family
in society.   The wife/mother, in contrast, is assumed to
be confined to the home and her role is seen as 'expressive'; it is implied that she is responsible for the
quality of the husband-wife relationship, the morale of
the breadwinner-husband and for all the domestic caretak-
ing activities.   According to this model, husbands and
wives (men and women) are perceived as complementary and
their task specialisation (presumed to be efficient for
social organisation) is seen as being based on potent
'bisocial' factors (Blood and Wolfe, 1960).   The model
was assumed not only to fit men's and women's biological
'givens' but to be the most adaptive or functional in the
social situation of industrial society.   With only one
provider, the family could adjust to changing labour
market conditions without conflict.   With only one expressive leader, the family atmosphere would minimise

tensions and conflicts, which would benefit children as well as husbands, who required a haven of comfort from the stresses of work.

In this stereotype of complementarity between women and men in their family sex roles, no room is left for the possibility that the men and women in families may *supplement* each other according to specific family requirements or values. Either the mother or the father or both can be tender or stern as they see fit and as the need arises.

The complementary model is based on the assumption that the specific form of the nuclear family described above is an adaptive response to an industrial situation. Where the individuals concerned did not fit it, it was they who were considered defective. Where alternative models were employed - e.g. mother as strong figure of discipline and father as nurturant homebody - this was seen as 'role reversal' and felt to be pathological and/or pathogenic. Indeed, some research supported this proposition (cf. the marital schism/skew literature), but it must be regarded as inconclusive in the long run because the conditions producing variant patterns in the past are different from those prevailing now, and the social sanctions and conflicts experienced by those who practised the variant patterns were great enough to form stressors in themselves. The point that is relevant here is that a specific type of family situation (the classical conventional family) was not only positively socially sanctioned in society, but it was described by sociologists in similar terms. 'Functional' came to imply 'natural', or normal; and 'deviant' (a perfectly neutral statistical term) came to imply 'pathological', 'deficient' or 'unnatural'.

At the beginning of the century many writers were concerned that the industrial revolution would lead eventually to the demise of the family as an institution. Social scientists like Zimmerman (1947) felt that the modern nuclear family was 'unstable' and that the emphasis on individualism would eventually lead to rejecting the burdens of family responsibility. Writers such as Louis Wirth (1942) and Ralph Linton (1959) also wrote with a negative image of urban life in mind, and were concerned about the potential collapse of the family. These writers were all concerned with the impact of modern technological society on culture and the personality of individuals. In traditional or folk society, personal attitudes and behaviour were shaped by familistic norms. Persons of a particular age, sex, family status were guided by prescriptions for behaviour that applied to all other people, according to age, sex and kinship categories. But in modern urban society these prescriptions are lacking. One may act in

many more areas according to individual preferences rather
than in terms of ascribed or ordained obligations.   Ultimately this individualism and removal of others from categories governed by humanistic equated with familistic
values may lead to a potential breakdown of all relationships, as Philip Slater and others have noted (Slater,
1970).

More specific to the sex-role issue, a position developed that held that familistic values were not necessarily
to be equated with humanistic values.   Family bonds based
on dependency and rigid role differentiation regardless of
individual differences came to be seen as particularly deleterious for women.   Early feminists (e.g. Charlotte
Perkins Gilman, 1903) saw the potential demise of the
classical family as an opportunity for the liberation of
women and children.

Parsons, though a contemporary 'bête-noire' of the feminist movement because of his paradigm of the functionality of the conventional family, actually presented an
analysis that seemed to offer a compromise solution to
this apparent conflict.   Parsons and his colleagues emphasised the strengths of the nuclear family in the context of modern society.   They maintained that although
the traditional family was changed by industrial society,
the new structure that emerged provided a stable family
environment in which to prepare children for their adult
roles in society and to maintain the psychological balance
of the men who faced the pressures of competition in their
work life (Parsons, 1965).   Rather than working with
polar oppositions - folk/urban, humanistic/technological -
Parsons concentrated on the modal pattern of a 'normal
American family' as a middle-class urban couple with young
children and reduced kin ties.   Within this set-up,
Bales' small-group dynamics model was assumed to apply;
with the husband seen to play an 'instrumental' role as
the breadwinner and the wife seen as following an 'expressive' role in the home (Parsons and Bales, 1955).   Parsons also believed that people came to want to do what was
required of them in their roles through the process of
internalising the appropriate sex-role models provided by
the parents during socialisation.   In this way families
created the conditions for conformity to the pattern.   As
this model was seen as consistent both with the requirements of industrial society and with the known dynamics of
small experimental groups, it was assumed to be healthy
and normal.   Other patterns were assumed to be socially
or personally pathological rather than alternative life
styles (Skolnick, 1973, p. 113).

But this model had a built-in static quality even

though Parsons originally saw it as an adaptive response
to a changed reality.   The model has led to a massive
stereotyping of sex roles in the family sociology literature.   Whether or not its architects intended this stereotyping to occur, it was an inevitable consequence of
the type of model and analysis that disregarded diversity
and variation in family life.

The model described above assumes as fact a picture of
marriage which is, at best, a hypothesis only partially
supported by research.   Many sociologists seem to confuse
hypothesis, ideology and empirical fact when they use this
model.   When the sociologist Ralph Turner wrote the following passage, he appeared to assume as fact what was a
conceptual model about behaviour:

> the solidification of the kind of mutual task bonds
> that create a sense of comradeship depends on the pre-
> sence of common goals and the development of a deci-
> sion-making pattern that minimizes the obstacles to
> collaborative activity.   The chances of such comrade-
> ship between mother and daughter are greatest when the
> daughter forms a somewhat traditional self-conception.
> The common interest in domestic activities permits a
> collaboration that can continue even into adulthood, so
> long as the daughter's self-conception does not move
> toward a repudiation of traditional feminine activity.
> Effective bonding is especially vulnerable to non-adap-
> tive division of labor.   (Ralph Turner, 1970, p. 387)

Thus a leading sociologist was still writing in 1970 as
though *all* mothers are involved in 'traditional feminine
activity', implying that if a daughter did not accept a
traditional self-conception, she could not develop or
maintain comradeship with her mother (effective bonding
breaks down) and that following non-traditional paths involves a 'nonadaptive division of labor'.   This is stereotyped thinking which presents at least two points of
concern.   First, it is potentially damaging to people who
derive their norms and self-conceptions partly from the
opinions of expert authorities.   Second, it is scientifi-
cally unsound and can be disproved.   An example of its
invalidity can be seen in the case of dual-career families
which are more adapted to certain conditions of modern
life than the mono-career family.   The point is that
Turner's statement, based not necessarily on malevolent
chauvinism but on stereotyped thinking which applied a
conceptual model as though it were empirical fact, represents the most widely used approach to the sociology of
the family.

It is the model that needs replacing and a contemporary
task is to do so without replacing one set of stereotypes

with another.   One route to doing this is by new research
conceived partly with this in mind and with the emphasis
on how people actually behave in the real world.   In research on sex roles and non-traditional marriages, it has
been found, for instance, that comradeship between parents
and their children can be maintained without traditional
self-conceptions.   The growing literature on dual-career
and other dual-worker families also provides grounds for
revision of the model.   In addition to the points made
above, this literature emphasises that non-traditional
paths may involve the development of new family structures
that are more adaptive to the needs of mothers and fathers
as people than are the traditional role models (Rapoport
and Rapoport, 1971a, 1976; Holmstrom, 1972; Lein et al.,
1974; Poloma and Garland, 1972; Gronseth, 1975; Bernard, 1975).

The set of stereotypes associated with the model described has also become a set of ideals for families to
conform to and for politicians and administrators to use
as assumptions on which to base family policies.   In Britain, the type of nuclear family in which mother (domestic
caretaker), father (economic provider) and children live
together apart from other kin is still regarded as 'normal' (See Land's chapter, this volume).   Oakley describes
the pressures to conform to this ideal:

> The family as an institution is a prescription for
> gender-role normalcy: one woman, one man and one or
> more children.   Families with adopted children count,
> but single-parent families do not.   They represent a
> social situation full of ambiguities, and are stigma-
> tised and ostracised.   There are strong economic,
> child-care and social pressures for the normalization
> of the family unit.   Within the gender-role structure
> of the family, women are reduced to a common social
> type: the housewife-wife-mother.   The woman doctor,
> shop assistant, professional engineer, primary school-
> teacher, ballet dancer, factory worker, all become Mrs.
> Y., the mother of Mr. Y.'s children, the support of Mr.
> Y.'s career/job, the washer of his clothes, the care-
> taker and creator of his home, the centre and symbol of
> his family life.   (Oakley, 1974a, p. 70)

Two additional sets of myths and stereotypes have accompanied and been used to underpin this model of 'ideal'
family life.   The myth of the biological basis for the
division of labour by sex, and the myth of the biological
basis for mothers (not fathers) caring for the young.
These myths, as Oakley and others have come to call them,
have gained great ascendency in the past few decades.
They are mutually reinforcing and their proponents under-

pin them with selected findings, interpreted statistical-
ly, from the crosscultural and ethological fields of knowledge.   It is from the latter that the idea that these
divisions are 'natural' ones (Parsons and Bales, 1955;
Murdock, 1949; Tiger and Fox, 1972).   It should be noted
that other research material from, for example, the cross-
cultural field, points to a different set of conclusions
(Whiting, 1972).

The *myth of the biological basis for the sexual division of domestic labour* stereotypes a married woman as a
'housewife'.   The housewife role is exclusively allocated
to women rather than to adults of both sexes.   Oakley has
documented how a housewife's work is seen as economically
non-productive and so has the status of non-work (Oakley,
1974a, 1974b).   The housewife role is a primary one for
women and has primacy over other roles.   The corollory of
this stereotype is that a man cannot be a housewife, which
implies that he cannot be responsible for domestic work.
If in fact he does do a great deal of the housework, he is
going counter to social custom and is likely to be seen as
a 'deviant'.   In English law, a man and a woman make a
'natural pair' and within this pair, it is 'naturally' the
woman who takes over the role of housewife.   A biological
male cannot legally take the social role of wife-house-
wife, and a biological female cannot legally take the role
of husband (Oakley, 1974a).   In societies which create
laws, policies and public opinion on the basis of archaic
stereotypes of biological capacities, individual choices
and inclinations may be thwarted or blocked.

For our purposes though it is the fact that social scientists perpetuate these stereotypes which is our concern.
Sociologists and social psychiatrists, in particular, tend
to work with *modal* conceptions when constructing their
models of the family.   In the Parsonian model, 'housework' is treated as a non-work role because society did
not define a wife's domestic work as part of the productive economy.   One may speculate that another facet of
this definition was that it was assumed that men did not
do housework.   Housework, in that context, was seen as an
expression for woman's 'natural' caring urge and as necessary for backing up men's work participation.   Housework thus became treated typically as only part of the
feminine role and was not analysed as work in its own
right (Oakley, 1974a, 1974b).   Recent research shows that
there is a great deal of variation in this.   This is related to a structural change process (e.g. that more married women are involved in paid work outside the home) and
also to changes in structure which reflect new perceptions
of domestic work (Oakley, 1974b; Lopata, 1971), new con-

ceptions of sex roles and new relations between men and women.   These new conceptions are part of ideas in our society about equality, equity, self-expression and real-isation of individual potential.   They have relatively recently been applied to sex roles (Rapoport and Rapoport, 1975).

More and more married women with children do paid work outside the family.   Some do so for economic or other practical reasons, others do so to express some felt psy-chological needs.   In either case, balances within fam-ilies are altered when women work outside.   New issues arise, such as how much a wife will tolerate her wishes being constantly subordinated to those of her husband's or how much her husband feels that the occupational sys-tem he is in should have so fundamental an effect on his family's life style.   The whole phenomenon and its cor-relates make it clear that many families do not fit the stereotyped model of sex roles and new conceptualisations are called for.

A second major set of sex-role stereotypes within the family relates to the care of children, particularly very young ones.   This gets us into the area of the *parent-child relationships*, and how they fit into the stereotyped model of family functioning.   It used to be that marriage itself provided a major turning-point in a woman's occu-pational career.   Studies dealing with parent-child rela-tionships have mostly assumed that mothers enjoy their children so they have not questioned how satisfying child-care is for mothers;   similarly, fathers have not been asked whether they enjoy being away from their children so much.   More recently it is the assumption of parenthood that provides this turning-point (Le Masters, 1957, 1974; Rossi, 1968).   The myth which places women as the only people who can mother exerts powerful pressures on women to give up major commitments outside the home when a child is born.   Thus, an extraordinary situation has developed in our society where parenting has come to be equated with mothering (Rutter, 1974).

An outstanding feature of the sociological literature on the transition to parenthood is the gender-differentia-ted pattern that is implicitly or explicitly assumed to accompany this process of transition.   Becoming a parent is seen as a very different experience with different con-sequences for women and men.   The nature of gender-dif-ference, its sources and consequences are usually taken for granted and not questioned or explored (Rapoport and Oakley, 1975).

A book that presents a thoughtful analysis of modern family life, but which follows the conventional sociologi-

cal model, is Christopher Turner's 'Family and Kinship in
Modern Britain'. Turner's section of the advent of
parenthood is a clear statement of the prevailing emphases
on gender-differentiation and the 'family' location of
parenthood:

> The arrival of the first child, in particular, makes
> not only the beginning of a new generation, but also a
> radical change in social commitment.... The incorpor-
> ation of the position of mother alongside that of wife
> clearly amounts to a substantial modification in the
> structure of household relationships. The restric-
> tions of pregnancy, and subsequent recurrent needs of
> the new infant during the first few months after birth,
> serve to curtail the mother's activities outside the
> home. The working wife normally gives up her job, and
> finds her freedom to engage in leisure activities
> severely circumscribed. The new mother-child rela-
> tionship is intensified by the obvious dependency of
> the infant, and the period just before and after birth
> is one of considerable emotional involvement for the
> mother. The birth of the first child thus generates a
> new family position for the mother, and one which has
> considerable repercussions, not only on her other kin-
> ship positions, but also on her multiple societal posi-
> tions as well. The development of the relationship
> between father and child tends to be somewhat detached
> from the immediate circumstances of gestation, birth
> and early physical dependency. (Turner, 1969, p. 64)

The model of normality implied here presupposes a situation in which parenthood only occurs within marriage,
where the mother is ready and willing to exchange her
occupational commitment for an exclusively maternal one,
but her husband's major identification is with his occupational role outside the family. The model is also characterised by consensus (husband and wife agree as to the
rearrangement of roles and activities that parenthood incurs) and lack of personal conflict (the mother is easily
able to switch from the worker role to the mother role,
and the father experiences no ambivalence about his position as breadwinner rather than actively involved father).

Sociologists lean heavily on psychology, psychiatry and
ethology for the validation of the myth. Most writers
still assume that mothers and children are 'both intrinsic
to each other; they are really part of each other's being
.... Nature intended mother and child to be together....
The mother is totally essential to the well-being of the
child ... (Tiger and Fox, 1972, p. 56). In 'Housewife',
Oakley (1974a) sums up the content of the myth in her
critical review of it:

Of all the rationales offered for women's presence in the home, the myth of motherhood seems the most persuasive and the least questionable in its premises and conclusions, for even if the housewife role and the wife role are capable of change, the maternal role is not. Women's position in the family is founded in their maternity, now and for all time. Simple logic produces the conclusion that since women's maternal role is unalterable, their oppression as housewives might just as well continue. As with other myths, the function of the myth of motherhood is a validation of the status quo. The myth of motherhood contains three popular assertions. The first is the most influential: that children need mothers. The second is the obverse of this: that mothers need their children. The third is a generalization which holds that motherhood represents the greatest achievement of woman's life: the sole true means of self-realization. Women, in other words, need to be mothers. 'Need' here is always vaguely specified, but usually means damage to mental or emotional health following on the denial of mothers to children, children to mothers, or motherhood to women.

The three assertions together form a closed circle: all women need to be mothers, all mothers need their children, all children need their mothers. Popular fiction, pseudo-psychology, and the pronouncements of the so-called 'experts' faithfully reproduce them as facts rather than as unevidenced assumptions. (Oakley, 1974a, p. 186)

So the woman who does not wish to have children, or does not wish to spend most of her time with them, is perceived as unfeminine and deviant.

The most recent empirical research concerned with sex roles and 'non-traditional' forms of marriage suggests that a lot of so-called mothering can, in fact, be performed by fathers. Other than breastfeed, there is little if nothing that men cannot do for young children that women can. Whether a person is nurturant enough to give a young child the closeness and affection and attention it needs is related to individual variation and practice rather than gender. In fact, it may be said that the orthodox model of family life and parenting straitjackets parent-child relationships. It forms the basis of sex-role socialisation theory throughout the life cycle and has been used extensively in the USA and other western countries since Parsons and Bales (1955) first formulated it. Both within the family and in institutions outside - such as schools - sex-role socialisation practices focus

on 'expressive' tasks that girls will have to perform and
the 'instrumental' ones that are perceived as appropriate
for boys.   As a result, sex-role socialisation prepares
girls inadequately for their instrumental tasks, even when
they lead conventional married lives, and boys inadequately for their expressive tasks which may be associated with
fathering (Rossi, 1964;   Cohen, 1966;   Bernard, 1975).
The paradigm also implies that children have no choice or
diversity in their role models.

Different options for participation within *family and
other institutions* in fact become available to men and
women at different stages of the life-cycle and the orthodox model assumes that they do not exist.   Some recent
research findings indicate that the option to participate
in spheres other than the domestic one is necessary for
women's personal and marital happiness.   Thus Cohler et
al. (1962), in a large study of child-rearing attitudes
and behaviour, found that mothers who coped well with maternity permit themselves more activity outside the home.
Other studies have shown that parent-child behaviour and
marital satisfaction may be positively affected by women
working outside the home if they want to and negatively if
they have to or do not want to;   or want to and do not do
so (Bailyn, 1970;   Ordern and Bradburn, 1968;   Rapoport
and Rapoport, 1971b).

Because women were so long exluded from developing
their potential in the outside work situation, and because they have begun to go to work in such large numbers,
they now constitute a 'problem' and consequently many
studies have been done on women's 'two roles' (Myrdal and
Klein, 1956).   It is only recently that the converse
'problem' has been defined for males - that they have had
to work full-time all their lives.   As men *and* women are
recognised to have at least two major role sets - at work
and in the family - both may be seen to have various options.   The options open to men at different stages of
the life cycle have not been investigated in any detail up
to the present, but they are now coming into focus in this
way.   As with women, their personal and marital happiness
might well be affected by a social climate which allows
various options in combining work and family life.   Many
men might prefer to stay home with their young children
part of each day or the whole day every other day, or some
other pattern which would fit their situation.   Such patterns would certainly affect father-child relationships
and allow for the possibility that inputs between fathers
and mothers could be supplementary rather than complementary.   It remains an open question as to what the effects
of such patterns will be on children.   They would have

their role model repertoire increased and the potential
for more choice.   These issues are not included in research designs even though it is assumed that children's
social and emotional development is affected by the quality of the mother-child and father-child relationships.
Where they are taken up, there is often a stress on bi-
polar measurement, so that two extremes only of parental
behaviour, for example, are considered.   An instance is
the work by Ainsworth and her colleagues which selects the
'sensitivity-insensitivity', 'acceptance-rejection', 'co-
operation-interference' and 'accessibility-ignoring' dimensions of maternal behaviour (Ainsworth, Bell and Stayton, 1974).   Variables that may be less important than
the quality of the relationship - such as the amount of
time spent with children, the activities engaged in with
children - are also focused on (Safilios-Rothschild,
Parents' Need for Child Care).   The satisfaction of
mothers and fathers in their parenting will affect the
quality of these relationships.   Fertility - or maternity
or paternity - does not guarantee quality parenting.
Quality parenting has many demands; it may be so onerous
that it needs to be shared with persons outside the family.   If it is, parent-child relationships will once more
be affected.   We know that women who are unwilling
mothers have negative effects on themselves and those
around them.   Rossi (1964) described the way in which
such mothers' stresses reverberate on their children.
Rheingold (1964) has suggested that unwilling mothers are
involved in a cycle of destructiveness in their relations
with their daughters, who then have destructive relations
with their daughters, and so on.   This research does not
deal with the ambivalence that may exist in 'willing'
mothers.   The stereotype is that 'normal' mothers are
not 'unwilling'.   It is only in very recent years that
books and articles on parenting have not been concerned
exclusively with mothers.   But social scientists have
not studied fathers or fathering and this is only beginning to emerge as an area which may be regarded as worthy
of attention.   Until now, it has only been father's role
as breadwinner and factors that affect this, that have
interested professional writers.
     Writers in the family and marriage field frequently
stereotype 'the family' as an isolated structure.   'Indeed a major fault of the marriage literature (and one
source of its conservatism) is the intellectual fallacy
of treating the family - particularly the marital dyad -
as a closed system' (Laws, 1971).   Thus, for instance,
viewing marriage as a closed system has gone side by side
with not seeing variations among couples as to how much

of each individual is included in the marital transaction, and it has precluded exploration of cultural expectations and stereotypes that marriage subsumes more of the wife than the husband. Instead of assuming that the woman is bounded by the family and should be, and that the man is mainly involved in the occupational system, we need to look at the variation that occurs. With what degree of intensity and with what constraints are individual men and women linked to other systems in society? The impact of dual linkages to the occupational system (Safilios-Roths-child, 1975) will be different from the consequences of only one spouse/parent being linked to the occupational system. Such variation affects availability and inter-action patterns within the family. It also affects the possibility of sharing the load in the family. The availability of other resource systems in the community - such as satisfactory daycare - also impinge on inter-rela-tions within families. A communal structure of household life perhaps shows the greatest differences in internal structure and the impact on parent-child relations. For instance, parent-child relationships in a communal house-hold are reported to be affected by:

the parents diminished sovereignty over the household, the presence of an audience and potential coalition partners, the pressures for individuation and autonomy. For parent-child units as well as couples, the communal household replaces the nuclear family's limited ex-change of goods and services with a market place. Since the family's exchange is usually one-sided, with many more goods and services flowing from the parent to the child than in the other direction, many parents ... come to communal households seeking the market place: a sharing of child care responsibilities, a provision of inputs from other adults, the presence of others to take over when the parent is depleted - that is, a change from obligatory exchange, in which the parent must give to the child because he or she is one of a number of resource-holders.   (Kanter et al., 1975)

In conclusion it can be seen that some of the new writ-ings on families emphasise *variation* and the possibility of achieving new kinds of *balance* in the ways in which men, women and children define and enact their family roles (Rapoport, Rapoport and Strelitz, 1976). This in-volves changes in the stereotyped patterns of relations between wives and husbands, parents and children, and families and other institutions.

7 Sex-Role Stereotyping at Work

Oonagh Hartnett

Good luck. This· is the dawning of the Age of Artemis - Diana, goddess of the hunt. And when it's in full bloom, I hope to God it's characterised by people working together - and having fun doing it - in organisations that are just. (Townsend, 1970)

Light years out, Mr Townsend! This is the space age - the age of women's liberation. However, we have the same hopes for organisations.

INTRODUCTION

There is much evidence which indicates that society as a whole, organisations in general and work organisations in particular are pervaded by a 'taken for granted' matrix of beliefs and behaviour concerning the sexes and their role (Broverman et al., 1972; Bushby, 1975; Mednick and Weissman, 1975). The main focus of this chapter will be upon some of the ways in which this belief system manifests itself in work organisations and upon some of the steps which can be taken to reduce its impact and replace it by an equal opportunities, person orientated ethos. Despite the concentration upon work organisations, much of what is discussed can be applied to other types of organisations such as professional associations, churches, trades unions, political parties and educational institutions.

Work organisations in common with other organisations and indeed with society itself are complex and dynamic psycho-socio-technical networks. They are composed of individuals all striving for their own private ends as well as co-acting with other individuals, within the limits imposed by the technical environment, in a collec-

tive effort aimed at achieving a goal or goals which need
not always be explicit and which can be conflicting as
well as compatible.   The belief systems of the individuals involved inevitably permeate the formal and informal, the overt and the covert aspects of these networks
and reciprocally the climate and structure of these networks influence the beliefs and behaviour of individual
members.   Change in either will effect some changes in
the other.   Individual systems of belief, whether justified or not, will be reflected in the types of organisational goals and values espoused; the distribution of
resources and power; the allocation of material and symbolic rewards; the content and style of communication,
written, verbal and non verbal (the politics of touch);
the nuances of informal interpersonal relationships and
influence; recruitment; training and promotion policies;
the temporal and technical structuring and design of work
and the division of labour.   Furthermore, as well as behaviour within organisations, these systems of belief will
reveal themselves in the type of exchange which takes
place between the organisation and its environment, i.e.
in the quality and style of contact with clients and customers; in the use or abuse of the eco-system; in service to or exploitation of the community; in the use of
patronage and buying power; in the extent to which an
organisation may be thought of as a 'greedy institution'
demanding total commitment from its members and refusing
to recognise the duties of roles which do not contribute
directly to its particular goals (Coser, 1974).   In the
case of work organisations such comparatively unacknow-
ledged duties would include home responsibilities and
civic and community activities.

In short, most aspects of an organisation are fabrica-
ted upon and shot through with the belief systems of its
individual members and these beliefs in turn are influenced by the organisational environment in which individuals
work.

One of the most powerful belief systems in existence is
that which may be called the 'sex-role system'.   Briefly,
it consists of at least three main strands or components
together with the interactions between them.   The main
components comprise: the assignment, on the basis of sex,
of one of two different series of personality traits; the
division of labour on the basis of sex, when sex, per se,
has nothing to do with the work requirements; and the investing of the male with a higher value than the female
(Rosaldo and Lamphere, 1974; Holter, 1973; Mead, 1935;
Davis, 1973).   These components interact with each other
in such a way as to give rise to institutional 'sexism' in

work and other organisations. The assignment of traits,
and the division of labour interact with one another so
that jobs themselves are stereotyped according to the sex
of the people performing them. Since males are invested
with higher value than females, 'masculine' traits are
accorded higher prestige than 'feminine' ones and thus
tend to dominate the value system of the entire culture of
an organisation, making it a patriarchial one. Also
activities performed by males tend to be rewarded and regarded more highly than even identical activities, when
these are carried out by females.

All societies agree that, in addition to the sex-linked
differences associated with procreation, there are or
ought to be other differences between the sexes. However
there is considerable disagreement about the nature and
extent of these differences. The masculine stereotype in
one culture may resemble the feminine in another. Societies are also not uniform in the type or degree of role
differentiation which they adopt. In some societies
there is little differentiation, with males and females
sharing most tasks, while in others there is little overlap in the activities assigned to the sexes. This lack
of uniformity has meant that the precise manifestations of
the 'sex-role system' have varied from culture to culture
and from era to era depending upon the versions of the
stereotypes and division of labour which happen to have
been current at the time.

In western society the traditional sex-role stereotypes
are such that traits like aggression, dominance, competitiveness, independence, objectivity and decisiveness are
seen as masculine and thus appropriate for the male only
while empathy, tenderness and consideration are thought of
as feminine and thus rightfully characteristic of the
female only. Additionally the division of labour is such
that it involves woman's place being 'in the home' while
man's is 'out at work' usually as a member of a work organisation.

These particular stereotypes, division of labour and
overvaluation of the male vis-à-vis the female, result in
work organisations which are typically characterised by a
symbiosis of unfair discrimination based upon sex and an
instrumental attitude towards employees which reveals itself in prejudice in general, in authoritarian structures,
the poor quality of much of working life and in a dearth
of a sense of responsibility to the wider community.
That is, such organisations are characterised by institutional 'sexism'. Were the stereotypes simply to be reversed, the result would be equally disastrous. The
'tyranny of structurelessness' would then hold sway

(Freeman, 1973).   Consequently there is no alternative
but to evolve an   adult ideal which combines the better
traits of both sexes in a way characteristic of creative
people (Suter and Domino, 1975).   In short it means
transforming the 'sex-role system' as it presently manifests itself so that it emerges instead as a meeting of
people.   This requires the elimination of unfair discrimination whether based on sex or anything else.

As far as work organisations are concerned, such action
will necessitate, on the part of both sides of industry, a
critical analysis of current modes of thinking and behaviour in work organisations in order to pin-point the form
and content of the attitudes and activities which are
aligned with discrimination.   It will require the development of action programmes designed to counter such discrimination and foster equal opportunities.   Personnel
policies and practices will obviously be of central importance in any analysis or action programme of this kind if
it is to be effective.   This chapter will look at the
ways in which some of the activities associated with the
personnel function   can hinder or contribute to the growth
of equal opportunities for men and women.   These activities include research, education, counselling, selection, training, promotion and career development, job
evaluation and job and organisation design.   Inevitably,
in the long term, if an equal-opportunities, person-
centred ethos is to supersede present manifestations
of the 'sex-role system', then the design of work organisations will be predicated upon a new definition of the
term   'work' and upon replacing present demands for mono-
organisational commitment (Coser, 1974) by an accommoda-
tion to pluralistic commitments, on the part of both
sexes, to a number of different roles and responsibilities.

ACTIVITIES ASSOCIATED WITH THE PERSONNEL FUNCTION

Research-education

Charity begins at home and undoubtedly at a very fundamental level there is a need for researchers themselves to
become conscious of the ways in which stereotyping may
permeate their own cognitive structuring of events and
lead to 'missionary-position thinking' becoming evident in
some of their conceptual models of behaviour in organisations.   At a less esoteric level, research is needed in
order to identify the motivations, attitudes and beliefs
that frustrate or alternatively facilitate equal opportu-

nities.   It will be necessary to distinguish the myth
from the reality both of sex differences and of the behaviour of women especially in the work situation.   Furthermore, it will be essential to disseminate this information to all concerned whether male or female, unskilled
or skilled, management or shop floor.

Reviews of the literature on the topic of sex difference are easily available.   Conclusions reached include
'it is by no means obvious that attempts to foster sex-
typed behaviour (as traditionally defined) in boys and
girls serve to make them better men and women' (Maccoby
and Jacklin, 1975) and that there is no reason why the
present division of jobs according to sex categories
should continue (Department of Employment, 1974b) and that
'to the extent that we encourage sex role stereotyping we
repress many of our cross sex characteristics so that in
effect we are denying part of ourselves'.

Myths about women in the work situation abound.   A
paper by Bass et al. (1971) gives some idea of the attitudes which influence male managers' abilities to accept
women on an equal basis with men.   Male managers did not
feel that women made good supervisors.   This does not
appear to be because women are perceived as less capable
than men.   Rather, managers indicated that they felt that
they themselves and other men and women too would be un-
comfortable with a woman supervisor.   That the problem
seems to be one of societal norms is the conclusion drawn
by Bass.   In the same study it was also shown that male
managers felt that women were not as dependable as men because of women's 'biological and personal characteristics'.   A more recent study (Hunt, 1975) reaches not dis-
similar conclusions.   It was found that only a minority
of male personnel managers thought that it would be a
'good thing' if more women occupied senior posts.   It
was also found that males in personnel posts, responsible
for the engagement of employees, believe, a priori, that a
woman applicant is likely to be inferior to a man in respect of all the qualities considered important.   These
managerial judgments whether about supervisory positions
or dependability do not stand up to the evidence.   In one
survey three quarters of the male and female executives
who had worked with women managers reacted favourably.
Studies have shown (United States Civil Service Commission, 1972) that most of the men who object to women
supervisors have never worked for a woman and that women
have no preference in the matter.   Another study (Boehm,
1974), reported at the 1974 Annual Convention of the American Psychological Association, supports the notion that
women are acceptable as managers.   It delineates evidence

obtained from the implementation of an affirmative action
programme in a very large American concern.   The data
covers about ten companies and nearly 5000 women.   It
consists of ratings of acceptability for management positions.   The data for women is compared with similar data
for men drawn from another study.   The ratings were as
follows:

Table 7.1   % Acceptability for management positions

Rating	Men	Women
More than acceptable	7.2	6.1
Acceptable	25.6	28.1
Questionable	32.7	29.0
Not acceptable	34.5	36.8

There simply is no meaningful difference.
    To turn now to the question of women's dependability,
the evidence indicates that once again managerial judgments are unsound.   Evidence from this country and the
USA indicates the following about turnover: higher turnover rates are true of all employees, irrespective of sex,
who are under 25 and are in low-income clerical jobs.
Evidence to the House of Lords by Sir William Armstrong
indicated that while turnover in certain clerical groups
was high for females, it was even higher for males (The
Select Committee on the Anti-discrimination (no. 2) Bill,
1972).
    A study quoted by Maier (1965) concerning labour turn-
over among men and women clerks shows that women with high
IQ scores were likely to leave.   The conclusion reached
is that inadequate promotion of women was responsible for
such turnover because for low-scoring and average individuals, where comparison with men in the same job was possible, turnover was lower among women.
    A survey of women's employment (Hunt, 1968) indicates
that in Britain, half of working women have been in their
present job for more than three years;   that married
women are at least as likely as single ones to remain in
one job for long periods;   that qualifications, skill and
responsibility encourage women to remain in their jobs.
The study concludes that women are not inherently less
stable employees than men.   The evidence showed that men,
who had worked during the previous ten years, had 2.3 jobs
on average compared with a figure of 2.1 jobs for women
over the same period.   Additionally, recent figures from
Britain, the USA and Canada indicate that the trend is for
the 'illness gap' between men and women (difference in

time lost from work due to illness) to all but disappear
or reverse direction (European Parliament, 1975; Women's
Bureau, 1971; Sinclair, 1971).

Another myth that results in women being judged less
dependable than men claims that women don't need to earn
money. This assumption has been called 'the myth of the
male breadwinner' or the 'cake-winner' fallacy. Land
(1975a) in a paper to the British Association quotes
census figures which show that, in Britain, 'nearly two
million women under retirement age are the chief economic
supporters of their households' and that 'the majority of
these households contain either children or adult depen-
dents, including husbands'. Furthermore, other evidence,
which she quoted, shows that the number of two-parent
families having incomes at or below supplementary benefit
scale rates would have trebled if earnings by the mother
had not been combined with those of the father. American
statistics tell the same story for that country (Women's
Bureau, 1971).

Yet another myth is that women will go out to work only
until they marry. Statistical trends for Britain and
other countries for which comparable figures are available
(Department of Employment, 1974a; OECD, 1975) indicate
that married women make up the majority of working women
and are increasing as a proportion of the work force.
Not only are women joining the paid work force in ever
increasing numbers, but attitudinal studies indicate that
they wish to do so. A recent EEC survey (Commission of
the European Communities, 1975b) found that 'a majority of
women be they single or married' would positively prefer
to be in paid employment and that men have always 'seriously' underestimated the strength of this preference.
One survey in the USA (Tavris and Jayaratne, 1973) to
which 120,000 women responded found that fewer than 2 per
cent of the respondents thought that most women could
develop their potential by being good wives and mothers
ONLY. Other studies indicate that in contrast with earlier findings, percentages of female students who agree
with the traditional views of women's role are very small.
Most look forward to having a career combined with marriage and a family. Furthermore, over half the women in
one of these studies demonstrated a preference for what
have been traditionally stereotyped as non-feminine occupations (Epstein and Bronzaft, 1972; Klemack and Edwards,
1973).

In Britain the census for employment for 1972 showed
women to be 38.5 per cent of all employees. The proportion of married women who work has increased from 10 per
cent in 1931 to 42 per cent in 1971 so that in that year

they formed just over 62 per cent of all female employees.
In 1966, less than 20 per cent of married women, in households with children under five, worked.   In 1971, 30 per
cent of married women with two dependent children worked
more than thirty hours a week (Department of Employment,
1974).   The 1970 figures for the USA are similar and show
that 42 per cent of all mothers worked outside the home
and that two out of five working mothers had children
under six years of age.
The OECD Report (1975) concludes 'The rising participation of young married women ... reflects the fact that
contrary to common belief, a sizeable and growing number
are developing a highly stable attachment to the work-
force.'
A final myth which behavioural scientists are in a
position to criticise is that which preaches that a woman
who works outside the home necessarily damages her children and degrades marital relationships.   The most recent
evidence indicates that child studies have confounded separation with deprivation and that bond disruption is not a
necessary consequence of separation (Rutter, 1972; National Child Development Study, 1972; Baruch, 1972;
Arnott, 1972).
To summarise then, there is in existence a body of
knowledge which can be used to dispel the stereotypic
myths which abound about the motivation and capacities of
women and which according to recent findings are still
espoused by 'gatekeeper' males in personnel departments
who are in a position to exert a powerful influence on
selection and promotion procedures (Hunt, 1975).

Counselling

Career and vocational guidance could be designed to encourage people to act more freely upon occupational alternatives and to transcend the pressures which limit the
sexes to traditionally stereotyped aspirations.   Additionally, personal counselling can take on a new dimension
by providing help and advice on how to survive and emerge
successfully from the 'lonely, expensive and emotionally
trying experience of women who protest sex discrimination'
(Prendergrass et al., 1976).
There is evidence that career counsellors are not free
from the pressures which society imposes in order to encourage conformity to sex-role stereotyping (Oliver, 1975;
Thomas and Stewart, 1971).   In these studies it was found
that neither male nor female counsellors approved of
career goals which deviated from the stereotypes as much

as they approved of conforming goals.   Clients holding
deviate career goals were reported as needing further
counselling concerned with 'self understanding' and
'choice of career'.

Another source of bias can be found in the use of sex-
stereotyped publications purportedly providing career information.   An analysis of two series of American career
books (Heshusius-Gilsdorf and Gilsdorf, 1975), indicated
that males were over-represented even when compared with
the present sex composition of the work force not to speak
of the potentially equal participation by both sexes.
Almost universally, males and females were shown in traditionally stereotyped occupations.   A related bias issue
concerns counsellors' use of sex-stereotyped vocational
interest measures which are based upon a socialisation
dominance hypothesis which reinforces the status quo.
Some interest blanks offer a more limited range of options
to females than to males (Strong, 1966;   Miller, 1968).
In the case of one test it has been acknowledged that 35
per cent of the items emphasise sex roles - for instance
'tool maker' is not on the female version anymore than
'typist' is on the male.   Another includes 'company secretary' and 'farmer' among the choices offered to males
whereas 'private secretary' and 'agricultural worker' are
the options with which females are presented.   Prediger
and Cole (1975) argue that the socialisation dominance
hypothesis should be replaced by an opportunity dominance
one which 'can facilitate career opportunities which are
only just developing'.

In addition to vocational guidance, personal counselling could develop a new dimension so as to include sex-
discrimination counselling.   This point has been made
strongly in papers published in 'The American Psychologist' and in the 'Personnel and Guidance Journal' (Pender-
gass et al., 1976;   Jeghelian, 1976).   Both papers include reports of case studies which illustrate the psychological stress to which a woman who protests discrimination may be subjected.   Such stressors comprise: sud-
denly being excluded from all but the most routine information;   multiple transfers;   being isolated in a separate cubicle;   and being given no duties.   Administrators
may insinuate that her problem is 'the result of a personality conflict, not sexism'.   The administrative 'run
around' may be used against her in a delaying tactic which
involves bouncing her case from one committee to another.
Rewards and insinuations may be used in such a way as to
make another sector of the work force, notably males but
also many females, feel threatened by her complaint and
thus to turn her co-workers against her.   'The woman may
also simply be ignored.'

By the time a woman comes for counselling she may have had one or more fiery and/or hostile interchanges with her boss.   She may have been ostracised by embarrassed or uneasy co-workers, and she will have been reminded of every past failure no matter how remote.   She may have already lost a few early skirmishes because of naivety or lack of backing.

Any guilt which she may have about not conforming to the notion that 'women's place is in the home' will probably have been played upon as no doubt will any stereotypically inculcated uncertainty that she may have about the competence of women and herself in particular.

In addition to advice on how to file a complaint, sex-discrimination counselling will need to concern itself with assuaging depression and anxiety about the value of women's skills and prospects for future employment.   What a woman needs in discrimination counselling is 'to be believed, to be encouraged and to be trusted'.

Selection

Sexism is a feature of many selection procedures and of the language of job advertisements.   Indeed, it is a feature of personnel language as a whole (Stephenson, 1975).   The selection base should be broadened with advertisements being placed in papers and journals known to be read by women as well as men.   The biased use of credentials and the collection of background data on candidates are two more items which introduce sexism into selection.   For instance, the qualifications specified may not be essential for a job but by using rigid qualification requirements a selector may be able to exclude women because on the whole they have not had the same opportunities for access to formal education and training as have men.   Also a woman may have had experience in voluntary work and running a home which an employer will refuse to accept though he will take the experience of military service and perhaps the organisation of a rugby club into account when recruiting a man.

A study by Cecil (1973) provides evidence that different variables are used to evaluate male and female job applicants.   The following variables were perceived as being more important for males: 1. Ability to change mind on an issue. 2. Persuasive individuals. 3. Capable of withstanding a great deal of pressure. 4. Exceptional motivation. 5. Aggression. A qualitatively different set of variables was perceived as being desirable for females: 1. Pleasant voice. 2. Excellent clerical skills.

3. Finished high school.   4. Excellent computational skills.   5. Immaculate in dress and person.   6. Ability to express self well.   The instruction to subjects specified that all applicants, irrespective of sex, were being interviewed for the same job.   However the job was described, rather vaguely, as a white collar one thus allowing the subject to project his image of the average male and female onto the job.   It is clear that the male was perceived as more of a typical administrative management employee and the female as more of a clerical employee.

Other studies bear this finding out.   Professional interviewers as well as male college students were found to discriminate among applicants for a managerial position not only on the basis of scholastic standing but also on the basis of sex and physical attractiveness.   Subjects revealed a strong bias in favour of males and the greatest discrimination occurred in deciding who was to be assigned the first rank (Dipboyee, 1975).   A further study (Cohen and Bunker, 1975) shows that it is not only women who suffer discrimination.   So also do men if the job is stereotyped as feminine.   Even so, obviously the overall discrimination against men will be much less than against women since the range of jobs stereotyped as feminine is smaller than the range stereotyped as masculine and since 'women's work' is assigned a low status and is poorly paid.

A variety of tests are used as criteria in selection as well as in vocational guidance and there is nothing in the Sex Discrimination Act which precludes the use of tests as such.   However where a test has a discriminatory impact it should be demonstrably related to job performance. Procedures to test such relatedness include criterion, content and construct validation.   Also differential prediction studies may need to be carried out.   For instance the ability to lift heavy barbells may be a more successful predictor of job performance for policemen on patrol than for police women on patrol (Malbin, 1973) since they are likely to use different techniques for achieving the same ends.   A similar form of reasoning also applies to interest tests, namely, women and men in the same job may not have the same vocational interests.   As was said earlier, jobs as well as people become stereotyped, yet there may be no reason why a job cannot be done equally well or even better by using styles, strategies and tactics other than those stereotypically associated with it.

It is of some interest that the '1975 Annual Review of Psychology' reports that in the USA some 15-20 per cent of the 70,000 complaints against discrimination (not only based on sex but also race) alleged discrimination by unfair testing (Ash and Krocker, 1975).

Interviewing practices also require examination and
improvement.   The 'United States Civil Service Journal'
(Junker, 1973) suggests rules to go by, some of which
include:
    It is improper to give consideration to the following
    factors:
    (a) that supervisors or managers might prefer men,
    (b) customers/clients would not want to deal with a
    woman,
    (c) co-workers might object,
    (d) the job involves unusual working conditions.
    (One should add that it is equally improper to give
    consideration to these factors in the case of men
    also.)
    It is improper to place undue emphasis on certain con-
    ditions of employment in order to solicit declination.
The general rule is that one should treat women and men
applicants in the same way and both of course with respect
and courtesy.   It does not make it right to go through
the motions of asking men about their prospects for parenthood.   Males have little reason to believe that any
improper significance would be attached to the answer
whereas women do.   Finally, more women should be involved
in selecting, as well as in being selected, for all levels
of jobs in the organisation.

Career development, training and promotion procedures

Even if a woman manages to break through the discrimination which characterises the vocational guidance and selection stages of her career, she will still have further
discrimination to face at later career stages.   Barriers
to women's career development need to be identified and
countered.   Studies show that male administrators discri-
minated against females in decisions involving promotion,
career development and backing from superiors.   Not only
were equally well-qualified females less likely to be pro-
moted but they were also less likely to be chosen to
attend a professional training conference.   Furthermore,
'superiors' were less likely to support decisions believed
to be made by female subordinates than the same decisions
purportedly made by males.   Additionally, evidence indicates a dislike of women considered to be competent and
recognised as such (Hagan and Kahn, 1975).
    I have suggested elsewhere (Hartnett, 1976) that tac-
tics for countering these discriminatory practices include
the removal of dead-end jobs, by building promotion
ladders from unskilled to skilled and from clerical and

secretarial to executive and administrative work;   the
establishment of special training grades;   the creation of
part-time career opportunities with pro rata training,
travel and conference funding;   monitoring time to promotion for males and females;   reviewing the qualifications
of all staff thus creating a promotion pool of women and
men also of course, without their having to apply.   They
can withdraw if they wish.   Application for promotion is
based upon expectancy of success and since women have
every reason to have lower expectancies they will be less
likely to apply even when well qualified.   The creation
of a promotion pool can help counteract this understand-
able hesitancy.

In addition to improved access to training as it presently exists, the development of new types of training
programmes will also be required if men and women are to
enter into areas of employment from which hitherto they
have been virtually excluded.   The Sex Discrimination Act
permits positive discrimination in the area of training
presumably in an effort to compensate for the effects of
past discrimination.

An example of what might constitute a compensatory
training programme can be gleaned from looking at educational programmes for the deprived (Eyde, 1972).   In this
context, it has been noted that mechanical talent appears
to be a skill largely learned through a variety of out-of-
school experiences.   Special curricula have been devised
for girls and boys who have not been exposed to 'Barnyard
Physics'.   In these curricula girls tended to gain more
than boys so that it would seem that if females have equal
exposure to learning opportunities in technological areas
they are equally capable of developing these basic vocational talents.   It has been suggested that such programmes might be adapted for women seeking training in a
variety of fields including appliance repair and automo-
bile mechanics.

More effort should be made by training and educational
institutions to cater for needs of women desiring to
return to employment after an interruption.   These needs
may well include assertive as well as skill training.
Provisions for funding and help with child-care will also
be necessary (Brandenburg, 1974).

More women also need to be included in management
training schemes, and a paper in the 'Harvard Business
Review' (Orth and Jacobs, 1971) makes the point that organisations should look beyond the number of women employed to the need for women on the training staff who
can serve as mentors for women trainees.   The paper goes
on to say that many successful young men have worked under

the tutelage of older men but that women find few women
mentors and that it is a rare occasion for a woman to be
tapped for such special tutoring.   A recent report of a
study of women interested in management (Ecternacht and
Hussein, 1974) makes the same point.   The study showed
that 'women believed that graduate business education is
designed and administered by men for men students'.

Programmes of management training for women are now
being developed (Heinen et al., 1975; Alpander and Gutmann, 1976).   As well as teaching basic managerial
skills, these programmes are concerned to develop an
understanding of achievement-related conflicts and role
conflicts and in general to increase an awareness of the
interaction between sex-role stereotypes and self-con-
cepts.   'For the woman who is attempting to fill a role
which has been traditionally associated with the masculine
role identity, an integral part of any training needs to
focus upon her self concept.'   She will also need special
training in conflict management in order to be able to
deal constructively with the negative attitudes she is
likely to encounter from those men who regard management
and decision-making as a male preserve.

A report (Woods, 1975) of a series of interviews with a
number of American women who have 'made it' in management
positions is instructive and also somewhat depressing.   I
consider it to be evidence of the strength of the pressures upon the isolated statutory woman to adopt a masculine stereotypic style of management behaviour.   It
highlights the need to be very aware of the dangers of co-
option if one is going to attempt to be a role innovator.
However, the report crystallises some of the difficulties
and gives some sound advice like 'don't wait around for
someone to tell you what to do.   If you do they'll give
you something that's not very interesting', 'let management know that you are really serious' and finally 'don't
try to imitate men'.

Evaluating, defining and designing work and its environment

'Sex-role stereotyping' is indissolubly bound up with the
ways in which work is evaluated and designed and with the
demarcation between what is considered to be 'work' and
'non-work'.   A schoolboy was recently asked to write
down what he thought was the difference between 'work' and
'non-work'.   He wrote 'Work is what men do', 'Non-work is
what women do'.   This division of labour combined with
the higher valuation placed upon the male results in work

typically done by males being evaluated more highly than
work done by females. Attitudes and beliefs such as
these underly the selection of criteria used in job-eval-
uation schemes. A report by a NALGO Working Party
(NALGO, 1975) states that 'job evaluation as such does
nothing more than legitimise the status quo' and its use
unamended would 'ossify the difference between "men's
work" and "women's work" rather than reduce them'. Heavy
weighting assigned to formal training and education mili-
tates against women who often develop their skills on the
job without benefit of formal training. The NALGO report
advises a proper analysis of the skills content and responsibility in jobs traditionally performed by women.
Pressure of work and manual dexterity are two factors
which, they suggest, are not given due weighting. Others
might include *lack* of physical exercise, one-sided demands
from machines, coping with the peculiarities of customers
and clients, not to mention the boss. Furthermore, it
is not only on the shop floor that work which women do is
undervalued. This undervaluation extends to what are
known as semi-professional and professional jobs (Eyde,
1970; Prather, 1971) - and also to the home.
    Sex-role stereotyping also affects the way in which a
job is carried out. It influences the choice of style,
strategy and tactics. Being a manager is 'male' stereotyped and is thus seen as ideally requiring dominance and
aggression even though these traits may well be inappropriate, especially today when values are shifting away
from the traditional hierarchical roles characteristic of
bureaucratic structures. It is not a little fascinating
that, when the language of expertise is translated, it
transpires that improvements, in the climate and structure
of work organisations, recently being suggested by organisation development experts (Friedlander and Brown, 1974),
bear an uncanny resemblance to the characteristics specified by a member of the Women's Liberation Movement as
being necessary, from the other end of the spectrum, in
the organisation to which she belongs (Freeman, 1973).
    Besides influencing job content and job evaluation,
stereotyping, as we know it, reinforces the fantasy that
employment is a male demesne despite the fact that women
form 40 per cent of the working population. Bell (1974)
states that:
    In general, however, most investigators of the effects
    of environmental variables and working conditions on
    the performance and well being of workers have com-
    pletely ignored the presence of women at work. This
    has been true of both laboratory and field studies.
The consequence is that temporal and technical structuring

of work is designed to suit males and the present male
life pattern.
Broadly speaking two alternative approaches to the
design of work are available.   This first may be regarded
as the 'status quo' approach.   The male life pattern will
not be required to change.   Women solely will continue to
remain responsible for work inside the home but will be
faced with fewer obstacles to combining home responsibilities with employment.   The second alternative is a radical approach and will involve the emergence of a culture
with a person-orientated matrix of beliefs and behaviour,
characterised by a broader and more varied range of occupations and styles of life being available to both sexes
so that both may have greater freedom of choice in how
they arrange their lives.
Whichever approach is adopted more communal help with
child-care will be required.   Responses to the EEC Survey
(1975) indicate that both sexes believe that women's sole
responsibility for family commitments is the greatest
obstacle to equal opportunities.   Also required will be
adjustments in the work situation like flexitime, job
sharing and recognition of home responsibilities.   The
status quo approach requires that these facilities be
available to women only.   The radical approach would require their being available to men as well as women.
This approach is exemplified by the Swedish provision for
'parenthood' leave.   The male as well as the female has
a right to 'time off' in order that he may care for the
child and additionally, while the mother is giving birth,
the father may have leave to look after any other children under ten years of age.   Sweden and the EEC countries on mainland Europe generally make better provision
for nursery-school places than does Britain where provision is poor (OECD, 1975;   Tizard, 1976).
The radical approach will be essential if the EEC
Social Policy Directive 'Equality of Treatment between Men
and Women Workers' is to become a reality.   The directive
calls for a social policy which will facilitate the reconciliation of family responsibilities with professional
aspirations (Commission of the European Communities,
1975).
Such changes will probably result in a redrawing of
the boundary between what we at present regard as 'work'
and 'non-work'.   This would be in line with trends towards a preference for pluralism (Thomas and Bennis, 1972;
Davis, 1971) which is beginning to manifest itself in our
society and might also eventually help solve what we at
present perhaps wrongly regard as a problem of work motivation.   It would not be outside the bounds of possibil-

ity if one were to suggest that these changes in our cultural values could be interpreted not so much as a questioning of the value of work per se but rather as a demand
for a wider definition of what is regarded, rewarded, protected and encouraged as work of value.   Such work might
be thought to consist of a balanced contribution to the
three main spheres of activity in adult life - the Home,
the Civic demesne and Employment.   This pluralistic role
pattern is a prerequisite if our society is to adopt person-orientated values and thus cease to depend for its
continuance upon 'wage slaves' and 'housebound' women.

CONCLUSIONS

Sex-role stereotyping pervades work organisations.   It
manifests itself in a symbiosis of discrimination based on
sex and an instrumental approach to all employees irrespective of sex.   This symbiotic relationship implies that
any programme aimed at improving the quality of life, and
working life in particular, must include the elimination
of institutional sexism and thus facilitate for both sexes
the reconciliation of the roles of Parent, Citizen and
Worker in a more varied and flexible life-style.

8 Women and Psychiatry

Susan Lipshitz

> All human individuals as a result of their bisexual
> disposition and cross-inheritance, combine in them-
> selves both masculine and feminine characteristics, so
> that pure masculinity and pure femininity remain theo-
> retical constructions of uncertain content. (Freud,
> 1925)

INTRODUCTION

Women are more likely than men to manifest symptoms of
what we diagnose as 'mental illness'. These seem at one
level to reflect particular stresses and contradictions
of the life of a woman living in a twentieth-century in-
dustrialised society and patriarchal culture, and at
another level to be entirely 'natural', and determined by
the female role in reproduction. In this chapter I shall
discuss how implicit beliefs about women contribute to the
diagnosis and treatment of their illnesses by western
doctors, psychiatrists and therapists.
    As it is psychology that informs and reflects these
practices, I link my analysis of female illness to psychological theory and research. The documentation produced
by psychological research into existing male and female
gender stereotypes can, by definition, only describe the
status quo. For psychology does not originally found but
invariably redescribes its objects of investigation in a
way that is bounded by a cultural context, in which female
sex and feminine gender are thought of as inextricable.
Partly as a result of direct challenge from feminists and
female patients (Mind Conference, Women and Psychiatry
Workshop, for example), some psychologists have recently
questioned their own phallocentrism in the practice of
their profession (Chesler, 1970; Broverman et al., 1970;

Levine et al., 1974; Lipshitz, 1975; Litman, 1975;
Weisstein, 1969).   In addition to the changes in treatment structures they call for, I think it essential to
reinterpret familiar information like hospitalisation
statistics, or the reports of general practitioners' work
with female patients, in the light of an analysis of the
sort of knowledge that psychology propagates in relation
to sex differences.

If we confine ourselves to the present perspective of
psychology, we can only get a documentation of the existing situation and since sex-role stereotypes tell us
nothing about the history or origins of male and female
psychology, we are unable to analyse the processes whereby
they are maintained and reproduced.   It is the family,
medicine and psychiatry, education and the legal definition and enforcement of particular ideas of gender and of
health, that institutionalise and perpetuate familiar
notions of masculinity and femininity.   Since it is
theory as well as practice that determines the emphases
and hypotheses of our research, we need to rethink our
data if the apparent concern among psychologists, feminists and patients is really to lead to change.

HISTORICAL EXAMPLES

Both cross-cultural comparisons (Lipshitz, 1975) and
recent historical studies suggest there is an association
between 'femininity' and 'illness' that is long-standing
and does not vary simply with the social and economic
status of women in particular societies and particular
periods in history (Rosen and Rosenthal, 1975).   However,
the phenomenal form of 'feminine' illnesses does vary.
In nineteenth-century America, for example, women were
feared as carriers of disease (Ehrenreich and English,
1974).   Working-class women, cooks and prostitutes, were
seen as potentially passing on tuberculosis, typhoid,
venereal diseases and just plain germs.   Upper-class
women had hysterics (womb fever) or suffered interminable
lethargies.   In the literature of the English medical
profession of that time (Skultans, 1975) women were re-
corded as having particularly strong predispositions to
lunacy at certain times in their life-cycle - like pregnancy, or menopause - which were obviously related to
their sexuality.   Medical theory, however, discussed the
cause of maladies, some of which like hysteria were considered as close to insanity, in terms of imbalances in
the sexual organs or as due to women not exercising their
brains.   For despite some recognition that social, econo-

mic and psychological conditions, whether of suburban
isolation, financial deprivation, lack of contraception
or absence of sexual satisfaction, were associated with
such disorders, there was a tendency to see them as con-
firming evidence for the prevalent belief in female moral
inferiority or as deriving directly from aspects of the
female physique. The classic example of this must be
Jordan Furneaux's description of the battered-wife type,
when he argued, in 1886, that assaulted women have characteristically bent head and convex spine, clear and
delicate complexion and sharp tongues, a configuration
that in and of itself engendered violence in their
husbands.

CURRENT DEFINITIONS OF ILLNESS AND HEALTH

Although the symptoms of women patients are seen as less
somatic and more psychosomatic, it remains an open question as to what extent current definitions of 'illness'
are dependent on alterations in the conditions of women's
lives, and how much the tradition of diagnosis and treatment, though still operating a predominantly medical model
of madness, tends now to interpret symptoms in a more
psychological way.

   The existence of mental hospitals, as such, dates from
the end of the eighteenth century (Foucault, 1967), thus
limiting our perspective on what was publicly recognised
as illness and treated in the public domain as disease
rather than poverty, unemployment or crime. I suggest
that although such shifts may contribute to the way in
which women as a group are perceived as ill, there are
more fundamental links between femininity and madness
still to be elucidated (Mitchell, 1974; Chesler, 1972).
The course of development of a girl or boy-child must be
influenced by a culture, in which all terms, even language itself, are male referent (Lacan, 1958). The possible effects of such a culture cannot be ignored.

   Just how different is the diagnosed 'mental health' of
men and women? We get some indication of the official
situation from figures of diagnoses at hospital admission
in Britain (DHSS statistics - table 8.1). The figures
for all admissions in England 1970-1 are given.

Table 8.1 Diagnoses of psychiatric disorders of males and
females on admission to hospital (1)

Diagnosis	1971		1972	
	Male	Female	Male	Female
Schizophrenia	15,506	17,149	15,266	16,755
Depressive psychoses	7,331	16,623	7,200	16,206
Senile psychoses	3,014	6,632	2,727	6,429
Other psychoses	4,821	7,335	4,902	7,522
Personality and behaviour disorders	8,348	8,316	8,492	8,592
Psychoneuroses	7,821	16,038	7,998	16,089
Alcoholism	5,169	1,384	5,736	1,607
Drug addiction	1,035	567	1,141	555
Other diagnoses	1,780	2,427	2,565	3,433

The figures indicate that women are categorised more
often than men as depressed, psychoneurotic, psychotic, or
as suffering from non-specific disorders. That is to say
they turn feelings in on themselves rather than expressing
them openly, and are characterised by *states* of retreat
like the psychoses. These statistics are not surprising
if we think of the image of women in our society. For
stereotypic femininity describes women as more passive,
weak, expressive of emotion, dependent, illogical and
living in a world of feelings and far more concerned with
their own appearance than are men. The male stereotype
emphasises competence, activity, analytic ability and
independence - all characteristics that are considered to
be both socially desirable and adult. Broverman et al.
(1970) investigated American clinicians' perceptions of
healthy functioning and its relationship to the patient's
sex, using a questionnaire that listed stereotypic characteristics of both sexes. They were able to show that
male and female clinicians shared an implicit model of the
female. There was a contradiction between the demands of
femininity and the demands of adult health. A 'healthy
woman' was implicitly expected to be a non-coping childish
being in need of protection, emotionally volatile and thus
not an independent adult. Female patients suffering
partly from the restrictive definition of the feminine
stereotype are confronted with treatment which may not
only reinforce these restrictions but presents them as
ideals.
In the light of this, the DHSS figures cited above can
be explained by the different standards for male and

female health and by the different opportunities offered
by the stereotypes for the expression and display of particular symptoms and illness.   Women's illnesses conform
to the stereotyped ways in which women are expected to
handle anger and frustration, and women coming into hospital unable to cope, are diagnosed in accordance with
what would be expected in terms of the stereotype.   This
raises the question not only of the function of the stereotype as ideology, but also the function of hospitalisation.   This will be discussed in more detail in a later
section.   The comparable stereotypic 'deviance' for men
seems to be their criminal behaviour;   from the age of
fourteen onwards more males commit criminal offences.
However, it would be oversimplifying the issue of illness
or criminality to argue that a similar dynamic can be said
to underlie both.

Women are more frequently diagnosed as mentally ill
than are men, both in the community and in hospitals.   Of
all the agencies in Britain who encounter such illness,
perhaps the most influential group of professionals are
medically trained doctors.   Women frequently consult
their general practitioners, presenting with symptoms and
complaints of panic, fatigue, sleep disturbance, moodi-
ness, indecisiveness and weight loss.   One survey (Shepherd et al., 1966) showed that about one quarter of these
women, under forty-five years of age, reported menstrual
disturbances that have, for example, a fairly common mani-
festation in pubertal girls as anorexia nervosa.   There
are also the familiar crises of depression or minor psychotic episodes that are particularly likely after childbirth or at the time of the menopause.   Other psychosexual disturbances like frigidity, infertility or uncon-
summated marriages are reported but never included in
statistics (Friedman, 1962).

General practitioners are consulted by women most often
between the ages of fifteen and forty-four;   up to fourteen and after forty-five there is the same rate of consultation for both sexes.   Women tend to be hospitalised
for mental illness more after the age of twenty-five years
and many hospitalisations occur when nothing specific
seems to be *the* problem.   Most psychiatric symptoms are
reported by women when they are at the time of life to be
getting married, having babies and caring for their pre-
school children alone at home.   The General Household
Survey of a sample of the general population showed that
some women prescribe for themselves by retreating to bed,
as frequently as three days a week.   The times at which
most symptoms are manifest seems to suggest that puberty,
pregnancy, childbirth and the loss of the capacity to

reproduce at the menopause, are critical times for a woman
and those around her.   What is the meaning of these symptoms to women themselves, to their doctors, psychologists
and others?

EXPLANATIONS: BIOLOGICAL

Some psychologists like Gray (1971) and Hutt (1972a) have
claimed that greater male mental health is related to
biological differences and have assumed that genetic sex
determines the sequential unfolding of development from
the brain, the body and hormones to abilities and personality.   The personalities of the sexes are entirely different, it is claimed, because they are based on immutably
different genetic material.   The 'female brain' and hormone system are said to develop in such a way as to cause
the growth of an 'emotional' (i.e. over-emotional in the
sense already described as 'ill') feminine personality.
This simple biological determinism is reflected in that
psychological determinism (Deutsch, 1945) which sees character structure as functionally related to the female reproductive role.   Masochism, a pleasure in pain psychology, Deutsch claims, is useful to women who have to
endure menstruation and childbirth and who cannot enjoy
sex.

> The whole psychology of women suggests that this
> juncture between pleasure and pain was organised in
> the course of phylogenesis and that it created some
> measure of constitutional readiness in every woman,
> something we might call a masochistic reflex mecha-
> nism, ... it accompanies woman's reproductive func-
> tions and endows the psychologic component of child-
> birth with a definite character.

Presumably passivity and narcissim (love directed towards
an imaged ideal of oneself), that like masochism in extreme are pathologically 'feminine', would be said on
this argument to derive simply from the experience of
having a female body.   Chemical changes, like hormonal
fluctuations after childbirth or at menopause, can then
be said to *cause* states like depression but to say this
is to ignore that such associations are only correlations
and that hormonal fluctuations are responsive to external
as well as internal events.

EXPLANATIONS: PSYCHOLOGICAL AND SOCIAL

Clearly this deterministic chain is oversimplified since
it dismisses both the social influences on the production
and identification of symptoms and, at another level, ignores the contribution of the unconscious to their formation. Once located within a wider social and economic
context, women's illnesses have to be described as partly
the effect of situational pressures in a culture which
defines women relative to, and inferior to, men and partly
as experience with a culturally as well as individually
constructed meaning of life changes. In this view depression after childbirth would be seen as related to the
difficulties faced by a woman taking on the mothering role
for the first time (Melges, 1972), and menopausal difficulties would be seen in the context of the loss of what
is defined as a woman's primary social value - the capacity to reproduce (Bart, 1971a). A recent study of how
the unconscious contributes to the resolution of a woman's
experience of having her first child (Breen, 1975) suggests something of how complex the process is by describing its reverberations in the woman's inner world. Good
or bad adjustment to the mother role depends on many aspects of the woman's history such as her relationship to
her own mother, her body image and other conscious and
unconscious experiences that accompany the physiological
changes of pregnancy and post partum. Specifically,
Breen found that the women who were able to cope well with
becoming mothers were those who were able to see themselves as active and creative.

THE FAMILY AND ILLNESS

    The man who in consequence of his unyielding nature
    cannot comply with the 'culturally' required suppres-
    sion of his instincts, becomes a criminal, an outlaw,
    unless his social position or striking abilities
    enable him to hold his own as a great man, a 'hero'.
    (Freud, 1908)
    These psychological and social explanations of the
genesis of mental illness in women force us to place in a
wider context what are usually cited as 'sex differences'
in an unchallenged psychiatric classification system.
That context is complex, but it is particularly through
family life that definitions of permitted female psychosexual identity are instituted. The kind of stress that
the World Health Organisation report on 'psychosomatic
disorders', indicated as a key factor in the aetiology of

illness, for women clearly is related to the experience of
the family.   Hinkle and Wolf (1958) for example, found
that there was a positive relationship between the amount
of stress a woman reported and whether she was married
with children, living in a nuclear family situation.
Since the same relationship did not hold for men, it seems
that family life has particular strains for women (Gove
and Tudor, 1972).   Perhaps men act out their frustrations
in the sphere that leads them to the courts or to heroism,
rather than to hospital.   To say this is in no way to
equate the frustrations of the sexes, but rather is to
indicate a specific route to the suppression of instincts
that may be open for men only.   For women, there is no
option of heroism in the public domain.   Furthermore male
illnesses may be covered byaa wife's care whereas such
care would be unlikely to be reciprocated.   There is also
a sex difference in the rate of medical consultations;
women's maximum rate occurs when they are concerned with
the daily cares of life in their own families between puberty and menopause, whereas men show no such fluctuation
in their consultation rates (Shepherd et al., 1966).

If we consider the housewife's situation and its precise contribution to illness, we may get an idea of how
women's work affects their health.   Many women are housewives; most spend a few years of their lives being housekeepers and taking care of children under school-age,
full-time in the home.   Traditional descriptions of the
life of a housewife reflect the female sex-role stereotype.   Her house is made in her image and is judged as a
showcase of her personality, her marital relationship and
her fulfilment in this role.   The realities of the tasks
comprising housework define a woman's place in culture,
her economic role in society and her relationships to a
particular man and children.

It is part of the ideology of romantic love that women
should provide material and emotional services *over and
above* those which are necessary for her own and her
family's survival.   This ideology obscures the fact that
housework is an economic necessity (Mackintosh et al.,
1974) and is located within the unequal power relationship
of every marriage.   This lack of recognition affects the
quality of the experience of working in the home, doing
what is often repetitious, tiring and continuous work.
Since the work is not recognised as labour, or as ever
being skilled, and indeed is said to be preferable to work
outside the home which is called productive labour, the
woman's experience of frustration, exhaustion and narrowed
scope is negated.   It is this experience which contributes to the creation of those psychosomatic illnesses

previously discussed.   The frustration, psychologically,
is due partly to the fact, as Oakley (1974a) points out,
that housework is ill-defined and the term housewife is
misleading in so far as it implies the existence of a role
with specified obligations and rights.   Clearly this can
lead to extreme reactions of disorientation.   On the one
hand there are women who give up doing housework and
instead eat, watch television, drink or sleep their days
away.   On the other hand are those women who constantly
repeat their cleaning, expanding the work to fill the
hours available, unable to stop their constant activity.
It follows that mental illness can be seen as an active
process, rather than a thing, a disease passively borne.
For being ill carries not only stigma but is a quite
powerful way of getting attention, and relief from the
daily demands for care made of women in families.   Illness is an acceptable incapacity.   I suggest that the
symptoms sometimes express the deep rage and anger felt
in this and other situations of oppression, where the
overt expression of these feelings is unsanctioned.
Women are not simply victims;   their own and others' belief in their vulnerability is the counterpart of the
doctors' diagnoses and is reinforced by their experience
with medicine and psychiatry in ways too complex to be
called collusion and certainly through activities that
are not entirely conscious.

PRESENT FORMS OF TREATMENT: HOSPITALISATION

Since for some women the strains of ordinary living seem
to be coped with by a retreat to bed and by pills, perhaps we should see admission to hospital as a similar retreat, but in crisis situations.   An extreme but appropriate example is the hospitalisation of battered wives
which functions as a last resort when the issue is one of
life or death, and thus is defined as a health problem
rather than a social one.   Violence in marriage is not
new, but has recently become publicly recognised with the
provision of sanctuaries (initially in the form of Chis-
wick Women's Aid refuge) to which women can escape
(Pizzey, 1974).   No other state apparatus, neither
police, law, doctors nor hospitals, had helped these
women previously since it would have meant violating the
'sanctity' of a husband's legalised private ownership of
his wife and home.   While the battered wife is no longer
automatically seen as the 'guilty victim' described by
Furneaux, the suggestion still lingers in the research
reports of today, that women bring violence upon them-

selves (Gayford, 1975a, 1975b).   The problem may also be
seen as one of extreme male pathology, developed in the
context of violence in their own families, where the
fathers often beat the wives, and offered only this model
of how men related to women.   While obviously these individual childhood experiences contribute to the transmission and repetition of violence, it ought to be recognised that these marriages are close to the stereotypic
ideals of masculine and feminine sado-masochistic relationships prevalent in our culture.   This characterisa-
tion is given here, not to suggest that these marriages
are simply unhealthy in a limited sense, as it is evident that they are destructive, but rather to suggest
that they are extremes of the common cultural construc-
tion of masculinity and femininity.   These marriages can
be construed as a particular deadlock created in the
image of the ideal.   To *understand* that a woman can pro-
voke violence by nagging, and that a man can be provoked
by his own fears that she can evade his control (hence
the common accusation of infidelity), or be involved with
someone other than himself (hence many attacks occur when
the women are pregnant), is not to explain the problem
away nor to condone it as inevitable.   It does indicate
that this dynamic is the underlying potential of every
marriage.

In America hospitalisation seems to serve custodial
purposes (Chesler, 1972).   For not only, as in England,
are women hospitalised mostly between the ages of twenty
and thirty-seven, 'the prettiest years', but state asy-
lums are apparently used as 'dumping grounds' for women
considered redundant by society.   These hospitals have
been described as containers for the social problems of
the poor and black women who are most of the inmates.
That is to say, state hospitals are used as part of a
punitive process.   In England it seems rather that hospitalisation in some cases acts as a refuge for women
who are thus extracted from the stresses of their environment for a brief moment.

A comparison of the results from two studies is particularly relevant to this argument.   The first carried
out by Angrist et al. (1968) studied a group of female
patients and ex-patients.   The second (Brown et al.,
1958) studied male patients.   In the case of the males it
was shown that more patients returning, after hospitalisation, to their parents' homes did better in terms of
psychological adjustment than did patients returning to
the conjugal home.   It was concluded that mothers are
more tolerant of their sons' illnesses than are wives and
that the presence of his father freed the patient from

confrontation with his own inadequacies in relation to his
gender role.   For the women in Angrist's study, for whom
gender role is also a central aspect of their illness, the
option of going home to their mothers did not seem to be
open.   The patients studied were of the group previously
described as being at high risk of illness (age: twenty
to forty-nine, occupation: housewife) and the majority
were diagnosed as psychoneurotic.   Fifteen per cent of
the patient group re-entered hospital within six months
of their release with the same symptoms.   These patients
returned from the family situation of living with their
husbands, one that seems to have been little altered by
their presence or absence, so they were faced with the
forced choice of either repeating a pattern of illness or
of leaving home, again.   Re-admission in Angrist's study
seemed to be precipitated by incidents of 'bizarre behaviour', a curious mixture of conventionally unfeminine behaviour (what was considered by others to be excessive
swearing, sexual 'misbehaviour', violence towards others
and fears that others might harm her) as well as symptoms
I have already called stereotypically feminine (self-
attack, etc.).   Clearly none of the problems dealt with
here are purely physical or confined to a particular
group of sick people.   Rather they are recurrent and
widespread in the general population and relate to culturally defined psychological sex differences.

DIAGNOSIS AND TREATMENT RE-EXAMINED

The interpretation of symptoms will depend on the doctor
involved.   Most doctors are men (Table 8.2).   They
occupy the highest positions in the medical hierarchy as
consultants, a fact that is linked to the age structure
of the profession and to more men than women being involved in full-time careers.   In England in 1972 about
one twelfth of all hospital staff specialised in adult
mental illness.

Table 8.2 Sex ratios of medical staff

	General practitioners	Hospital staff	Total
Males	18,291	21,648	39,939
Females	2,738	3,821	6,559
All doctors	21,029	25,469	46,498

of unequal power.   This seems to imply that therapy
simply repeats the pattern of family relationships.   I
consider that a crucial additional aspect of the therapeutic process is that the therapist interprets the
relationship as it proceeds, thus offering the possibility
of complex, habitual functioning being understood and
changed.

This is just not possible in a group, whose basis for
meeting is primarily an attachment to some simplistic
notion of the democratic process.   While consciousness-
raising groups provide support for the exploration of
painful emotions as well as freeing anger and making private emotions accessible to comparison with those of other
women, they do not abolish the need for a structured long-
term commitment with a therapeutic aim, any more than they
abolish the need for theory to integrate the insights of
political group activity with strategic demands.

The initial rejection by feminists of all professional
psychology was based on more substantial grounds than
simply that it tried to make *tolerable* what are really
intolerable aspects of capitalism and patriarchal culture.
There was a desire to see the spread of democratic, self-
help practices, that seemed to necessitate rejecting *all*
situations of inequality.   So sometimes groups rejected
psychotherapy because it was assumed to perpetuate unequal knowledge, an argument that is based on drawing a
very crude analogy between hypnosis, said to be the exploitation of a powerless subject, and the psychoanalytic
situation ('Red Collective', 1973).   In Szasz's work the
solution offered for this perceived imbalance of power
was said to lie in making therapy another service paid
for by a consumer, in order to give both participants
equal interest in the interaction and to prevent abuses
of power.   Szasz's ideas about mental illness, like those
of Chesler who warned of the danger that therapy for women
with a male therapist can become a repetition of the worst
exploitative aspects of the marital situation, seem to
refer to a specifically American experience and ideology
in several ways.   In the first place, psychotherapy in
the tradition of ego psychology, is the common experience
of many American, urban middle-class women.   While obviously at times the relationship is abused and this must
not be ignored, it is a facility that many women in other
countries might well envy and prefer to the physical
treatment they, at present, receive.   At least it offers
the potential for change and insight within a relationship
with another person.   Second, the way to counter such
abuse does not seem to me to make it yet another free
enterprise situation, but rather to see that struggles for

better conditions as inaugurated by patients' unions or
other organisations, ensure the protection of civil
rights.   If my earlier distinction between hospitalisation as custodial or curative is tenable, then it is
clear that the struggle over each set of conditions of
treatment will be different, just as it will vary through
history depending on the prevalent ideology, technology
and the state's interest in who gets defined as 'ill'.
For example in the nineteenth century there was good
reason to struggle for the recognition of the physiological ('scientific') basis of 'mental illness' against it
being defined as moral aberration.   Perhaps today the
emphasis is on struggling for recognition of psychosexual
factors in the aetiology of female illnesses rather than
regarding the issue as mythic, and struggling for the
wider availability of treatments other than physical
ones.   There has been debate recently about the forms
of therapy that could be considered 'feminist'.   The
assumption at first, that women treating other women
would be better than men treating women, was based on a
simple faith that all women had similar experiences and
would be prepared to admit to this, identify with each
other and share their pain in a way men could not.   Pat-
ently this is not the case since women as well as men
share a particular view of their sex, and there seems no
reason to assume that female solidarity is easier to
create than any other bond.   Women have the potential
for understanding female problems but it does not necessarily follow that such a consciousness develops, and to
rely on immediate feeling experience to fight ideological
formations is to ignore that this is their terrain.   That
is to say, what is experienced as 'natural' is not necessarily, in fact is unlikely, to be indicating what is
really problematic.   Similarly, identifying with someone's experience may not help them, and could indeed
hinder them from articulating their difficulty.   This is
a problem with self-help therapies.   Rather than explain-
ing illnesses away, or denying or validating experience
by joining the patient, we should use our insight into
the genesis of illness to recognise its complexity and
its basis in persistent cultural structures and in the
unconscious.   The preconditions now exist for rethinking
the situation of women's illnesses within a patriarchal
order, whose effects are visible in the marks of the
symptoms and features of feminine psychology like low
self-esteem, covert expression of anger and frustration,
etc.   Clearly drugs and hospitalisation perform an often
necessary holding operation, but one that is particularly
unsatisfactory because it does not challenge the source of

the problems manifest in women as mental illness.   It is
asking too much of psychiatric and psychological treatment
to expect that it should make this challenge.   So long as
psychological theory, on which psychological treatment is
based, does not include the analysis of symptoms in the
context of their social and historical conditions, and the
myths and stereotypes of our gender ideals, we shall not
begin to see how to make changes.

NOTE

1   The diagnostic categories in table 8.1 are not as
    clear-cut as would appear from the table, but roughly
    speaking schizophrenia comes from the Greek for split
    mind and is classically said to be characterised by
    incoherence, disorganisation of thinking, feeling and
    action, and the living of life in phantasy rather than
    reality.   The psychoses are disturbances in relation
    to reality and include paranoia, manic depression and
    schizophrenia.   The neuroses are psychical conflicts
    with origin in childhood and neurotic symptoms are
    compromises between wishes and defence against them.
    Neuroses include physical disorders of presumed psy-
    chogenic origin.

9 Clinical Aspects of Sex-Role Stereotyping

Gloria K. Litman

INTRODUCTION

In the preceding chapter, Susan Lipshitz has argued that
implicit cultural beliefs in the 'essential' nature of
women directly affect their diagnoses, treatment and dis-
posal when they are presented, or present themselves, as
being ill. In this chapter, I will discuss the processes of sex-role stereotyping in relation to two specific
diagnostic categories: depression and alcoholism. The
contention of this chapter is that the processes of sex-
role stereotyping play a crucial, albeit subtle, role in
the aetiology and maintenance of depression in women and
that these same processes operate more explicitly in the
clinical perception and management of the female alcoholic.

DEPRESSION IN WOMEN

An overview

What is characterised as depression presents a major
problem in terms of the number of people presenting for
treatment. It also has the highest mortality rate of
any personality disturbance (Becker, 1974). In addition
to psychiatrically diagnosed depression, there is some
evidence from Brown's (1975) work that depression may be
prevalent, although undiagnosed and untreated, in women
in the general population, particularly those in lower
socio-economic groups.
    In the clinical setting, the depressed woman presents
as dejected, sad and apathetic. Tears may be frequent
and copious, although some women have described themselves
as being beyond tears - too empty even to cry. The

appetite is usually greatly diminished and sleep is disturbed.   Sexual interest is lost.   Physical symptoms such as aches and pains may be reported, but the outstanding physical symptoms are fatigue and inertia.   Concentration is poor and there is a preoccupation with hopelessness and helplessness.   Speech may be slow and halting and the conversation usually revolves around an exaggeratedly negative self-punitive concept of worthlessness, inadequacy and uselessness.

Despite the multitude of theoretical, empirical and popular publications dealing with the subject of depression, many workers (Grinker et al., 1961; Wittenborn, 1965; Mendels and Cochran, 1968) agree that in fact we know very little about its essential nature, how to define its diverse manifestations nor how to categorise, classify and diagnose various types of depression. Indeed it has not yet been established whether there are several depressive illnesses or whether depression as an illness syndrome exists at all.   However, there does seem to be agreement that depression is regarded by professionals as a complex rather than a unitary phenomenon. The consensus is that depression is comprised of complicated phenomena which manifest themselves in a variety of ways in diverse populations.   It is also generally agreed that, aside from alcoholism which will be discussed in a later section, there are few forms of psychological distress which produce the same degree of debilitation and misery as does depression.

Incidence

Women have been found to have a higher incidence of depression than men (Beck and Greenberg, 1974).   The findings of higher rate of psychological disorders for women than for men have been questioned by Phillips and Segal (1969) on the grounds that these results do not reflect real sex differences in frequency of disturbance but only the greater reluctance of men to admit to unpleasant affects and sensations.   In other words, they attribute these findings to the fact that it is culturally more acceptable for women to admit their difficulties than for men.   This 'expressiveness of women' argument has been challenged by Gove and Tudor (1973) on the grounds that (a) their data indicate that men probably had higher rates of mental illness prior to the Second World War;   (b) there is a consistent finding that in certain marital categories men continue to have higher rates;   and (c) the pattern of differential rates in mental breakdown holds

constant regardless of whether the selection is made by
the professional community, by self-selection or by dis-
interested researchers in community surveys. Clancy and
Gove (1974) looked at such sources of response bias as
perceived trait desirability, need for social approval,
etc. on a psychiatric rating scale by a general population sample. They hypothesised that if sex differences
in rates of mental illness were primarily the result of
the differences in the social desirability of reporting
symptoms between men and women, this should be reflected
in the perceived social desirability of the symptoms on
the rating scale. When sources of response bias were
examined, it was found that perceived undesirability of
symptoms and the need for social approval had little
effect on the relationship between the sex of the respondent and the number of symptoms reported. Their results
indicated that the higher rate of treated mental illness
among women is not a product of women being more willing
to discuss their problems. In fact, their results on
'naysaying' or denial suggest these statistics may even
tend to mask higher rates in women.

If we consider some of the theories about depression
in the context of women's roles in western society, the
culturally approved readiness of women to admit symptoms
of distress as an explanatory framework seems much too
facile and simplistic. Based on Broverman's (1970) research, it has been noted that there might in fact be an
actual greater incidence of mental illness in women related to greater sex-role conflict experienced by them
(Fodor, 1974). On the other hand, it has been suggested
(Beck and Greenberg, 1974) that if depressions in males
'masked' by physical symptoms were accurately diagnosed,
the discrepancy between male and female rates for depression would be diminished. Despite these speculations,
the fact remains that the large numbers of women seeking
help for affective disorders clearly indicates that depression is a serious health problem for women.

Theories of depression

It is not within the scope of this chapter to review
models of depression which are biologically or biochemi-
cally based and the interested reader is referred to
Becker's (1974) review. However, since no concrete
evidence has been adduced to identify an underlying meta-
bolic, genetic or constitutional basis to distinguish
depressive 'disease' (Wittenborn, 1965) recent approaches
emphasising socialisation and learning processes in the

aetiology and maintenance of depression seem far from
appropriate for the study of what remains a gender-related
disturbance.

Exaggerated feelings of low self-esteem and self-worth
are among the outstanding characteristics of depression.
According to such social psychiatrists as Sullivan (1953),
self-evaluation is largely a reflection of the appraisals
of significant others during the early socialisation process. If the significant others, who largely serve as
mediators of reality for the uncritical child, provide
conflicting identification models and reinforce appraisals
which are excessively low or excessively high of the
child's worth, then self-esteem is more irrationally and
crudely regulated with a strong susceptibility to reality
distorting moods (Greenson, 1954).

According to Jacobson's (1953, 1957) analysis, these
moods pervade all aspects of personality function: feelings, ideas, overt behaviour, physiological processes and
the perception of oneself and the world.   I have discussed elsewhere (Litman, 1971) the mechanisms by which
depressed moods serve to reduce drastically the range of
cues assimilated and thus bias thought and perception so
that feelings of low self-esteem and low self-worth are
maintained.

Following Freud's analogy between mourning and melan-
cholia Chesler (1972) maintains that many women are in
mourning for something they never had - a positive conception of their own potential.   Her line of argument implies that historically women have been relegated to roles
of low and servile social status.   Therefore, women
share an attitude of resignation with which the hopelessness of depression can be equated.   Chesler believes
that the symptomatology of depression is merely an inten-
sification of those traits which normal socialisation
processes in our society induce in women: passivity,
dependence, self-deprecation, self-sacrifice, fearfulness, failure and helplessness.

Feelings of helplessness as the core of depression have
been stressed by many theorists.   In a classic work,
Bibring (1953) conceptualises the basic mechanism of
depression as the 'ego's shocking awareness of its helplessness in regard to its aspirations'.

Depression and 'learned helplessness'

In a series of carefully controlled experiments, Seligman
and his colleagues (1975) have investigated the correlates
of helplessness.   The central idea of Seligman's work is

that there are many aspects of depression which can be
equated with 'learned helplessness'.   Learned helplessness was first explored in the laboratory where animal
and human subjects were exposed to unpleasant conditions,
shock, loud noise, insoluble problems, etc. which they
could not control.   In other words, any response they
made was futile.   No matter what they did, the shock or
noise could not be terminated by their action.   According to Seligman, it is not the trauma itself which produces the symptoms, but the learning that there is no
response which they can make in order to alleviate or
control that trauma.   This learning undermines the incentive to respond and produces profound intereference
with any motivation to act at all.

In a typical experiment, three groups of students were
exposed to a loud noise.   The first group could learn to
turn off the noise by pressing a button.   The second
group had uncontrollable noise, that is, there was no
connection between their pressing the button and the ces-
sation of the noise.   The third group were not subjected
to noise at all.   After several exposures to a specific
condition the students were then place in a situation
where they could learn to control the noise.   In order
to escape the noise, they had only to move their hands
from one side of the shuttle box to the other.   The
group which originally had the option of turning off the
noise and also the group which received no noise soon
learned to control the new situation.   In contrast, the
group which originally received 'uncontrollable noise'
sat passively and failed to learn how to escape.   Similar results were obtained in experiments using animals.

In the laboratory the most important factor which produced 'learned helplessness' was the repeated experience
of being in uncontrollable situations.   There were also
two other factors which seemed to affect the results to
some extent.   If people were *told* that their performance
was governed by chance, the probability that they would
attempt to learn to control the stimuli was lessened,
regardless of the actual conditions.   Second, it was
found that people who believe that their rewards and
punishments in life occur by chance and are beyond their
control were more readily rendered helpless than people
who believe they can control their rewards and that skill
will count.

How can these findings be related to the phenomena of
depression?   According to the learned helplessness model,
depression is not generalised pessimism but pessimism
specific to the ineffectiveness of one's own actions.
The results of another series of experiments carried out

by Seligman supply evidence which supports this model.
In this series of studies, groups of depressed and non-
depressed people were placed in tests of skill and chance.
In both tests, the subjects were exposed to the same
pattern of success and failure.   Initially depressed and
non-depressed people did not differ in their expectations
of success.   However, they differed greatly once the two
groups had experienced success and failure.   The non-
depressed people, believing that their responses mattered
in the skill task, showed much greater changes in their
expectations for success for that task than they did in
the chance task.   In contrast, the more depressed people
were, the more likely they were to believe that their
responses mattered no more in tests of skill than they
did in tests of chance.

A third series of experiments indicates that depression
and laboratory-induced helplessness may impair some types
of problem-solving ability in a similar manner.   Again
three groups of people were used: half of each group were
depressed, half were not.   One group was given escapable
noise, the second inescapable noise, the third no noise at
all.   On a subsequent problem-solving task, depressed
subjects who were given no noise did very badly as did
non-depressed persons given uncontrollable noise.   For
depressed subjects who had experienced escapable noise,
this experience seemed to reverse their negative cognitive
set during the remainder of the experiment.   This depressed group did far better on the task than the depressed
group who were given no noise at all.

The deficits shown in depression and the deficits produced in non-depressed subjects by uncontrollable events
were parallel.   In the laboratory, learned helplessness
in animals produced the following symptoms: (a) passivity, a generalized lack of response; (b) difficulty in
learning that response brings relief; (c) lack of agres-
sion; (d) weight loss, loss of appetite, sexual deficits.
In humans, the symptoms produced were passivity and reduced problem-solving ability.   These characteristics are
parallel to those of depression as outlined at the beginning of this section.

Thus there is strong support for the learned helplessness model, perhaps not of all types of depression, but
certainly of many of the types of depression seen clini-
cally and also those experienced by women in the general
population who were interviewed by Brown and his colleagues (1975).

Sullivan's (1953) view of feelings of self-worth as
reflections of early parental attitudes coincides with
Seligman's view that in order to 'immunise' against

depression, infants must be taught that there is synchrony
between their responses and their environment.   The model
would predict that those individuals who are particularly
resistant to depression or who are resilient and recover
easily from depression would have exercised a large degree
of mastery over their lives.   People who have had extensive experience in controlling the course of their own
lives will tend to see the future optimistically.   A life
without mastery, on the other hand, would produce vulnerability to depression.   The learned helplessness model
would also predict that people who are rewarded constantly, regardless of their response, may be rendered similarly helpless since there is no synchrony between their
responses and their environment.

Learned helplessness and sex-role stereotyping

If we examine sex-role stereotyping within the framework
of the learned helplessness model, the greater incidence
of depression in women does not seem surprising.   During
the early socialisation process, when sex roles are
learned, many female children are taught that their personal worth and survival depends not on effective responding to life situations but on physical beauty and appeal
to men, i.e. they will have no direct control over the
circumstances of their lives.   In all too many instances,
the only control they are taught is to manipulate men,
originally the father, to obtain their needs.   Therefore
their response is not only indirect but also the results
are unpredictable since their needs are interpreted and
mediated secondhand.   Throughout childhood and adolescence, they are subjected not necessarily to physical
trauma, but to parental and institutional supervision
that both restricts their alternatives and shelters them
from the consequences of any disapproved alternatives
they choose to pursue.   This restriction is also experienced by boys, but to a greater extent by girls, as the
Newsons (see chapter 4) have described when discussing
'chaperonage'.
    In adulthood, the social roles allotted to most women -
namely secretaries, nurses, assistants and particularly
those duties inherent in the roles of housekeeping and
motherhood, while not necessarily subservient in themselves, are in current practice organised so that the
actual decision-making and power are dissociated from
them.   Therefore, they afford very little direct or
relevant control over the environment.   It is reasonable
to argue that women who have learned that their own be-

haviour is unrelated to their subsequent welfare, lose their ability to respond effectively and to learn that responding produces relief.

Summary: women and depression

This section has attempted to examine the part played by sex-role stereotyping in the aetiology and maintenance of depression in women.   Early socialisation processes for women set up stereotypic role expectations which emphasise passivity, helplessness and dependence as appropriate feminine behaviours and attitudes.   When viewed within the context of the 'learned helplessness' model of depression these roles will tend to lead to an inability to respond directly and effectively to the environment and therefore to subsequent pessimism and despair about personal effectiveness, adequacy and self-worth.   The social roles allotted to women further reinforce feelings of inadequacy, helplessness and low self-worth since opportunities for gaining direct control over the environment are limited by a structure which assigns tasks and positions to women, but from which the crucial decision-making and power have been removed so that the results of actions are unpredictable.   There is a synchrony between responses and outcomes.

WOMEN AND ALCOHOLISM

> Women represent important social and moral symbols that
> are the bedrock of society.   And when angels fall,
> they fall disturbingly far.   We would rather have them
> in their place which is another way of saying that they
> define and make our own place possible and even more
> comfortable.   (Hirsch, 1962)

The current conceptualisations and treatment of women and their abuse of alcohol represents, in microcosm, the stereotype which is attached to women in society generally.   The woman alcoholic, the 'fallen angel', has violated popular stereotypic conceptions of what is considered suitable and appropriate feminine behaviour.   The consequences of this deviance from expectations are harsh.

Incidence

The incidence of alcoholism among women has been changing over the last sixty years.   There were very severe prob-

lems of alcoholism and heavy drinking at the beginning of
the century, with the gin shops contributing heavily to
the abuse of 'mother's ruin' among the 'dangerous'
classes.   With the First World War and the passage of
legislation to control licensing hours, the number of
cirrhosis deaths dropped sharply for both women and men.
The decline in cirrhosis deaths (1) among women continued,
particularly during the Second World War but started
rising again during the 1950s.   This rise has continued
until the rates for cirrhosis deaths among women almost
match   those of men in the 1960s and 1970s (Office of
Home Economics, 1971).

Table 9.1   Psychiatric hospital admissions by sex and
diagnostic group 1971

Diagnosis	All admissions			First admissions		
	Total	Male	Female	Total	Male	Female
Alcoholic psychosis	1,208	892	316	374	279	95
Alcoholism	6,309	4,977	1,332	1,942	1,569	373

Source: Regional Hospital Board statistics

The figures in table 9.1 show the numbers of men and
women admitted to regional hospitals who were diagnosed
as alcoholics or suffering from alcoholic psychosis.
What these figures suggest is that alcoholism is primarily a male problem, but this situation is by no means as
clear-cut as the figures would indicate.   Reports published by various Councils on Alcoholism (Merseyside,
1976;   Glasgow, 1975;   Manchester, 1975) report that the
ratio of women to men seeking help for excessive drinking
problems has   increased sharply.   The ratio is now reported as 1:3 as compared with the 1:6 ratio reported
five years ago.   It is estimated that the ratio may be
1:1 in private practice (Lindbeck, 1972).

Some sources have suggested that there is a direct
relationship between the changing roles of women in society and the rising incidence of alcoholism among women -
that 'alcoholism represents the ransom woman pays for her
"emancipation"' (Massot et al., 1956).   This is not
borne out by the figures at the beginning of the century
when the more traditional roles of women did not prevent
them from drinking.   Another explanation might be that
changing social norms serve to 'emancipate' the hidden
drinker so that she may present herself for treatment if
the threat of stigmatisation is reduced.

Perception of the female alcoholic

That this stigmatisation still exists is evident from a
recent general population survey carried out by the
Maudsley Alcoholism Pilot Project (Cartwright et al.,
1975).   Two hundred and forty-four people were asked
the following questions:
(a)   What were the effects of someone regularly drinking
too much?
(b)   What were the particular effects of women drinking
too much?
Only 43 of the 244 respondents thought the effects of excessive drinking were the same for men and women. (2)
The vast majority clearly saw women as being less likely
to experience health problems or to become aggressive but
more likely to experience marital difficulty and loss of
personal esteem and respect.   Perhaps most significantly,
there was much more likelihood of moral judgements being
made about women who drink excessively than about their
male counterparts.   There was clearly a double standard
being used.   Women who drink to excess were seen as
being vulnerable to becoming sexually promiscuous and this
was felt to be more disgusting and degrading than violent
behaviour in men.   This is supported by a Finnish study
(Haavio-Mannila, 1967) which shows that fidelity and tee-
totalism are the characteristics required of women.
From an historical perspective these attitudes are not
surprising.   From earliest times, Biblical injunctions
and Roman law linked women's drinking with sexual 'irreg-
ularities'.   Although lurid case histories have been reported (Karpman, 1948) there is no real evidence that
promiscuity or homosexuality is characteristic of alcoholic women (Johnson, 1965).
Because the role of women has been equated with the
stabilising functions of wife and mother, the drunken
woman seems to present a special threat.   The stereotype
is very clear: a woman who has deserted her feminine role
to the extent that she has become an alcoholic is considered to have deserted respectability in every area of her
life.   This has been confirmed elsewhere (Litman et al.,
1976).   Using a person-perception technique, the results
indicated that a general population sample held the female
alcoholic in low esteem.   These perceptions in the general population may indicate that professionals, too, may
hold a deprecatory or negative attitude towards female
alcoholics.   This follows from the observation (Bloombaum et al., 1968) that strongly held cultural beliefs
tend to colour the attitudes of both therapists and researchers, even when there is research data which contra-
dicts the cultural belief (Stotsky, 1955).

Psychopathology in female alcoholics

There is widespread belief among many professionals in
the field (Johnson, 1965; Johnson et al., 1966; Lisansky, 1957) that women alcoholics are far more abnormal
and show far greater personality and emotional maladjustment than do men alcoholics. This view is based on the
rationale that since excessive drinking is a far greater
social taboo and has a far greater social stigma for
women than for men, only deeper emotional pathology could
elicit its expression. If we take a closer look at what
these statements actually mean there would appear to be a
serious lack of definition in this area. When the woman
alcoholic is labelled as 'much more abnormal' and 'more
emotionally disturbed' than her male counterpart, does
this mean that men and women were compared on the same
norms of behaviour, or as seems more likely from other
evidence (Broverman et al., 1970) that women alcoholics
deviate more from the norms of what is considered 'feminine' behaviour than male alcoholics do from 'masculine'
behaviour?

Three indicators of emotional disturbance have been
used to support the argument that female alcoholics are
more disturbed than males: (a) the number of psychiatric
admissions; (b) the number of suicide attempts; and (c)
the incidence of marital breakdown (Curlee, 1968; Rathod
and Thompson, 1971).

The argument that a greater number of psychiatric admissions is proof of greater emotional maladjustment is
suspect. If 'woman alcoholic' qua 'woman alcoholic' is
automatically seen as being more emotionally disturbed,
it is likely that she will be hospitalised more quickly
and more frequently than her male counterpart. It should
also be taken into account that women in general have a
higher probability of being labelled 'sick' and that there
is a tendency for labels also to reflect deviations from
socially acceptable stereotypic behaviour patterns (Fodor,
1974). However, Horn and Wanberg (1973) have shown that
in their group of women alcoholics there was a good level
of social integration and, of those who were employed, 80
per cent never missed work because of drinking and managed
to retain their jobs.

This contradiction highlights the fact that there may
be a valid distinction between the 'public' and the
'secret' woman alcoholic (Lindbeck, 1972). Those who
drink in public are more likely to be labelled alcoholic
by hospitals, alcoholism clinics or outpatient clinics
and it is these women who are included in the official
reports. The woman who drinks in secret is more likely

to be seen in private clinics or by general practitioners.
This type of secret drinker usually performs well socially.   She is rarely seen drunk in public, and does not
come to the attention of the law, is seldom included in
the statistics and is a problem primarily to herself and
to her immediate family.   There may be a long conspiracy
of silence on the part of the husband and other members
of the family.   When the husband does acknowledge to himself that his wife is drinking excessively, he tends to
keep this knowledge secret for fear that disclosure will
reflect on his own masculinity and his ability to control
his wife's behaviour.

There is conflicting evidence about the number of suicide attempts among alcoholic women.   Rimmer et al.
(1971, 1972) did report a greater frequency of suicide
attempts among alcoholic women than among alcoholic men,
but attributed this finding to the higher incidence of
these attempts in those women with affective disorders.
On the other hand, Glatt (1961) found no significant differences in the frequency of suicide attempts between the
men and women alcoholics in the group he studied.   But
even if it could be demonstrated that women alcoholics
have a high ratè of suicide attempts could we attribute
this solely to greater emotional disturbance without
taking into account the pressures from social stigmatisation and disapprobation which the woman who is labelled
an alcoholic must endure?   The social isolation of these
women has been discussed by Beckman (1975) who describes
how alcoholic women in family settings are kept hidden by
their families.   Even Skid Row women show more solitary
drinking patterns than their male counterparts and tend
to remain sensitive to the social disapproval associated
with public drinking (Garrett and Bahr, 1973).

The marital instability of alcoholic women has been
cited as an indicator of emotional disturbance (Rimmer et
al., 1971, 1972; Curlee, 1970).   Marital discord and
domestic stress have been reported (Sclare, 1970) as pre-
cipitating factors for hospitalisation in women, while
employment stress was reported by men.   This would suggest that regardless of the upheavals and distress which
the alcoholic male in the family may create, he is considered a serious case for treatment only when his job is
in jeopardy.

This use of marital instability as an indicator of
greater emotional disturbance in the alcoholic woman
simply does not take into account the fact that the marital relationship is an interaction.   To highlight this,
let us consider the marital patterns between the non-
alcoholic wife and alcoholic husband versus the non-

alcoholic husband and alcoholic wife (Curlee, 1968;
Orford, 1975).   The wife of an alcoholic seems to be
more likely to stand by her husband and, unless an unusually pathological relationship exists, devote herself
to helping him recover, at least as far as her own understanding enables her to be helpful.   On the other hand,
the husband of the alcoholic woman is more likely first
to shield her and deny her illness until he can no longer
tolerate it, then to leave her.   The reason for this
difference is partially economic.   The husband is more
likely to be filling the role of wage earner, at least
to some extent, and the wife is dependent on him, particularly if there are children.   Even more important, the
wife is expected to adjust to her husband's and children's
needs and problems and to maintain the home.   Failure to
meet the needs of her family and to maintain the home is
a mark of failure for a woman, both psychologically and
socially.

The attitude of professionals and the layman to the
spouses of alcoholics is markedly different.   The non-
drinking spouse of the alcoholic husband is regarded with
suspicion in that she may be in some way contributing to
her husband's drinking - 'she drove him to drink' - 'she
has an unconscious investment in his continuing to drink'
- while the husband of the alcoholic wife is seen as a
long-suffering, deprived person who deserves much sympathy
for putting up with his wife's inadequacies.

Treatment and prognosis in alcoholic women

An important correlate of the perception of the woman
alcoholic as being more emotionally disturbed than her
male counterpart is that she is also seen by professionals as being more difficult to manage or to treat in
clinical settings and her prognosis is judged to be
poorer (Bateman and Peterson, 1972;   Curlee, 1971;   Glatt,
1961;   Pemberton, 1967).   There is some evidence that
treatment regimes which were designed specifically for
male patients simply do not transfer successfully to
females (Curlee, 1971).

Most treatment facilities and approaches are modelled
to meet the needs of men and very little has been done to
adapt them to the needs of women.   It is hard to tell
whether the underlying assumption is that what is thought
will work for men will work for women, or whether it is
simply a sign that treatment centres have been generally
unwilling to accept fully the problem of alcoholism among
women.   In any case the emphasis in the treatment of

alcoholism has been placed on group therapy.   In group
settings, great attention is paid to identifying with the
group, establishing strong group ties and loyalties and
self-esteem through a sense of belonging and being accepted.   Women alcoholics rarely seem to find the meaningful comradeship and warmth which seem to help the men
so much.   Women may sometimes relate well to relatively
few people within the group but, in general, the feeling
of real membership and participation seems to be missing.
A part of the explanation may be the attitudes of the men
in the group, who are not completely immune to society's
harsh judgment of the female alcoholic.   But this does
not entirely explain away the problem.   Whatever the
reasons, much of the evidence which exists suggests that
group therapy is more effective with male patients and
that women are less responsive to group therapy but look
for individualised one-to-one relationships (Curlee,
1971).   However, behavioural techniques focused on the
modification of low self-esteem in groups of women alcoholics are being developed (Burtle, Whitlock and Franks,
1974).   The preliminary findings indicate that using all-
women groups and focusing on building up self-esteem may
be a fruitful approach.

Sex roles and alcoholism

Sex-role confusion has been postulated as a factor in the
development of alcoholism in women (Lisansky, 1957;
Mogar et al., 1970) with Sherfey (1955) suggesting that
about 10 per cent of these women have a strong masculine
identification.   However, it has also been found that
alcoholic women consciously accept traditional female
roles and express concern about their inability to perform the traditional roles of wife and mother and are particularly concerned about failure to maintain viable marital relationships (Kinsey, 1966).
    The evidence for sex-role confusion emerges from
studies which attempt to look at preconscious or unconscious levels of personality.   Wilsnack's work (1973)
indicates that while alcoholic women appear to value the
mother role more significantly than non-alcoholics, their
drawings on the Franck Drawing Test were more like the
drawings of men.   Wilsnack concluded that while there is
great desire to be more feminine, the unconscious sex-
role confusion causes them to feel inadequate as women.
On the other hand, Parker (1972) reported that conscious
femininity, as measured by role-relevant preferences, was
lower in alcoholic women.   However, 'unconscious femi-

ninity' as measured by terms relating to anger, fear and
pity was higher in women alcoholics. It seems apparent
from studies cited above that the notion of sex-role confusion per se and the instruments designed to measure this
confusion are muddled indeed. The assumption that a
drawing test can possibly measure unconscious pre-verbal
sex-role identity is indeed a tenuous one, but the measurement of 'unconscious femininity' in terms of emotion-
ality makes far more of a statement about the stereotypic
prejudices of the researcher than anything he can say
about his subjects.

Female physiology and alcoholism

The findings of physiological associations with the development of alcoholism seem relevant to this discussion.
It has been reported (Podolsky, 1963; Wilsnack, 1973;
Belfer et al., 1971) that the onset of excessive drinking
in some women is associated with pre-menstrual tension,
menstrual difficulties, post-partum depression or menopause.   There is apparently a relationship between alcoholism and a high incidence of gynaecological-obstetrical
problems like infertility, miscarriages and hysterectomy.
As with most other features of alcoholism in women, the
interpretation of these relationships becomes highly complex.   Did these difficulties in fact cause the excessive
drinking or is it that the same social mores which may
make it difficult for a woman to accept her distinct physiological functions also may predispose her to alcoholism
in an attempt to solve a wide range of problems?   Until
researchers have adequately separated the effects of excessive drinking on physiological functioning from primary difficulties in physiological functioning that may
precede or cause excessive use of alcohol, this remains an
open question.   It is possible too that women may link
'female troubles' and the onset of alcoholism in an
attempt to excuse their alcoholic state and make it more
palatable to the often male medical therapist.

Self-esteem, identity and life stages

Some studies (Kinsey, 1966, 1968; Wood and Duffy, 1968)
have indicated that the self-concept of alcoholic women
is characterised by low self-esteem and feelings of inadequacy.   Even among alcoholic women themselves, it is
not unusual to hear the judgment that there is nothing so
disgusting as a drunken woman (Litman, 1975a).   In fact

Blane (1968) has postulated that the source of alcoholism
in women may well be the preoccupation with being inadequate and inept.   In this regard the   connection between
alcoholism and the 'empty nest syndrome' has been explored
by Curlee (1969).   For many women, both depression and
alcoholism seem to be triggered by the middle-age identity crisis when there is a dramatic change in their role
as mother and wife.   For women who may be unusually dependent upon their husbands and children for their identity
and feelings of worth and purpose in life, the children's
growing up and leaving home can be traumatic indeed.
Alcohol may be used to blur the feeling of emptiness,
purposelessness and no longer being needed.

This illustrates the fact that an 'identity crisis' is
not something which one experiences in adolescence and
then has solved for all time.   It can occur at many
periods of life and, for many women, may frequently be
associated with the menopause, which is itself often co-
incidental with their children leaving home.   Women who
seem to be particularly at risk are those who are not
clearly defined as persons in their own right - many never
seemed to have thought of themselves except in relation to
their husbands or children.   Until very recently our culture has fostered the belief that women could only find
'real happiness' by devoting themselves sacrificially to
their husbands and children and by living vicariously
through them.   Bart (1971a) argues that implicit in this
was the guarantee that such self-sacrifice would reap
rewards.   When this payoff doesn't appear, the women who
have lived by the 'rules' are bewildered and bereft.
Their whole life-pattern seems meaningless.   They have
been 'conned' and there is no pot of gold at the end of
the rainbow.   Whatever the merits of the argument, much
more attention needs to be devoted to the problems which
result when a woman forms an identity by defining herself
in terms of others and what happens when these defining
relationships are altered.

In contrast to women who find their identity only
through the wife-mother role, there are a number of women
who strive to take their place on their own merits in
what is still a masculine orientated society.   For the
woman who is seriously pursuing a career, there are many
problems which could contribute to excessive drinking and
to alcoholism.   Women who are, in a sense, competing
with men on their own terms may also find special pressure
to 'drink like a man'.   Women engaged in highly competitive, high risk occupations are subjected to the same
pressures as their male colleagues to indulge in heavy
male drinking patterns, thus putting themselves at risk.

Recently, with the entrance of married women into full-
time occupations, the burden of carrying the dual role
of full-time employment and major responsibility for the
management of the home may also add stress.

Summary: women and alcoholism

It is clear that the 'woman alcoholic' is as gross a
stereotype as any other and is further contaminated by
moral and punitive judgments concerning what is appropriate female behaviour in our society. The professional
view of greater emotional disturbance and difficulties in
management of these women may deleteriously affect their
treatment. Considering the accumulating evidence that
expectations influence outcomes (Rosenthal and Jacobson,
1968; Sutherland and Goldschmid, 1974) this 'set' or
assumption concerning female alcoholics has counterpro-
ductive implications for treatment and its outcome. The
lay person's view of the female alcoholic as immoral and
promiscuous may equally diminish the chances of successful prognosis in the case of these women. After treatment, which may be carried on by professionals with a
biased view, these women are returned to a society which
regards them with suspicion, scorn and condemnation.
What is urgently needed is the development of treatment
modalities which enables these women to regain their
self-esteem and feelings of self-worth and furthermore a
concerted campaign geared to attitude change towards
these women not only in the general population but also
at the political level, so that suitable allocations for
treatment and rehabilitation tailored to their needs are
made.

CONCLUSIONS: WHAT CAN WE DO?

As has been shown in this chapter, depression and alcoholism in women represent strategies which are used in
an attempt to cope with social roles and cultural expectations that are narrow and inhibiting. Both depression
and alcoholism in women are characterised by low self-
esteem and an exaggeratedly punitive self-concept. Self-
reliance and self-respect in the long run can be engendered only by changing early socialisation processes and
their stereotypic conceptions of sex-role norms. However, this is no solution for the women who are now
suffering and debilitated. Expanded role repertoires
(e.g. by using assertive training techniques) must be

taught and the acquisition of these repertoires must be
constantly reinforced.   Furthermore awareness of alternative life-styles should be encouraged and support for
these provided.

NOTES

1 While cirrhosis of the liver deaths are not a precise
   measure of alcoholism within a population, they can
   serve as a broad indicator of changes over time.
2 While it would be more precise to state that women
   were actually compared with a hypothetical 'someone',
   the results indicate that this 'someone' was interpreted by respondents as being male.

10 Sex-Role Stereotyping in the Social Security and Income Tax Systems

Hilary Land

'The social view that the woman's place is at home in the unpaid care of household and family finds its expression in the tax rates and social security benefits set forth in the legislation of many countries' concluded a recent report of the Manpower (sic) and Social Affairs Committee of the OECD (1975, p. 113).   The United Kingdom, although a member of the OECD, was not one of the ten countries who chose to participate in this study.   Nevertheless, an examination of both its social security system, which includes contributory national insurance benefits and means-tested supplementary benefits, and the range of fiscal policies which enables the taxpayer to offset allowances against his (or less often, her) taxable income in respect of some specified family responsibilities, will reveal similar underlying assumptions.   These assumptions have been modified only slightly by the changes contained in the Social Security Benefits Act 1975 and the Social Security Pensions Act 1975.

'The family is not a word of precise significance' wrote the Royal Commission on the Taxation of Income and Profits (1955, p. 54) twenty years ago.   Nevertheless, precise or not, for decades our income tax and social security systems have embodied assumptions about the extent and nature of family relationships, in particular the economic relationship between husband and wife, and parents and children.   Some of the assumptions are different.   For example, the anthropologist looking at our social security system might be forgiven for concluding that the extended family died in 1948.   Then under the National Assistance Act (superseded by the Social Security Act in 1966 which created the Supplementary Benefits Commission) children ceased to be responsible for their old and infirm parents and the national insurance legislation limited adult dependants to one per family.   Turning to

the tax system s/he would find extended kinship networks
still flourishing in the system of allowances and reliefs
which recognise that children do support their elderly
parents as well as other more distant relatives.

Some differences are not surprising because until the
Second World War income tax payers (of which there were
only four million) belonged exclusively to the middle-
and higher-income groups.   (In 1938, average male earnings were £180, the single person's tax allowance was
£220.)   The means-tested public assistance (the fore-
runner of national assistance, now supplementary benefits) and the contributory national insurance scheme only
covered the poor and the lower, middle-income groups.
(The earnings limit for membership of the National Insurance Scheme was £250 in 1919 increasing to £420 in
1940.)   Today, however, income tax payers and social
security recipients are not distinct groups and the numbers of individuals involved in both systems are far
greater.   For example, in 1974 there were over 21 million
income tax payers, more than 10½ million recipients of
national insurance benefits, and in any month 2¾ million
claimants of supplementary benefits.   Both single people
and married men now start paying income tax when their
earnings are well below not only those of the average
male worker but below the income of those on supplementary benefit which is often taken to be the 'official'
poverty line.   (The single person's tax allowance for
the year 1975/6 was £625.   The average earnings of the
male industrial worker during that year was over £2,500.)
As the two systems now overlap there are pressures to
avoid duplication.   It is likely in the future that the
special needs of some groups will be met by cash benefits
instead of by relief in the tax system.   It is important
therefore, both from the point of view of equity and consistency to examine new developments in social security
benefits and to see what assumptions about men's and
women's roles are being made.

Some of the assumptions common to the income tax and
social security systems will be examined.   These relate
to the needs and responsibilities presumed to arise from
marriage for it is here that the strength and persistence
of the concept of female dependency in every social class
is revealed.

THE MARRIAGE RELATIONSHIP AND THE TAX SYSTEM

The income tax system has treated husband and wife as a
single taxable unit since William Pitt first introduced

taxes on income in 1799.   The tax was a proportional
one so such treatment made no difference to the total
tax bill.   At that time a woman retained virtually no
control over her property on marriage so the Finance Act
of 1842 stating that for income tax purposes the 'profits
of any married woman living with her husband shall be
deemed the profits of her husband', was consistent with
the position of women in law.   However the Married
Women's Property Acts passed between 1882 and 1907 gave
married women the right to control their own property,
income and earnings but this had little impact on the
treatment of women in the income tax system.   The Board
of Inland Revenue justified this on the grounds that 'the
Crown is not mentioned in the [Married Women's Property]
Act and is consequently not bound thereby' (Royal Commission on the Income Tax, 1920, Evidence, vol. 1, p. 332).
The tax system has, therefore regarded married women as
'incapacitated persons' along with infants, lunatics,
idiots and insane persons (Income Tax Act, 1918, S. 237).
This has meant that the liability for payment of a married woman's income tax has rested upon her husband, and
for tax purposes a woman's unearned income is still regarded as her husband's, although since 1972 husband and
wife have had the choice of being separately assessed and
taxed on their earnings.

The principle of aggregation has not disappeared from
the tax·system.   It was defended by the Royal Commission
on the Taxation of Income and Profits in 1954 on the
grounds that the family constitutes a common spending
unit and shares a common standard of living.   However,
they defined 'family' very narrowly because the majority
of the Royal Commission were opposed to extending the
principle of aggregation to include children's income,
apparently having some doubts as to whether children in
fact shared the same standard of living as their parents.
In other words marriage was, and still is, regarded as
the key relationship and the assumption that husband and
wife have an equal share in the 'joint purse' created by
their combined income has gone unchallenged.   It is interesting to note that the practice for apportioning the
marital property when the marriage ends has in the past
more often been based, not on equal shares, but on giving
the wife one third and the husband two thirds.

Lloyd George introduced a system of graduated rates of
tax in 1909.   This had important consequences for the
operation of the principle of aggregation.   If a married
man is taxed on his own and his wife's *joint* income, the
married couple pay more tax than two single people living
together unless the husband is allowed to offset a bigger

allowance against his taxable income than his single col-
league. A system of the former kind might be held to
penalise and therefore discourage marriage. Arguments
along these lines were used in favour of giving a bigger
personal allowance to married men than to single men at
the end of the First World War. However, the stronger
argument appeared to be that the presence of a wife should
be recognised as a burden which reduced a man's 'taxable
capacity'. The Chancellor of the Exchequer told the
House of Commons when introducing his Finance Bill in
1918, 'I propose to make the children's allowance apply to
a wife also ... and to extend a similar allowance to all
dependants who are incapacitated' (H.C. Debates: vol.
105, col. 708, 1918). One Member suggested that a wife
was worth two children, but the House seemed satisfied
with equating a wife with a child or disabled person and
that year £25 (the value of the child allowance) was
added to the personal allowance of any married income
tax payer whose earned income together with his wife's
earnings was less than £800 a year. By 1920 the allowance in respect of a wife had been increased to £90, the
single person's allowance being £135 (which was almost
equal to a male semi-skilled manual worker's annual
income). Neither changed much over the next twenty
years. During the same period, the husband of a woman
who was in paid employment was allowed a maximum of £45
earned income relief to offset against her earnings for
it was recognised that expenses were incurred in having
paid employment. Marriage therefore made little difference to the tax position of the couple who were both
earning moderate incomes but it increased the husband's
tax bill when both had unearned incomes.

The entitlement of all married men to the married
man's allowance irrespective of whether their wives are
in paid employment or not, is not in fact consistent
with the principle of aggregation. In giving evidence
to the Royal Commission on the Income Tax in 1920 (vol.
1, p. 127), the Assistant Secretary to the Board of Inland Revenue argued in defence of aggregation that:

It is beyond question that in the immense majority of
cases where the wife has a separate income she contributes to the common funds either by the actual
merger of part or all of her income, or by bearing
expenses which would otherwise fall upon the husband.

If that is so, and there is considerable evidence to show
that this is and has always been the case (ever since
1882 when a woman's income and earnings ceased automatically to belong to her husband from the moment she married him), then it cannot also be argued that, as the

Tax-Credit Study group (Select Committee on Tax Credit,
1973, p. 360) recently did that 'a man with a wife to
support has clearly a lower capacity to pay tax than a
single person'.

This view of the dependent wife was however in accord
with the prevailing assumptions about women's proper
role and reflected the situation of many middle-class
women during the inter-war years.   By the end of the
nineteenth century marriage had become something 'to be
afforded' by middle-class and respectable working-class
men.   Marriage bars had been introduced in the Civil
Service, in teaching and in many professions: many educated women had to choose between marriage and a career.
The 'idle' wife was a symbol of prosperity and success
and those women who attempted to combine marriage with
paid employment were accused of being less efficient
workers.   For example, in 1925 it was argued in defence
of the marriage bar in teaching that 'the duty of a married woman was to look after her domestic concerns ...
it was impossible for her to do so and act effectively
and satisfactorily as a teacher at the same time' (Reiss,
1934, p. 257).   This remained the situation until the
beginning of the Second World War.   Nevertheless, women
comprised a third of the labour force throughout this
period although the majority appearing in the official
statistics were single.   (For a discussion of the
reasons why the extent of married women's paid employment
was under-estimated see Land, 1975b.)

The Second World War brought about an increased demand
for labour, and women, including married women, were required to meet this demand.   For the first time, therefore, the income tax system had to take account of married women's incentives to work outside the home.   This
applied to women from all social classes for tax thres-
holds had been reduced and tax rates increased, thus
bringing the average working-class couple within the
clutches of the income tax collector for the first time.
Increases were therefore made in the amount of earned
income relief a married woman's earnings could attract
so that in effect, while the husband continued to claim
the married man's bigger allowance, the equivalent of a
single person's allowance could be offset against the
wife's earnings.   As an official historian of the Second
World War (Sayers, 1956, p. 113) later wrote:

> As a concession to stimulate the movement of married
> women into employment the Chancellor in his 1942 budget
> accepted a proposal, originating in the TUC, that the
> married woman's earned income allowance should be
> raised from £45 maximum to £80 maximum.   At most

income levels that mattered for the attraction of
married women into war production, *husband and wife*
would henceforth be treated more favourably than if
they were single people.   (My italics)

However, notice that incentives for married women to take
up paid employment were not made in a way that recognised
any reduction in their dependence on their husbands.   It
was the tax position of the *man*, not the woman, which improved upon marriage and he continued to benefit whether
or not his wife continued in paid employment.

The influx of married women into the labour market
during the Second World War was not a temporary phenomenon.   In 1951, one in five or nearly 3 million married women were counted as being in the labour market
compared with one in eight in 1931 and one in seven in
1938.   During the next two decades the number increased
dramatically.   By 1971 the numbers and proportions had
doubled so that in over 5½ million households both husband and wife were earning.   In 1975 a Government review
of women and work (Department of Employment, 1975a, p. 3)
concluded:

the prospect of being continuously available for employment over a period of 20 or 30 years is now the
normal pattern, and no longer the rarity it was, say,
between the wars ... whereas in 1931, the older married woman in employment was a rarity, it is now normal
for married women to work, and withdrawal from the
labour market and return to it is the general pattern.

Throughout the post-war period the tax position of the
married couple in which both husband and wife are earning
has remained better than that of the 'cohabiting' couple
except for a minority attracting high rates of tax.   The
justification for this was seen in the 1950s by the Board
of Inland Revenue, for example, to be based entirely on
the needs to attract married women into the labour market.

The present favourable treatment of the married woman
at work is the result of successive concessions made
on incentive grounds.   The position under which the
husband retains the full married allowance although
the single allowance is given to the wife in addition,
is difficult to defend either on grounds of logic or
of taxation principle.   (Royal Commission on the Taxation of Income and Profits, 1951/5, Evidence, vol. 4,
p. 198)

It is interesting to see that it is the married woman who
is perceived to be favourably treated, rather than her
husband, although the opposite is the case.

Those concerned with the tax system remain aware of
the need to retain incentives for married women to take

paid employment.   The Green Paper on Proposals for a
Tax-Credit System in 1972 (p. 18), stated 'the needs of
the economy require the continued employment of large
numbers of married women and the system must be such
that they feel it is worth their while going to work'.
It is also argued that a household with two earners
incurs more expenses than a household with one and so it
is appropriate that given the same total earnings the
former should pay less income tax than the latter.   Thus
irrespective of whether or not his wife is contributing
to the household income a married man claims the larger
personal allowance, and the equivalent of single person's
allowance is offset against any earnings his wife has.
(This has the undoubtedly unintended consequence that
in theory the tax position of the couple with *one* earner
only is more favourable if the earner is the wife, for,
with her husband's consent, she can offset against her
earnings the married man's allowance *and* earned income
relief to the value of the single person's allowance.
He can only offset the married man's allowance.   However, this effect is practically negated by the fact that
women's earnings are still considerably lower than men's
earnings, and so, especially if there are children, the
total value of tax allowances will probably exceed her
earnings but not his.   Therefore in order not to 'waste'
the tax allowances it is better that the husband is the
earner, particularly when there are dependent children
in the family.   In practice then the tax system does not
encourage role reversal.)
     Although the value of the married man's allowance rela-
tive to the single person's allowance declined during the
1950s and 1960s, until 1970 when reduced rates of tax were
abolished and the taxpayer started paying tax at the standard rate, reduced rate relief could be claimed against
both husband and wife's earnings.   (Not to have done so
would have been administratively complicated for employers
operating the PAYE scheme because they would have had to
have distinguished between married and single female employees.)   In 1974 the cost of the married man's allowance was £1,100 million in foregone revenue.   (The
allowance has increased since then so the cost for the
year ending April 1977 may well be of the order of £1,500
million (H.C. written answers, vol. 887, col. 397, 1975).)
Under the Finance Act 1971 married couples were given the
choice of being separately taxed on their earned income
but in the first year only 17,000 couples took the option
because unless their joint income is very high, to choose
independence increases their tax bill (H.C. written answers, vol. 868, col. 475, 1974).

The assumption that the husband is and should be the primary breadwinner is underlined by a number of other practices.   For example, even if the house is jointly owned it is assumed that the husband will claim the tax relief on the interest element of the mortgage payments. The father claims the tax allowances in respect of his legitimate children unless he agrees that the mother may claim them.   The deserted wife may find that her husband continues to claim these allowances although he is contributing nothing towards the children's maintenance. In such circumstances the Board of Inland Revenue may exercise their discretion and allow the mother to use these allowances.   However, they do not require evidence that a father is actually contributing to his children's keep.   Proof that they are his legitimate children or that he has custody of them is all that is required. Only the husband can sign their joint income tax return unless the wife has opted for separate taxation.   Should too much tax be deducted from a woman's pay, the rebate may be sent to her husband because legally it belongs to him.

The way in which dependent relatives allowances operate provides further evidence that it is the marriage relationship which makes a woman a dependant as far as the Board of Inland Revenue is concerned.   Under the present system a taxpayer supporting a dependent relative may claim tax relief on up to £100 a year.   Normally, a dependent relative must be either incapacitated by old age or infirmity, have an income the same as the national insurance basic pension, and be in receipt of some income from the taxpayer concerned.   However, the taxpayer's mother-in-law, irrespective of her age or state of health, is by definition a dependent relative if she is widowed, divorced or legally separated.   The unmarried mother, however, is not.   She will have to prove old age or infirmity, on the grounds that because she has never been dependent on a husband, then her son or daughter cannot be regarded as replacing the maintenance provided by a former or deceased husband.   In 1973, tax relief was claimed in respect of 1¼ million dependent relatives at a cost of £35 million in foregone revenue.   This was three times the cost of the family income supplement for that year (Select Committee on Tax Credit, 1973, p. 60).

This treatment of unmarried mothers is not just a hangover from the past when attitudes toward this group were more punitive.   Two recent tax concessions make the same distinctions.   In 1974 tax relief on mortgages for second homes was abolished except for the son or daughter buying a house for a mother or elderly or infirm father.

Once again mothers of any age are included provided they
have been married and the marriage has ended. Similarly, when sold, second homes are subject to Capital Gains
Tax, and this will include the dwelling bought by the son
or daughter of an unmarried mother. The dwelling bought
for a separated, divorced or widowed mother will be exempt
from this tax. Motherhood alone then does not make a
woman dependent in the eyes of the Board of Inland
Revenue: marriage does.

There are many other ways in which the assumptions
about men's and women's roles are embodied in the tax
system. The development of housekeeper's allowances
illustrates this very clearly. The allowance, which was
introduced in 1918, was initially only for widowers with
dependent children, and the housekeeper having care of the
children had to be a female relative and resident in the
taxpayer's home. The allowance was £25, the same as
that for a wife. A year later a widower without children could claim for a female relative acting as his
resident housekeeper.

The reason for this extension appears to have been the
largely sentimental one that when a man's wife dies he
cannot be expected to give up his home and therefore
he must have someone to look after him ... [the widow]
... is already accustomed to look after the home herself,

explained the Board of Inland Revenue in their evidence
to the Royal Commission on the Taxation of Profits and
Income 1951-5 (vol. 4, p. 55).   In 1920, however,
widows with children were allowed to claim such an allowance and rather surprisingly in 1924 childless widows
were included.   This last measure was regarded later
as an anomaly for which it was 'difficult to find any
rational purpose' as the Inland Revenue Staff Federation
told the same Royal Commission, (vol. 3, p. 18) because
'it is not the death of a spouse but the lack of a *wife*
who can keep house which may necessitate a housekeeper'
(my italics).

During the Second World War the housekeeper's allowance was extended to include any taxpayer with children
who employed a resident housekeeper. The definition of
housekeeper was broadened to include non-relatives but
she still had to be female. The married man could only
claim if his wife was permanently incapacitated and if
the taxpayer was a woman with children then to claim she
either had to be totally incapacitated or supporting herself by full-time paid employment. Kingsley Wood,
Chancellor of the Exchequer at the time, resisted pressure to include other persons besides widows or widowers

without children because he too considered that extension
had been 'unwise'.   The condition that the housekeeper
be resident was thought to be important because if it
were removed 'it is likely that the allowance would become a vehicle for assisting the employment of charwomen
and daily helps for purposes unconnected or only remotely
connected with the care of children' (Royal Commission
on the Taxation of Income and Profits 1951-4, evidence,
vol. 4, p. 56).

By 1960, these views had changed, but only slightly.
Amory in his budget in the House of Commons (H.C. Debates, vol. 621, col. 61-2) in 1960 introduced

a new allowance of £40 for a widow or widower who has
a child or children eligible for child allowance and
who has no resident housekeeper.   The new allowance
will be available also to single persons who are responsible for young children or who have no housekeeper
but would qualify for housekeeper's allowance if they
had one.   [The housekeeper's allowance at the time
was £75.]

The Government refused, however, to consider giving a
married woman an additional allowance if she had an incapacitated husband.   As Boyle explained to the House
of Commons (H.C. Debates, vol. 621, col. 1558):

though the work of looking after an invalid husband
may be a serious tie to the wife, it does not prevent
her from undertaking *the normal responsibilities* of
looking after the children and it is the fact that
some wives are unable to perform these responsibilities that lead to the housekeeper allowance being
given in the first place.   To give an allowance
where a man is incapacitated would be to give an
allowance not for the care of the children, but in
respect of the husband's disability.   (My italics)

There is little doubt that married women are assumed to
be responsible for domestic work and moreover, this work
should remain *unpaid*.

Seven years later the £40 allowance for single parents
was increased to £75 and now following the proposals of
the Finer Committee on One-Parent Families, they receive,
in effect, the same personal tax allowance as a married
man.   The resident housekeeper's allowance remains and
she still has to be female.   In 1973, allowances on behalf of 100,000 housekeepers were claimed at a cost in
foregone revenue of £1½ million.   Another allowance
introduced in 1920 also remains.   This was an early
form of constant attendance allowance because it was for
the taxpayer 'who by reason of old age or infirmity is
compelled to depend upon the services of a daughter

resident with and maintained by him or her' (Finance Act
1920, S. 22).   The allowance has only ever applied to
daughters, other relatives even if female do not qualify.
However, this particular form of tax relief is very
little used now and in effect has been replaced by the
cash constant attendance allowance introduced in 1972
and the new non-contributory invalid care allowance.
The poor have had to wait rather longer than the rich
before their specific needs were recognised.

THE MARRIAGE RELATIONSHIP AND THE SOCIAL SECURITY SYSTEM

The origins of the social security system and the circumstances of the majority of its beneficiaries provide
little justification for the automatic definition of man
as paid worker, woman as full-time housewife.   Skilled
working-class men were able through their trade unions
to bargain for wages high enough, in the words of a
speaker at the TUC Annual Conference in 1875, 'to bring
about a condition ... where their wives should be in
their proper sphere - at home - instead of being dragged
into competition for livelihood against the strong men
of the world' but the many unskilled, casual and irreg-
ular labourers could not do so.   For example, Rowntree
(1922) in his first study of poverty in York at the end
of the nineteenth century decided to classify families
according to family income rather than by the wages of
the male earner because the wages of wives and children
'frequently amount to *more* than the earnings of the
head' (p. 56, my italics).
     However, the first national insurance scheme started
by Lloyd George in 1911 copied the Friendly societies
whose membership was drawn mainly from the more skilled
and regularly employed sections of the labour force.
Their normal practice was based on the concept of the
male breadwinner, paying benefits to the sick or injured
man but excluding benefits for his wife and family.
     Thirty years later Beveridge revised and extended the
national insurance scheme to all income groups in his
report which forms the basis of much of the post-war
social security legislation.   The expanded scheme was
still firmly based on the assumption that marriage permanently removed women from the labour market.   Housewives were treated as a special class, a dependent class,
and were given the choice of not paying full contributions, relying instead on their husbands, each of whom
contributed (Beveridge, 1942, p. 50) 'on behalf of himself and his wife, as for a team.'   Ignoring the not

inconsiderable evidence that neither women themselves,
nor the economic policy-makers, regarded women's war-
time employment as a temporary measure, Beveridge states
(1942, p. 50) 'the attitude of the housewife to gainful
employment outside the home is not and should not be the
same as that of a single woman.   She has other duties.'
     Under the Social Security Pensions Act 1975 the choice
of not paying the full contribution (known as the married
woman's option) is to be gradually withdrawn.   In 1978
when this Act will be implemented, for the first time a
married woman who pays full contributions will receive
unemployment and sickness benefit at the same rate as a
man or a single woman instead of at two-thirds the full
rate as at the time of writing.   She will also be able
to leave a widower's pension in some circumstances.
While women are at home looking after children, sick or
elderly relatives, they will continue to be included in
the insurance scheme.   Provided they contribute fully
for 20 years, counting their contribution record prior
to marriage as well as during marriage, they will get a
full pension in their own right when they retire.   If
they contribute less than 20 years their pension will be
proportionately reduced.   These changes remove some of
the inequalities which married women have experienced in
the social insurance system for over half a century.
     However, the concept of female dependancy has not been
weakened.
     The measures in the 1975 legislation do not recognise
that the majority of men and women already share the
economic support of the family.   (In 1971, in more than
half of all married couples both husband and wife were
in paid employment.)   At the same time it is still
assumed that a woman's primary tasks lie in the home and
so the sharing of child-care responsibilities is dis-
couraged.   At last it is recognised that families may
depend on a woman's earnings but only when the husband
cannot work.   For example, the widower's pension for
men of working age will only apply to the sick and disabled man whereas all widows regardless of age, health
or employment status receive a benefit.   A married woman
can only get additional unemployment or sickness benefit
for her husband and her children if he cannot work because, as a Minister of State to the Department of Health
and Social Security said (Brian O'Malley, 1975):
     it is normal for a married woman in this country to be
     primarily supported by her husband, and she looks to
     him for support when not actually working rather than
     to a social security benefit.
It is not sufficient to show he is not working as is the

case when the unemployed or sick man is claiming an
allowance for his wife and in any case he automatically
gets additional allowances for any dependent children.
The recognition of home responsibilities as being a
valid reason for being out of paid employment thus entit-
ling the person concerned to be credited with insurance
contributions will include women and single men.   However, although at the time of writing, the regulations
had not been published, it seems that the married man
who *chooses* to stay at home to look after the children
while his wife takes paid employment will not be credited
with contributions in these circumstances.   As Brian
O'Malley (1975) explained:

> What we are concerned with in national insurance terms
> is not to reflect role duplication, but merely to pro-
> vide for *the genuine case of involuntary role reversal.*
> (My italics)

The needs of men and women who wish to, and do, share
roles are ignored.

These rigid assumptions about men's and women's roles
within marriage are also incorporated in the new non-
contributory benefits included in the Social Security
Benefit Act 1975 to help the sick and those who care for
them.   Moreover, they extend them to those alleged to
be cohabiting.   The invalidity pension is for those too
disabled or ill to work, and the married woman or the
woman cohabiting with a man as his wife will have to
demonstrate that 'she is incapable of performing normal
household duties'.   (The DHSS are taking two years to
define 'normal household duties'.)   The invalid-care
allowance will benefit single men and women who have
given up paid employment (i.e. earn less than £6 a week)
to care for an elderly or infirm relative who is in
receipt of a constant attendance allowance and so is
considerably incapacitated.   This ignores the fact that
many (one in ten of all working women compared with one
in eight of full-time housewives) have to combine this
task with paid employment.   In any case the allowance
will not be large enough to live on.   But worse, the
married woman or the woman cohabiting with a man is excluded altogether.   The role of the married or cohabiting woman is clear: she must do the housework and care
for any children, or sick or elderly relatives.

The system of non-contributory means-tested benefits
also only supports men and women in particular roles.
For example, the sick or unemployed married woman or a
woman deemed to be living with a man as his wife has no
right even to apply for supplementary benefits, for it
is assumed the man in the household is supporting her.

A man when he is ill or unemployed has the right to apply
for supplementary benefits although his wife's earnings
will be taken into account in assessing his needs because
for the purposes of supplementary benefits as in the tax
system, a man's and his wife's resources are aggregated
and regarded as his.   The Family Income Supplement introduced in 1971 to help the low-wage earner and his or
her family specifies that, where there are two parents to
qualify for the benefit, it must be the father who is in
full-time employment.   Until 1975, a lone father was required to register for work in order to get supplementary
benefit.   A mother left on her own with children has
never been obliged to do so.   Women with children on
supplementary benefit have not been subject to the wage
stop, the device for reducing the level of benefit to
that of a person's 'normal earnings'.   Low-wage-earning
men were because

> it would be unfair to the man who was working but earn-
> ing less than the supplementary benefit level if his
> counterpart who was unemployed received a higher
> income. (Supplementary Benefits Commission, 1974, p.
> 77)

However, more women than men earn wages less than supplementary benefit levels.   This difference is only expli-
cable in terms of the assumptions made about men's and
women's attitudes to paid employment.   The preservation
of incentives to take paid employment are important for
a man, particularly if he is a low-wage earner, but not
for a woman with children, because as Beveridge (1942)
said 'she has other duties'.

It is clear then that the social security system like
the tax system only supports men and women in specific
roles.   Even role sharing, not to mention role reversal,
often results in heavier taxation or reduces entitlement
to social security benefits.   Throughout both systems
the assumption is that women become dependent on men once
they marry or cohabit: breadwinners are male and only
women have responsibilities for domestic work.   Reading
the social security legislation it would be difficult to
deduce that in 1971, one in six households (excluding
pensioner households) relied on a woman's income for
support and that the majority of these households contained dependants (see Land, 1976).   It would also be
hard to realise that the 'typical' family consisting of
man in full-time employment, woman full-time housewife
and two dependent children, is at any point in time a
minority of families (about 10 per cent in 1971).   The
needs (if any) arising from marriage are confused with
the needs arising from parenthood.   For example, is

there really a justification for subsidising the basic
rate taxpayer to the tune of £2 a week just because he
is married when child benefits are too low?   That is
just one issue of many which needs to be raised.

CONCLUSIONS

The British social security and income tax systems ori-
ginated in response to the perceived needs of quite separate income groups.   Nevertheless, one of the major
underlying assumptions common to both schemes is that
the marriage relationship is an unequal one.   The direct
economic contribution that most wives and an increasing
proportion of mothers (over half of all mothers with
children of school-age were in paid employment in 1971)
make to the family in the form of their earnings (quite
apart from the value of their unpaid work in the home)
does not justify this assumption.   Neither does the
legal relationship between husband and wife.   In the
first place the legal obligation to maintain is not as
one-sided as it is often presented.   Ever since the
first Married Women's Property Act in 1882 (and remember
before that time a wife had no control over her property)
any woman who had property of her own could be asked by
the Poor Law authorities to reimburse them if her husband, children or grandchildren became dependent on
relief.   Under the present supplementary benefit system
the obligation to maintain may rest on the wife if she
is in employment and the husband she has deserted becomes
sick or unemployed.   Since 1970, in the divorce courts
the duty and ability to maintain each other and their
children can be shared between the spouses irrespective
of any notions of 'guilty' and 'innocent' parties.   In
the magistrates courts since 1960, the wife of a physically or mentally disabled man may be required to support
her husband if the couple should legally separate.   In
theory then, *both* men and women take on obligations to
maintain each other and their children on marriage.   The
difference between these obligations is (Brian O'Malley,
1975): 'a husband who is capable of work has a duty to
society as well as to his wife, to provide the primary
support for his family', whereas a woman with children
does not have such an obligation to take paid employment
in order to support either herself or her husband.   In
other words, the man's obligation to maintain his family
is as much concerned with preserving work incentives for
men as with his family's welfare.   In practice the obligation affords wives very little financial security either

before or after the marriage has broken down for it is
difficult to enforce.

Why then, do the state's income-maintenance schemes
still only support men in the role of chief breadwinner
and woman as man's dependent housewife?   The answer
must lie in the fact that there are enormous advantages
to the economically powerful groups in our society in
sustaining the belief that men are breadwinners and
women, at most, are supplementary earners, whose primary
duties lie in the home.   In this way work incentives
for men are preserved even among low-wage earners whose
wives also have to work to support the family.   At the
same time it justifies paying women lower wages than men.
Women when they enter the labour market do so in the
belief that they do not need as high a wage as a man.
Moreover, their paid employment must take second place
to their unpaid work in the home.   They, therefore,
form a very cheap, docile and flexible section of the
labour force and the majority confine themselves to the
less secure and less rewarding jobs.   At the same time
they continue to care for husbands, children, the elderly
and the infirm at a minimum cost to the state.   However,
it should not be forgotten of course, that when we talk
of economic advantages, we have, as Eleanor Rathbone
pointed out forty years ago 'an economic structure devised by and for men' (Reiss, 1934, foreword).

11 Sex-Role Stereotyping and Social Science

Mary Fuller

while women have, legally, ceased to be minors, they
still have the mentality of minors in many fields and,
particularly in politics.... The man - husband,
fiance, lover or myth - is the mediator between them
and the political world. (Duverger, 1955)

The husband brings to his politics a certain patina of
realism, and in an interview a certain dialectical
facility, while his wife remains a femme couverte at
best able to repeat his views, without qualification
or critique. (Riesman, 1956)

The mindless matrons who followed their husbands' lead
or direction could scarcely be said to be exercising a
choice at all. They were, in every sense but the
physical, non-voters. Politics for them had the
character of a masonic or secret religious order.
(Burns, 1961)

I do not claim that females have no organisations;
obviously they join and are active in a great number
of social and service clubs. But female organisations affect political activity far less than male
ones ... women do not form bonds. Dependent as most
women are on the earnings and genes of men, they
break ranks very soon. (Tiger, 1969)

It is profoundly characteristic of the behaviour of
the more fortunate strata of the community that responsibility for widespread non-participation is attributed wholly to the ignorance, indifference and shift-
lessness of the people.... There is a better explanation. Abstention reflects the suppression of the
options and alternatives that reflect the needs of the
non-participants. (Schattschneider, 1960)

If psychology constructs the female as Weisstein (1969) and other writers since (see Hartnett, 1975; Litman, 1975b) have demonstrated, it is equally true that sociology and political science construct theories of society which are not capable of postulating political action by women. Moreover, these theories assume that conditions and life-styles for the sexes are such that a political challenge to them is unnecessary and undesirable. In this way mainstream sociology denies the possibility of the Women's Movement, is blind to the conditions which have treated it and, confronted with the actuality of political analysis and action by women, has shown itself unable to analyse its implications and potential importance. The growth in feminism and the development of an autonomous women's movement in America and Britain has not gone undocumented, but until recently the literature (Malos, 1972; Rowbotham, 1972, for Britain; Dixon, 1969; Freeman, 1969, for America) has mainly been ignored by so-called respectable academic journals.

THE GROWTH OF THE WOMEN'S MOVEMENT IN BRITAIN

The existence of the Women's Liberation Movement as an organisation in Britain can be dated from at least 1970, when the Women's Conference at Ruskin College, Oxford, brought together participants from a variety of backgrounds: the trade union based National Joint Action Campaign for Women's Equal Rights; left-wing political activists; those who had been involved in the student movement of the late 1960s or in such organisations as CND and the Vietnam Solidarity Campaign; and those with experience of or in contact with the American Women's Liberation Movement. Since that date the continuing analysis of women's position in advanced industrial societies has suggested remedies which have been formulated into a set of demands whose content is reflected in task-orientated campaigns: wages for housework; family allowance campaign; free abortion and contraception on demand; women's refuges from violent men (Women's Aid); analysis of sexism in the media (Women in Media); the Campaign for Legal and Financial Independence; Women in Education. A 'working women's charter' in which these and other demands (e.g. for greater nursery provisions) are set out has also created an organisation whose aim is to get the charter accepted and implemented particularly by pressure and activity within the trade unions. A Women's Research Centre has been set up to act as a focal point for research on and undertaken by women. The

consciousness-raising group is an integral part of the
women's movement.   This is an informal gathering of
women who meet to discuss and analyse their personal
situations and to provide mutual support.

If the British Women's Movement had emerged from a
vaccuum overnight the blindness of sociology to it as
a social and political movement might be more understand-
able.   And though as a form of radicalism the feminist
movement may be qualitatively different from other kinds
of radicalism (Weinreich, 1975), it is sufficiently like
other social movements to have discernible beginnings,
to have grown out of trends and events that were available knowledge to those who were interested.   Most
obviously there was the example of America where a
women's movement had been in existence for some years
previously and one of whose effects had been the setting
up of women's caucuses in a number of professional associations (Rossi and Calderwood, 1973; Bernard, 1973)
acting within and outside the professions as catalysts
for change in the material situation of women and to
their representation in the literature of the social and
behavioural sciences.

Second there was the existence in America of legislative measures to combat discrimination on the basis of
sex (Article VII, Civil Rights Act of 1964) which at the
very least might have alerted interest as to why such a
measure was considered necessary, who thought it to be
so and in what way that opinion was articulated.   Furthermore, when one considers that in America, discrimination on the basis of sex was made unlawful in a piece
of legislation originally drawn up to fight racial discrimination, and that the analogy between the situation of
blacks and women was being made in America and in Britain
(Rendel, 1968) where legislation to combat racial discrimination also already existed (Race Relations Act,
1965), it is all the more surprising that sociologists
did not pick up the suggested parallel between women and
blacks made as early as 1944 (Myrdal, and see Hacker,
1951) in the academic literature.

This is not to suggest that sociology could or should
have been able to predict the exact form of a feminine
perspective or the way in which a renewed interest in the
position of women would be manifested, nor to predict
precisely when this would happen.   Rather it is suggested that having had the example of the recent rise in
black militancy and the analogy of the status of blacks
and women pointed out, the possible meaning of other
events both in America and Britain should have been perceived and the potential for a women's rights lobby more
clearly recognised.

Though the relevance of trends in America is often
problematic for analysts of British social and political
life, in this instance discussions about the position of
women were being carried on at about the same time in
each country and the suggested means of remedying that
position were also similar.   In Britain, in 1967 Joyce
Butler MP introduced a Private Members Bill to make discrimination against women illegal and each year until
1973 similar bills were introduced, though none passed
a second reading.   Meanwhile a Labour Party Study group
was making interim reports on 'Discrimination against
Women' and on women and social security (Labour Party,
1968 and 1969).   At about the same time Conservative
Party reports dealing with women's position were also
published (Cooper and Howe, 1969; Conservative Party,
1969).   1970 saw the passing of the Equal Pay Act and
the next year the setting up of the House of Lords Select
Committee on the Anti-Discrimination (no. 2) Bill.   In
1972 Anti-Discrimination Bills were introduced into the
Lords by Lady Seear and into the Commons by Willie Hamilton MP, both of which passed their second reading but
were referred to Select Committees which reported in 1973
and concluded that legislation was required.   Evidence
to these Committees provides a great deal of information
about discriminatory practices and the depressed status
of women.   Later in the same year the Conservative government issued a consultative document setting out its
own proposals for 'Equal Opportunities for Men and Women'
and this was followed in 1974 by the new Labour government
White Papers 'Equality for Women' and 'Better Pensions'
which superseded their earlier opposition Green Paper
(Labour Party, 1972).
Britain's entry into the European Community during
this period also brought to public notice the differing
social, economic and political positions of women in
these countries as Britain was obliged to consider ways
in which its legislation and provision for social security, maternity leave, equal pay, pensions, etc. could
be harmonised with the standards prevailing amongst its
partners in the Common Market.   (In most, but not all
cases this required making better provisions than currently existed in Britain.)   What this has done is to
expose the differences and similarities in the way that
governments define women and dependency as well as making
available comparative data about women in Europe (see
Department of Employment, 1975a).

REASONS FOR MAINSTREAM SOCIOLOGY'S BLINDNESS TO THE GROWTH
OF THE WOMEN'S MOVEMENT

Structural weaknesses in the theories of society upon
which mainstream sociology relies are rapidly uncovered
when one looks at the way in which women are represented
or, indeed, remain unrepresented. Sociologists have
seemed unaware of women generally and women's political
activity specifically, because they have confined their
interest to institutions and structures in which men predominate. This is not through simple misogyny (though
there may be elements of that), but on the assumption
that in describing the behaviour of men or in analysing
those institutions and structures in which men predominate that they are able to make legitimate generalisations about women, too. Sometimes this is on the basis
that what is true of men is also true of women while at
other times it is assumed that what is true of men can
be reversed for a description of women.

Assumptions made about the way society is ordered are
related to assumptions made about women. It will be
useful to look at these in turn. First, *taken-for-
granted assumptions about the sexes* (sex-role stereotypes)
underlie analysis of women's role in society, so that
the *functionality of a sexual division of labour* is almost axiomatic. Consequently, *women have little or no
sociological reality outside the family*. Furthermore,
as the family is an institution in which, sociologically,
men are unimportant, analysis of it is relatively underdeveloped, at least so far as the conceptual apparatus
applied to other institutions is concerned. This leads
many sociologists to make *simple-minded accounts of the
genesis and meaning of change* within the family which
show a lack of acknowledgment of women's own perceptions,
definitions and assessments of their situation.

1 Sex-role stereotypes in sociology and political science

It will be sufficient to summarise a few of these stereotypes as they relate to women's supposed apathy and political passivity. Goot and Reid (1975) in their critique
of political sociology have clearly demonstrated the re-
sistance of this discipline to considering the meaning
of women's political activity which is manifested by their
lack of participation in formal politics. Hughes (1973)
has accused the discipline of relying upon 'folk myth and
stereotype' as far as this subject is concerned. Some of
these myths have already been referred to and others will

be discussed later.   That women are emotional and expressive is an assumption which in voting studies is interpreted as meaning that they personalise politics and are
fickle in their allegiances.   That men are instrumental
and rational is an assumption which leads political scientists to assert that men, by definition, know what the
real issues are and should they change their allegiances
it is because they can discriminate between issues.   Women's assumed dependency, so fiercely asserted in other
branches of sociology, occurs here, too, in the assertion
(often belied by the actual data) that women follow their
husband's lead and that the direction of influence from
one partner to another is entirely from the man to the
woman.

These add up to the notion that women are politically
immature, 'political minors' or 'mindless matrons' where
by contrast men are mature.   It is not surprising, then,
that the allegation that women do not participate in politics is meant as a statement about their 'nature' not a
comment on the nature of established politics or on the
definition of what constitutes political behaviour.
However, when men abstain from political activity this is
accounted for by assuming it has a 'political' cause and
is certainly not an assertion about men's 'nature'.

Women are presented as being not only politically backward, but because of their assumed role as moral guardians
in the family as being inherently, if not innately, conservative, traditional and conformist.   The 'conservatism' of women is one of the more dearly held beliefs
which is a useful catch-all 'explanation' for whatever
women do.   Women are conservative if they vote Tory;
they are conservative if they vote Labour, because it is
asserted that their reason for doing so is a 'traditional
attachment', unlike that of men, who in voting Labour
demonstrate their lack of conservatism (Goot and Reid,
1975).   Adducing different explanations for similar behaviour in women and men is a further way that political
sociology tries to establish women's a-political character.

As Goot and Reid themselves conclude 'too often where
voting studies have actually looked at women voters, prejudice has posed as analysis and ideology as science'.
The conservatism of women is not only asserted in political sociology.   This belief is just as deep-rooted in
other branches of the discipline.   In industrial sociology, for example, much has been written about the supposed lower degree of unionisation among women, which is
often accounted for by their being less interested in
politics or more conservative than male workers.   As

Brown (1974) in his review of the literature makes clear,
here, as elsewhere, the significance of a sexually divided
job market is ignored.   It is taken for granted that men
and women are employed in different work, and so it
appears to make sense to ask the questions 'are women less
unionised than men?', 'are women less likely than men to
engage in strikes?', etc.   Put in this way the answer is
'yes' and that answer is explained by recourse to pseudo-
psychological arguments about the differences between the
sexes.   If it is recognised that in many instances men
and women are not working at the same jobs, the questions
have to be rephrased: 'do women who are employed at the
same jobs as men show lower degrees of unionisation than
those men?' etc.   In which case the answer is 'no'.   In
other words, the stereotype that women are less political
than men leads sociologists to adopt personal-difference
type explanations and blinds them to the fact that men and
women are located at different points in the job-market -
which leads to structural explanations of the differences
in behaviour between the sexes.
    The inability of mainstream sociology to see the poli-
tical significance of feminism or of the women's movement
stems from these stereotypes which make it difficult to
consider that activities engaged in by women could be political.   Sociology is hampered here by its limited definition of 'power' which confines interest to the machinery
of government, state and political administration rather
than widening it to include an analysis of the political
dimension to behaviour - 'the exercise of constraint in
any relationship' (Worsley, 1964).   As Oakley (1974b)
points out a phenomenon such as gossip meets the criterion
of power (a means of controlling other people's behaviour)
yet is more or less totally ignored in the sociological
literature.   She suggests that, although gossip is not
actually the prerogative of women (as anthropological
literature attests) it is certainly considered as such in
the stereotypes on which sociology is based and it may be
for that precise reason that it has not been analysed as
power.

2 Functionality of a sexual division of labour

In the society which sociologists construct for study it
is assumed that segregation of roles by sex is functional
and acceptable.   Parsonian functionalist theory enshrines
the notion of segregated and mutually exclusive roles and
functions in its concept of the 'pattern variables' which
are used to designate the orientations of a person or

collectivity. The variables are actually polar opposites in which women are characterised (alongside underdeveloped societies) by the first, and men (together with
developed societies) by the second in the following list
of characteristics: ascription vs achievement (women
'borrow' status from whichever man - father or husband -
they are attached to, while men achieve their own status);
diffuseness vs specificity (women have woolly minds, men
are clear-headed); particularism vs universalism; collectivity orientation vs self-orientation (women put
others before themselves); affectivity vs emotional neu-
trality (this is sometimes expressed as women have expressive functions while men are instrumental). The
weakness of this conceptual schema lies in the fact that
what are presented as supposedly analytic categories,
which approximate to a greater or less extent to social
reality, also carry connotations of what is right and
proper, i.e. they are prescriptive.

And it is for this reason that sociologists, in desig-
nating housework, for example, as part of women's expressive role in the family, have been hindered in their
analysis of its meaning: because it is considered part
of the expressive role it is not instrumental, therefore
it is not work. Sociologists have thus been forced into
a position of suggesting that the skills required for its
execution are different in kind from those required in
the world of 'real' (i.e. paid) work (Oakley, 1974b).
This is only one example of the way that mainstream sociology's assumptions about the functionality of role segregation leads it to highlight supposed differences
rather than focus on the possible similarities between
the role, orientations and skills of women and men.

As part of its analysis of the functionality of a complex division of labour in advanced industrial societies,
sociology has contributed to the idea that a division of
labour based on sex is defensible. In the terminology
of the discipline there are two kinds of status - that
based on innate characteristics (sex, race, age) and
called ascribed status; and that which is based on some
achievement of its holder which is called achieved status.
The defensibility of a division of labour in advanced
industrial societies based on certain ascribed statuses
has long since been discredited. Few, if any, sociologists would defend as proper a division based on the
racial or ethnic origin of a group, nor would they attribute the existence of a racially structured division of
labour to the supposed different nature of blacks and
whites. But in its contention that men and women should
have different spheres of activity sociology is certainly
perpetuating this idea with regard to the sexes.

It further assumes that such sexually segregated roles
are equally important for the stability of society, that
they thus attract a similar value, or at the very least
do not lead to significant differences in evaluation.
Since the segregated roles are in some mysterious way
complementary there is no essential reason for conflict
between the bearers of the roles and thus no reason for
an exercise of power in this dimension of social life.
In this way mainstream sociology apparently believes or
anyway gives credence to the belief that equality between
the sexes exists. Of course inequalities in other
spheres of life are recognised and focused on, but by
sociology's definition the primary role of women is in
the family - the woman's fundamental status is that of
her husband's wife, the mother of his children - and so
different evaluations of the sexes is defined as unimportant for women. Therefore, by definition the burden of
inequalities is located mostly in the field of work, and
so perceived to fall more heavily on men.

3 Women have no reality outside the family

Not only does sociology define women as playing an expressive role in life, but they are confined to playing this
in the family. Women's main or only role is in the
family - as Comer (1974) points out sociology actually
assumes the synonymity of 'women' and 'the family':
    marriage is interpreted as serving the needs of indi-
    viduals, whereas it is so institutionalised as to
    serve the needs of society. The same is true of the
    family itself, many of whose apparently intimate func-
    tions are, in fact, performed directly on behalf of
    society ... any scrutiny of these functions focuses on
    the duties of the woman within the family ... as pro-
    vider of her husband's (i.e. worker's) physical,
    sexual, emotional and psychological well being, and as
    bearer and rearer of children ... if we look closer at
    the family as a refuge for the (male) worker, we can
    see how, what is regarded as the usefulness of the
    family is, in fact, the usefulness of *women*. (Comer,
    1974)
The assumption that women have no real existence outside the family and that within the family women are
dependent on men is quite explicit in that field of sociology which specifically applies itself to the analysis of
structured inequalities in society - social stratification
theory. Its starting point is that inequalities derive
from class, not gender, and that the family is the proper

unit of analysis of class; individuals derive their
status from the family to which they are attached by
birth or marriage; a convention stemming from the theory
has developed that the most efficient indicator of a
family's status or class is the occupation of the head
of household.   Heads of household are by definition or
usage male (Steinmetz, 1974).   So except in circumstances
when they cannot do so, sociologists present women as
entirely dependent on men - father or husband - for their
status while men are seen as defining their own status.
The ideological underpinnings of such a view are fairly
easy to see; as critics of this area point out (Acker,
1973; Hutton, 1974; Steinmetz, 1974) such formulations
bear little resemblance to the actual situation of men
and women and, moreover, leave out more people than they
include (those who do not live in families, female-headed
households) and take no account of women's presence in
the labour market.   To recognise that a majority of
women are employed outside the home presents some difficulties for stratification theorists, notably, why if a
man's job defines his socio-economic status a woman's job
does not have that meaning for her, and perhaps more
alarmingly for the axiomatic definition of women as dependent, why when a woman is employed in an occupation
ranked higher than her husband's - Hutton (1974) suggests
this applies to a sizeable proportion of women - his
status is not dependent on hers.   It is difficult to
avoid the conclusion that such theoretical confusions
arise because of the prescriptive nature of sociologists'
conception of the way society is ordered and that they
are more concerned to maintain the existence of this 'reality' than to look for or analyse situations which call
that reality into question.

4 Change within the family

Having assigned women their place in the home as part of
their schema sociologists might then be expected to have
given some consideration to the way that the family is
structured, how its members play their roles and how they
effect changes within it.   Certainly one would expect
that, since this is the primary area in which women are
assumed to operate, sociologists wishing to analyse
changes or challenges to the existing order, such as have
been made by the recent feminist movement, would look to
precisely this institution for their evidence.   Had they
done so they could scarcely have avoided some awareness
that here was a place where roles, structures and self-

definitions were indeed changing. However, such an
awareness did not emerge because this change is of a
different kind, brought about for reasons different from
those normally recognised by sociology. For another un-
tested sociological assumption is that the family does
and should change to keep pace with changes outside it
'in society', or more particularly to keep pace with
extra-familial economic and technological forces. A
more or less automatic fit between family forms and
technological change is one strand in this, while Young
and Willmott (1973), for instance, can talk of a new
'symmetry' in the family without any consideration of
the deeper structure of power dimensions within the
family itself or between family members. The family,
in short, is conceived as changing in reaction to forces
outside it.

Most literature on the family skirts the issue of how
change is effected within the family, blandly assuming
that it is accomplished smoothly and without greater personal cost to one member than another. This should not
be too surprising if it is understood that here as elsewhere in sociology we are dealing with male perceptions
of male-defined situations. By equating 'women' and
'the family' it is possible for sociologists to disregard
or even to be blind to the fact that when they talk of
the family accommodating to societal changes what they
mean is that women are being expected to accommodate.
Particularly, but by no means solely in this area, sociology fails to give consideration or credence to the meanings which women themselves attach to their roles. Such
meanings, if they were studied, might very well be at
variance with their 'sociological meaning'. In brief,
mainstream sociology tends to confound functionality - an
external assessment - with acceptability - a personal
assessment. By greater concentration on functionality
sociology has imposed limitations on its ability to
recognise the importance of changing ideas about the
acceptability of roles within the family.

It would be wrong to give the impression that all
sociologists have been uniformly dilatory in the matter
of stereotypic presentations of women for a number have
been applying themselves to different aspects. Some
(Ehrlich, 1971; Kirschner, 1973; Laws, 1971; McNally,
1974; Schneider and Hacker, 1973) have analysed introductory texts and other source materials for evidence of
the way the sexes are represented; others have looked
at substantive areas or sub-disciplines to uncover
assumptions made about women (Acker, 1973; Hutton, 1974;
Schwendinger and Schwendinger, 1971; Steinmetz, 1974;

Watson and Barth, 1964);   a few (Brown, 1974;   Frankenberg, 1974) have re-analysed their own or others' work in
the light of the feminist critique;   yet others have researched and written about discrimination within the
profession of sociology itself (Chubin, 1974;   Hughes,
1973;   Henandez et al., 1973;   Lorch, 1973;   Wolfe et
al., 1973) and there are, finally, the beginnings of new
substantive work from a feminist perspective (Comer, 1974;
Felson and Knoke, 1974;   Gillespie, 1971;   Oakley, 1974b).

These are mostly recent attempts, but there existed an
earlier paper (Mitchell, 1966) whose importance within
the women's movement is not paralleled in the academic
world of sociology.   In this paper, Mitchell set out a
'justification' for socialist theorists to look again at
the subordination of women.   Arguing that women's subordination had been of great theoretical concern to early
analysts such as Marx, Engels and Fourier, but had subse-
quently 'become a subsidiary, if not an invisible element
in the preoccupations of socialists' she traces the cause
of this to the fact that 'the liberation of women remains
a normative ideal, an adjunct to socialist theory, not
structurally integrated into it'.   She suggests a more
complex analysis of women's condition which would integrate that analysis more centrally into Marxist/socialist
theory.

This analysis was taken up by some left-inclined sociologists, but it is interesting to note that Frankenberg
in 1974 could still say, in his criticism of the left at
large, 'The relations of production at work are lovingly
and loathingly described;   relations of production in the
home and community are ignored with equal determination.'
It is precisely in the area of work, re-defining women's
role in the process of production (how to analyse housework as productive labour, what constitutes work, etc.),
that radical left sociologists have concentrated their
efforts to analyse women's condition and to locate women
more centrally in a Marxist analysis (Gardiner, 1974;
Secombe, 1974).   But Frankenberg is substantially right,
for while instructive accounts have been given of housework as unpaid but essential (for capitalism) productive
labour, these sociologists have left relatively unques-
tioned the assumptions that women are dependent on men
and that a class analysis which is predicated on such
assumptions continues to be fruitful.   And it is true to
say that among left-inclined sociologists the three other
related and interconnected elements suggested by Mitchell
- reproduction, sexuality and the socialisation of children - have continued to be ignored and underdeveloped.

The importance of focusing analysis on all elements of

women's situation in the family rather than defining the
family per se as the cause of women's subordination is
recognised within the women's movement and although there
are some sociologists who have pointed the way the challenge has not yet been taken up widely among left sociologists and hardly at all by mainstream sociologists.

The Women's Liberation Movement has implications in
all spheres of life, the academic disciplines included.
Its impact, as Weinreich (1975) points out, is potentially
very great. Women in the movement and commentators in
social science who are gathering information about the
material condition of women are likely to have a great
impact as 'any factual statement about women's position
in society creates a moral conflict in that the actual
situation of women is in direct contravention of the pro-
fessed morals and egalitarian principles of the culture'
(Campbell, 1973). The reason for sociology's failure to
apply itself to the issue can perhaps be inferred from
Campbell's second contention that

> because of cultural norms, reflected as we have noted
> in psychological research, any argument proposing even
> quite minor reforms is revolutionary because [for
> women] to question the norms is itself a violation of
> sex-role stereotypes, and it is bound to lead to major
> personal as well as social and political change.

As has been well demonstrated elsewhere (Tomlinson,
1974) sociology adopts the same stereotypes of women as
those perpetuated by psychology, notions which define
women as a-political, passive, non-instrumental, not part
of or concerned with the 'real' world of work. These
stereotypes make it difficult for mainstream sociology to
recognise women's activities in the Women's Movement as
political, for to do so would mean recognising that these
stereotypes are and have been a nonsense. Women have
analysed their environment and found it wanting. They
have suggested means for rectifying the situation and
banded together to implement these solutions and to give
support to each other. They are challenging a situation
in which they consider themselves to be oppressed even if
sociology does not see it that way. All of this con-
fronts sociologists with unavoidable evidence of political activity on the part of women and at the same time
evidence of the ideology of sociology - the kind of society which sociologists study and the caricatures of
those people who inhabit the society owes more to prescription than to testable hypotheses.

In Britain women's caucuses have been set up in sociology and psychology, aimed at monitoring the progress of
women in the professions and at eliminating the caricature

of women and men that passes for empirical truth in these
disciplines. Drawing their inspiration from the women's
movement and from the undeniable difference between the
way women are acting and the way they 'ought' to if their
representation by social science were correct, it is
likely that such groupings will have a lasting impact on
the disciplines.

Sociology traditionally views women in such a limited
light that it has been hampered from seeing the social
and political significance of the recent behaviour of
women. It has taken commentators, many of whom are considered marginal in the profession, to point out that the
stereotypic presentation of women probably always bore
more relation to men's fantasies of the ideal society and
their (central) place in it than to women's actual behaviour and self-conceptions.

The axiomatic taken-for-granted assumptions on which
sociology has relied hinders rather than aids its aim of
being able to analyse and comment on human social behaviour. In order to apply itself to a better analysis of
social reality it must stop relying on ossified perceptions of the sexes. First, it should take for analysis,
not for granted, differences between the sexes and in
doing so should avoid conceptualisations that assume a
polarity of characteristics, roles, functions and self-
definitions. By concentrating more on people's own perceptions of their situation rather than on external definitions it would become much more obvious that to disregard 50 per cent of the population makes a nonsense of
a purportedly *human* science: it would bring more to the
surface the limitations that are imposed on its efficacy
to comment on human social behaviour at present - by its
current automatic assumption that with men being the
ground plan, women can be omitted from study because inferences can legitimately be made by either assuming
that what is true for men is true for women as well or
by reversing for women what is established for men.

The need to study women is central to this enterprise,
as is the need to look at the differences among men and
among women. Sociology must give up the automatic or
near automatic assumption that where differences between
the sexes exist this is attributable to 'nature' rather
than to structured inequalities between the sexes.

It is strangely inconsistent for a discipline which is
concerned with the importance of environmental influences
on the person to continue to view women as being in some
way exempt from such influences and tied to a destiny
defined by their biology.

In giving prominence to the actor's definitions of the

situation sociology should find itself more able to effect a more complete analysis of the differing and complex ways in which humans attempt to integrate the many different roles, statuses and functions with which they are daily confronted.

Work has already begun in the area; some writers have begun to point the way to a less limited perspective in sociology. It is to be hoped that their voice will be heard and their message acted upon.

Epilogue

This book has attempted to give some insights into the factors and the complexities which the sex-role system embodies. We hope we have conveyed the message that, with the development of understanding of this system, we can replace it with a person-orientated ethos.

There is no doubt that some changes affecting the sex-role system are already evident in our society and that the main components of the system are being questioned. The notion that masculinity and femininity represent dichotomous and mutually exclusive classes of traits is beginning to be recognised as not merely inadequate but positively detrimental to creative thinking and to the development of mature adults capable of combining the more desirable traits from both stereotypes. Furthermore the division of labour on the basis of sex per se is beginning to be seen as a restrictive and unsound practice and the validity of investing the male with a higher value than the female is being constantly challenged.

In general the relationship between the components of the sex-role system and the entire value system of our society is being highlighted and explored. We hope that this exploration will continue and that future explorers will find this book of use to them in a venture which will be characterised by a symbiotic relationship between efforts to expand knowledge and endeavours to effect action at both the personal and societal levels.

Bibliography

ACKER, J. (1973), Women and social stratification: a case of intellectual sexism, 'Amer. J. Soc.', 78 (4), pp. 936-45.

AINSWORTH, M.D.S, BELL, S.M.V. and STAYTON, D.J. (1974), Infant mother attachment and social development: 'social-isation' as a product of reciprocal responsiveness to signals, in 'The Integration of a Child into a Social World', M.P.M. Richards (ed.), London, Cambridge University Press.

ALPANDER, G.V. and GUTMANN, J.E. (1976), Contents and techniques of management development programs for women, 'Personnel J.', 55 (2), pp. 76-9.

ALPER, T.G. (1973), The relationship between role orientation and achievement motivation in college women, 'J. Personality', 41, pp. 9-31.

ANDREW, R.J. (1972), Recognition processes and behaviour with special reference to effects of testosterone on persistence, in 'Advances in the Study of Behaviour', D.S. Lehrman, R.A. Hinde and E. Shaw (eds), vol. 4, New York and London, Academic Press.

ANGRIST, S. et al. (1968), 'Women After Treatment', New York, Appleton-Century-Crofts.

ARCHER, J. (1971), Sex differences in emotional behaviour: a reply to Gray and Buffery, 'Acta Psychologica' 35, pp. 415-29.

ARCHER, J. (1975), Rodent sex differences in emotional and related behaviour, 'Behav. Biol.', 14, pp. 451-79.

ARCHER, J. (1976a), Biological explanations of psychological sex differences, in 'Exploring Sex Differences', B.B. Lloyd and J. Archer (eds), London and New York, Academic Press.

ARCHER, J. (1976b), The organization of aggression and fear in verterbrates, in 'Perspectives in Ethology', P.P. P.P.S. Bateson and P. Klopfer (eds), New York, Plenum Press.

ARCHER, J. and LLOYD, B.B. (1975), Sex differences: biological and social interactions, in 'Child Alive', R.
Lewin (ed.), London, Temple Smith.
ARDREY, R. (1967), 'The Territorial Imperative', London,
Collins.
ARNOTT, C.C. (1972), Husbands' attitudes and wives' com-
mitment to employment, 'J. Marr. and the Fam.', November,
pp. 673-84.
ARNOTT, C.C. (1973), Feminists and anti-feminists as 'true
believers', 'Sociology and Social Research', 57, pp. 300-
6.
ASH, P. and KROEKER, L.P. (1975), Personnel selection,
classification and placement, 'Ann. Rev. Psychol.', 26,
pp. 481-507.
BAILYN, L. (1970), Career and family orientations of hus-
bands and wives in relation to marital happiness, 'Human
Relations', 23 (2), pp. 97-113.
BARNES, K. (1958), 'He and She', London, Darwin Finlayson.
BART, P. (1971a), Depression in middle-aged women, in
'Women in Sexist Society', V. Gornick and B.K. Moran
(eds), New York, Basic Books.
BART, P. (1971b), Sexism and social science, 'J. Marr. and
the Fam.', 33 (4), pp. 734-45.
BARUCH, G.K. (1972), Maternal role pattern as related to
self esteem and parental identification in college women,
paper presented at EPA, Boston, April.
BASS, B.M. et al. (1971), Male managers' attitudes toward
working women, 'Am. Behav. Scientist', 15 (2), pp. 221-36.
BATEMAN, N.I. and PETERSEN, P.M. (1972), Factors related
to outcome of treatment for hospitalized white male and
female alcoholics, 'J. Drug Issues', 2, pp. 66-74.
BAUMRIND, D. and BLACK, A.E. (1967), Socialisation practice associated with dimensions of competence in preschool
boys and girls, 'Child Development', 38, pp. 291-327.
BECK, A.T. and GREENBERG, R.L. (1974), Cognitive therapy
with depressed women, in 'Women in Therapy', V. Franks and
V. Burtle (eds), New York, Bruner, Mazel.
BECKER, J. (1974), 'Depression: Theory and Research', New
York, John Wiley.
BECKMAN, L.V. (1975), Women alcoholics: a review of
social and psychological studies, 'J. Studies on Alcohol',
36 (7), pp. 797-824.
BELFER, M.L. et al. (1971), Alcoholism in women, 'Arch.
Gen. Psychiat.', 25, pp. 540-4.
BELL, C.R. (1974), 'Men at Work', London, Allen & Unwin.
BELOTTI, E.G. (1975), 'Little Girls', London, Writers and
Readers Publishing Cooperative.
BEM, S.L. (1975), The measurement of psychological andro-
gyny, 'J. Consult. Clin. Psychol.', 42, pp. 155-62.

BERGER, P.L. (1966), 'Invitation to Sociology', Harmonds-worth, Penguin Books.
BERNARD, J. (1972), 'The Future of the Family', New York, World Books.
BERNARD, J. (1973), My four revolutions: an autobiograph-ical history of the A.S.A., 'Amer. J. Soc.', 78 (4), pp. 773-91.
BERNARD, J. (1975), 'Women, Wives, Mothers: Values and Options', Chicago, Aldine.
BEVERIDGE, W. (1942), 'Social Insurance and Allied Ser-vices' (The Beveridge Report), Cmnd 6404, London, HMSO.
BIBRING, E. (1953), The mechanism of depression, in 'Affective Disorders', P. Greenacre (ed.), New York, In-ternational Universities Press.
BILLER, H.B. and BORSTELMANN, L.J. (1967), Masculine dev-elopment and integrative review, 'Merrill-Palmer Quart.', 13, pp. 253-94.
BLACKSTONE, T. and FULTON, O. (1975), Sex discrimination among university teachers: a British-American comparison, 'British J. Sociology', 26, pp. 261-75.
BLANE, H.T., HILL, M.J. and BROWN, E. (1968), Alienation, self-esteem and attitudes toward drinking in high-school students, 'Quart. J. Stud. Alc.', 29, pp. 350-4.
BLOCK, J. VON DER LIPPE, A. and BLOOK, J.H. (1973), Sex-role and socialisation patterns, 'J. Consulting and Clinical Psychol.', 41, pp. 321-41.
BLOOD, R. and WOLFE, D. (1960), 'Husbands and Wives', Chicago, Free Press.
BLOOMBAUM, M., YAMAMOTO, J. and JAMES, Q. (1968), Cultural stereotyping among psychotherapists, 'J. Consult. Clin. Psychol.', 32, p. 99.
BLURTON-JONES, N. (1972), Characteristics of ethological studies of human behaviour, in 'Ethological Studies of Child Behaviour', N. Blurton-Jones (ed.), London, Cam-bridge University Press.
BOEHM, V.R. (1974), Changing career patterns for women in the Bell System, symposium on 'Employment Status of Women in Academic, Business, Government and Military', for APA Convention, New Orleans.
BOULTON, M. (1976), Report to British Psychological Soc-iety Conference, York.
BRANDENBURG, J.B. (1974), The needs of women returning to school, 'Pers. Guid. J.', 53 (1), pp. 11-18.
BREEN, D. (1975), 'Understanding the Birth of a First Child', London, Tavistock.
BROPHY, J.E. and GOOD, T.L. (1970), Teacher's communica-tion of differential expectations for children's class-room performance: some behavioural data, 'J. Ed. Psychol.', 61 (5), pp. 365-74.

BROVERMAN, D.M., KLAIBER, E.L., KOBAYASHI, Y. and VOGEL,
W. (1968), Roles of activation and inhibition in sex
differences in cognitive abilities, 'Psychol. Rev.', 75,
pp. 25-50.
BROVERMAN, I.K. et al. (1970), Sex role stereotypes and
clinical judgements of mental health, 'J. Consult. Psychol.', 34, pp. 1-7.
BROVERMAN, I.K. et al. (1972), Sex role stereotypes: a
current appraisal, 'J. Soc. Issues', 28 (2), pp. 59-78.
BROWN, G. et al. (1958), post-hospital adjustment of
chronic mental patients, 'Lancet', September.
BROWN, G.W. BHROLCHAIN, M. and HARRIS, T. (1975), Social
class and psychiatric disturbance among women in an urban
population, 'Sociology', 9 (2), pp. 225-54.
BROWN, R. (1974), Women as employees: some comments on
research in industrial sociology, paper presented at the
BSA annual conference, Aberdeen, April.
BUFFERY, A.W.H. and GRAY, J.A. (1972), Sex differences in
the development of spatial and linguistic skills, in
'Gender Differences, their Ontogeny and Significance',
C. Ounsted and D.C. Taylor (eds), London, Churchill.
BURNS, C. (1961), 'Parties and People', Melbourne Univer-
sity Press.
BURNSTYN, J.N. (1971), Brain and intellect: science
applied to a social issue 1860-1875, 'XIIe Congrès Inter-
national d'Histoire des Sciences', IX, pp. 13-16.
BURTLE, V., WHITLOCK, D. and FRANKS, V. (1974), Modifica-
tion of low self-esteem in women alcoholics: a behaviour
treatment approach, 'Psychotherapy: Theory, Research and
Practice', 11 (1), pp. 36-40.
BUSHBY, L.J. (1975), Sex-role research on the mass media,
'J. Communication', 25 (4), pp. 107-31.
BYRNE, E.M. (1975), Inequality in educational-discriminal
resource-allocation in schools?, 'Educational Rev.', 27
(3), pp. 179-91.
CADOGAN, M. and CRAIG, P. (1976), 'You're a Brick,
Angela!', London, Gollancz.
CAMPBELL, K.K. (1973), The rhetoric of women's liberation:
an oxymoron, 'Quart. J. Speech', 59, pp. 74-86.
CARTWRIGHT, A., SHAW, S. and SPRATLEY, T. (1975), 'Design-
ing a Comprehensive Community Response to Problems of
Alcohol Abuse', London, Maudsley Alcohol Pilot Project.
CECIL, E.A., et al. (1973), Perceived importance of selected variables used to evaluate male and female job appli-
cants, 'Personnel Psychol.', 26, pp. 397-404.
CHESLER, P. (1970), Patient and patriarch; women in the
psychotherapeutic relationship, in 'Women in Sexist Society', V. Gornick and B.I. Moran (eds), New York, Basic
Books.

CHESLER, P. (1972), 'Women and Madness', Garden City, New York, Doubleday.

CHUBIN, D. (1974), Sociological manpower and womanpower: sex differences in career patterns of two cohorts of American doctorate sociologists, 'Amer. Sociologist', 9 (2), pp. 83-92.

CLANCY, K. and GOVE, W. (1974), Sex differences in mental illness: an analysis of response bias in self-reports, 'Am. J. Sociol.', 80, pp. 205-16.

COHEN, M.B. (1966), Personal identity and sexual identity, 'Psychiatry', 29 (1), pp. 1-14.

COHEN, S.L. and BUNKER, K.A. (1975), Subtle effects of sex role stereotypes on recruiters hiring decisions, 'J. App. Psychol.', 60 (5), pp. 566-72.

COHLER, W., et al. (1962), Childbearing attitudes among mothers volunteering and revolunteering for pathological study, 'Psychol. Reps.', 23 (2), pp. 603-12.

COMER, L. (1974), 'Wedlocked Women', Leeds, Feminist Books.

COMMISSION OF THE EUROPEAN COMMUNITIES (1975a), 'Equality of Treatment between Men and Women Workers', COM (75), 36 Final, Brussels.

COMMISSION OF THE EUROPEAN COMMUNITIES (1975b), 'European Men and Women: a Comparison of their Attitudes to some of the Problems facing Society', Brussels.

CONSERVATIVE PARTY (1969), Cripps Committee Report, 'Fair Share for the Fair Sex', London.

COOPER, B. and HOWE, G. (1969), 'Opportunity for Women', London.

COSER, L.A. (1974), 'Greedy Institutions', New York, Free Press; London, Colliers MacMillan.

CROOK, J.H. (1970), Introduction - social behaviour and ethology, in 'Social Behaviour in Birds and Mammals', J.H. Crook (ed.), London and New York, Academic Press.

CURLEE, J. (1968), Women alcoholics, 'Federal Probationer', 32 (1), pp. 16-20.

CURLEE, J. (1969), Alcoholism and the empty nest, 'Bull. Menniger Clinic', 33 (3), pp. 165-71.

CURLEE, J. (1970), A comparison of male and female patients at an alcoholism treatment center, 'J. Psychol.', 74, pp. 239-47.

CURLEE, J. (1971), Sex differences in patients' attitudes towards alcoholism treatment, 'Quart. J. Studies on Alcohol', 32, pp. 643-50.

DALE, R.R. (1971), 'Mixed or Single-Sex School?', vol. 2, London, Routledge & Kegan Paul.

DARWIN, C. (1871), 'The Descent of Man, and Selection in Relation to Sex', London, Murray (1901 edn).

DAVIES, L. and MEIGHAN, R. (1975), A review of schooling

and sex roles, with particular reference to the experience
of girls in secondary schools, 'Educational Rev.', 27 (3),
pp. 165-78.
DAVIS, E.G. (1973), 'The First Sex', London, Dent.
DAVIS, L.E. (1971), Job satisfaction research: the post-
industrial view, 'Industrial Relations', 10 (2), pp. 176-
93.
DAWSON, J.L.M. (1972), Effects of sex hormones on cogni-
tive style in rats and men, 'Behav. Genet.', 2, pp. 21-42.
Department of Employment (1974a), 'Women and Work: A
Statistical Survey', Manpower Paper no. 9, London, HMSO.
Department of Employment (1974b), 'Women and Work: Sex
Differences and Society', Manpower Paper no. 10, London,
HMSO.
Department of Employment (1975a), 'Women and Work: A
Review', Manpower Paper no. 11, London, HMSO.
Department of Employment (1975b), 'Women and Work: Over-
seas Practice', Manpower Paper no. 12, London, HMSO.
DEUTSCH, H. (1945), 'The Psychology of Women', New York,
Grune & Stratton.
DIPBOYEE, R.L. (1975), Relative importance of applicant
sex, attractiveness and scholastic standing in evaluation
of job applicant resumés, 'J. App. Psychol.', 60 (1), pp.
39-43.
DIXON, M. (1969), The rise of women's liberation, 'Ram-
parts', 8 (6), pp. 57-64.
DOERING, C.H., BRODIE, H.K.H., KRAEMER, H., BECKER, H.
and HAMBURG, D.A. (1974), Plasma testosterone levels and
psychologic measures in men over a 2-month period, in
'Sex Differences in Behaviour', R.C. Friedman, R.M. Rich-
art and R.L. Vande Wiele (eds), New York, John Wiley.
DOTY, R.L. (1974), A cry for the liberation of the female
rodent: courtship and copulation in 'Rodentia', 'Psychol.
Bull.', 81, pp. 159-72.
DOUGLAS, J.W.E. (1964), 'The Home and the School', London,
MacGibbon & Kee.
DRAPER, P. (1975), !Kung women: contrasts in sexual
egalitarianism in foraging and sedentary contexts, in
'Toward an Anthropology of Women', R. Reiter (ed.), New
York and London, Monthly Review Press.
DUNLOP, (1970), cited in D.R. Lawrence, 'Clinical Phar-
macology', New York, Churchill Livingstone.
DUVERGER, M. (1955), 'The Political Role of Women', Paris,
UNESCO.
EBERT, P.D. and HYDE, J.S. (1976), Selection for agnostic
behaviour in wild female 'Mus musculus', 'Behav. Genet.',
6, in press.
ECTERNACHT, G.J. and HUSSEIN, A.L. (1974), Survey of
women interested in management, prepared for the Graduate

Business Admissions Council by Educational Testing Service, Princeton, NJ.

EHRENREICH, B. and ENGLISH, D. (1974), 'Complaints and Disorders', Glass Mountain Pamphlet, no. 2.

EHRLICH, C. (1971), The male sociologist's burden: the place of women in marriage and family texts, 'J. Marr. and the Fam.', 36 (3), pp. 421-30.

EIBL-EIBESFELDT, I. (1970), 'Ethology: the Biology of Behaviour', New York, Holt, Rinehart & Winston.

EPSTEIN, G.F. and BRONZAFT, A.L. (1972), Female freshmen view their roles as women, 'J. Marr. and the Fam.', 34 (4), pp. 671-2.

EUROPEAN PARLIAMENT (1975), 'Debates, Reports and Proceedings', 29 April, Luxembourg.

EYDE, L. (1970), Eliminating barriers to career development in women, 'Personnel and Guidance J.', 49 (1), pp. 24-8.

EYDE, L. (1972), Met and unmet needs of women: implications for continuing education of women, paper presented at the pre-conference workshop on the Professional Guide to Continuing Education Programs for Women, The National University Extension Association, Columbia, S. Carolina.

EYSENCK, H.J. (1975), Crime as destiny, 'New Behaviour', 3, pp. 46-9.

FAGOT, B.I. and LITMAN, I. (1975), Stability of sex-role and play interests from pre-school to elementary school, 'J. Psychol.', 89, pp. 285-92.

FEATHER, N.T. (1975), Positive and negative reactions to male and female success and failure in relation to the perceived status and sex-typed appropriateness of occupations, 'J. Personality and Social Psychol.', 31, pp. 536-48.

FEATHER, N.T. and RAPHEALSON, A.C. (1974), Fear of success in American and Australian student groups, motive or sex-role stereotype?, 'J. Personality', 42, pp. 190-201.

FEINMAN, S. (1974), Approval of cross-sex role behaviour, 'Psychol. Reports', 35, pp. 643-8.

FELDMAN-SUMMERS, S. and KIESLER, S.B. (1974), Those who are number two try harder; the effect of sex on attributions of causality, 'J. Personality and Social Psychol.', 30, pp. 846-55.

FELSON, M. and KNOKE, D. (1974), Social status and the married woman, 'J. Marr. and the Fam.', 36 (3), pp. 516-21.

FESHBACH, N.D. (1969), Student teacher preferences for elementary school pupils varying in personality characteristics, 'J. Educ. Psychol.', 60 (2), pp. 126-32.

FODOR, I.E. (1974), Sex role conflict and symptom forma-

tion in women: can behaviour therapy help?, 'Psycho-
therapy: Theory, Research and Practice', 11 (1).
FOUCAULT, T. (1967), 'Madness and Civilisation' (1961),
London, Tavistock.
FRANKENBERG, R. (1974), Community life and the interaction
of production systems: the source of sex differentiation
and the genesis of gender, paper presented at the British
Sociological Association's annual conference, Aberdeen.
FRAZIER, N. and SADKER, M. (1973), 'Sexism in School and
Society', New York, Harper & Row.
FREEMAN, B. and SIMMONS, C.G. (1963), 'The Mental Patient
Comes Home', New York, John Wiley.
FREEMAN, J. (1969), The new feminists, 'Nation', 208, p.
8.
FREEMAN, J. (1973), Informal elites or the tyranny of
structurelessness, reprinted from 'Second Wave' by Rising
Free Bookshop, 197 King's Cross Road, London, WC1.
FREUD, S. (1908), 'Civilised' sexual morality and modern
nervous illness, 'Complete Works', vol. 19 (standard edn,
1961), London, Hogarth Press.
FREUD, S. (1925), Some psychical consequences of the ana-
tomical distinction between the sexes, 'Complete Works',
vol. 19 (standard edn, 1961), London, Hogarth Press.
FREUD, S. (1933) (1973), 'Femininity in New Introductory
Lectures on Psychoanalysis', Harmondsworth, Penguin Books.
FRIEDLANDER, F. and BROWN, L.D. (1974), Organization dev-
elopment, in 'Annual Review of Psychology', M.R. Rosen-
weig and L.W. Porter (eds), California, Annual Review.
FRIEDMAN, L.J. et al. (1962), 'Virgin Waves', London,
Tavistock.
FRUEH, T. and MCGHEE, P.F. (1975), Traditional sex-role
development, and amount of time spent watching television,
'Developmental Psychol.', 11, p. 109.
GARAI, J.E. and SCHEINFELD, A. (1968), Sex differences in
mental and behavioural traits, 'Genetic Psychology Mono-
graphs', 77, pp. 169-299.
GARDINER, J. (1974), Political economy of female labour
in capitalist society, paper presented at the BSA Annual
Conference, Aberdeen, April.
GARDINER, J. (1975), Women's work in the Industrial Revo-
lution, in 'Conditions of Illusion', S. Allen, L. Sanders
and J. Wallis (eds), Old Westbury, NY, Feminist Press.
GARNER, J. and BING, M. (1973), The elusiveness of Pygma-
lion and differences in teacher-pupil contact, 'Inter-
change', 4 (1), pp. 34-42.
GARRETT, G.R. and BAHR, H.M. (1973), Women on Skid Row,
'Quart. J. Studies on Alcohol', 34, pp. 1228-43.
GARSKOF, M.H. (1971), 'Roles Women Play', California,
Brooks/Cole.

GAYFORD, J.J. (1975a), Wife battering: a preliminary
survey of 100 cases, 'Brit. Med. J.', vol. I, pp. 194-7,
25 January.
GAYFORD, J.J. (1975b), Battered wives, 'Medical Science
Law', 15 (4).
'General Household Survey' (1973), London, HMSO.
GILLESPIE, D.L. (1971), Who has the power? The marital
struggle, 'J. Marr. and the Fam.', 33 (3), pp. 445-58.
GILMAN, C.P. (1903), 'The Home: Its Work and Influence',
New York, McClure, Phillips.
GINSBERG, S. (1976), Report to the British Psychological
Society Conference, York.
GLATT, M.M. (1961), Treatment results in an English mental
hospital, 'Acta Psych. Scand.', 37, pp. 143-68.
GLUCKSMANN, A. (1974), Sexual dimorphism in mammals,
'Biolog. Rev.', 49, pp. 423-75.
GOLDBERG, P. (1968), Are women prejudiced against women?,
'Transaction', 5, pp. 28-30.
GOLDBERG, S. (1971), 'The Inevitability of the Patriar-
chy', New York, Morrow.
GOLDBERG, S. and LEWIS, M. (1969), Play behaviour in the
year-old infant: early sex differences, 'Child Devel.',
40, pp. 21-31.
GOOD, T.L., SIKES, N.J. and BROPHY, J.E. (1973), Effects
of teacher sex and pupil sex on classroom interaction,
'J. Educ. Psychol.', 65 (1), pp. 74-87.
GOOT, M. and REID, E. (1975), 'Women and Voting Studies:
Mindless Matrons or Sexist Scientism?', London, Sage
Publications.
GOVE, W.R. and TUDOR, J.F. (1972), Adult sex roles and
mental illness, 'Am. J. Sociol.', 4, p. 78.
GOVE, W.R. and TUDOR, J.F. (1973), Sex roles and mental
illness, in 'Changing Women in a Changing Society', J.
Huber (ed.), University of Chicago Press.
GRAY, J.A. (1971), Sex differences in emotional behav-
iour in mammals including man: endocrine bases, 'Acta
Psycholog.', 35, pp. 29-46.
GRAY, J.A. and BUFFERY, A.W.H. (1971), Sex differences in
emotional and cognitive behaviour in mammals including
man: adaptive and neural bases, 'Acta Psycholog.', 35,
pp. 89-111.
'Green Paper on proposals for a tax-credit system' (1972),
London, HMSO.
GREENSON, R.R. (1954), On moods and introjects, 'Bull. of
Menninger Clinic', 18, pp. 1-11.
GRINKER, R.R., MILLER, J.B., SABSHIN, M., NUNN, R. and
NUNNALLY, J.C., (1961), 'The Phenomena of Depression',
New York, Harper & Row.
GRONSETH, E. (1975), Work sharing families, to be pub-

lished in the Proceedings of the ISSBD Conference, Guild-
ford.
'Guardian', The (1972), Jill Tweedie, Ephesians 5:23 says
'A husband is head of his wife as Christ is head of the
congregation', p. 9, 26 June.
HAAVIO-MANNILA, E. (1967), Sex differentiation in role
expectations and performance, 'J. Marr. and the Fam.',
29 (3), pp. 568-78.
HACKER, H.M. (1951), Women as a minority group, 'Social
Forces', 30, pp. 60-9.
HAGAN, R.L. and KAHN, A. (1975), Discrimination against
competent women, 'J. App. Soc. Psychol.', 5 (4), pp. 362-
76.
HARMAN, W. (1972), The nature of our changing society, in
'The Management of Change Conflict', J.H. Thomas and W.G.
Bennis (eds), Harmondsworth, Penguin Books.
HARTLEY, R.E. (1959), Sex-role pressures and the social-
isation of the male child', 'Psychol. Reports', 5, pp.
457-68.
HARTNETT, O. (1975), Sex role stereotyping and occupa-
tional psychology, paper presented at the BPS Annual Con-
ference, Nottingham.
HARTNETT, O.,(1976), Affirmative action programmes,
'Women Speaking', April, pp. 9-13.
HAYS, H.R. (1966), 'The Myth of Feminine Evil', London,
Methuen.
HEINEN, J.S. et al. (1975), Developing the woman manager,
'Personnel J.', 54 (5), pp. 282-6.
HENANDEZ, J., STAUSS, J. and DRIVER, E. (1973), The mis-
placed emphasis on opportunity for minorities, and women,
'Amer. Sociologist', 8 (3), pp. 121-4.
HERBERT, J. (1970), Hormones and reproductive behaviour
in rhesus and talapoin monkeys, 'J. Reprod. Fertil.
Suppl.', 11, pp. 119-40.
HESHUSIUS-GILSDORF, L.T. and GILSDORF, D.T. (1975), Girls
are females, boys are males: a context analysis of career
materials, 'Personnel and Guidance J.', 54 (4), pp. 207-
11.
HINDE, R.A. (1974), 'Biological Bases of Human Social
Behaviour', New York and London, McGraw Hill.
HINKLE, L.E. and WOLF, H.G. (1958), Health and social
environment, in 'Explorations in Social Psychiatry', A.R.
Leighton et al. (eds), New York, Basic Books.
HIRSCH, J. (1962), Women and alcoholism, in 'Problems in
Addiction', W.C. Bier (ed.), New York, Fordham University
Press.
HMSO (1975), 'Social Trends', London.
HOFFMAN, L.W. (1972), Early childhood experiences and
women's achievement motives, 'J. Social Issues', 28, pp.
129-56.

HOFFMAN, M.M. (1975), Assumptions in sex education books, 'Educational Rev.', 27 (3), pp. 211-20.
HOLMSTROM, L. (1972), 'The Two Career Family', Cambridge, Mass., Schenkman.
HOLTER, H. (1973), 'Sex Roles and Social Structure', Oslo-Bergen-Tromso, Universitetsforlaget.
HORN, J.L. and WANBERG, K.W. (1973), Females are different: on the diagnosis of alcoholism in Women, 'Proceedings of the First Annual Alcoholism Conference, NIAAA', pp. 332-54.
HORNER, M.S. (1970), Femininity and successful achievement: a basic inconsistency, in 'Feminine personality and conflict', J.M. Bardwick, E. Douvan, D. Gutman (eds), Belmont, California, Brooks Cole, pp. 45-74.
HUGHES, R.M. (ed.) (1973), 'The Status of Women in Sociology, 1968-1972', Washington, American Sociological Association.
HUNT, A. (1968), 'A Survey of Women's Employment' (Government Social Survey), VSP 1, London, HMSO.
HUNT, A. (1975), 'Management Attitudes and Practices towards Women at Work' (Office of Population Censuses and Survey), Social Survey Division, London, HMSO.
HUTT, C. (1972a), 'Males and Females', Harmondsworth, Penguin Books.
HUTT, C. (1972b), Sex differences in human development, 'Human Devel.', 15, pp. 153-70.
HUTTON, C. (1974), Second-hand status: stratification terms and the sociological subordination of women, paper presented at the BSA Annual Conference, Aberdeen, April.
'Ink' (1972), Riding along on the crest of a wave, 7 January, p. 12.
JACKLIN, C.N. and MISCHEL, H.M. (1973), As the twig is bent - sex-role stereotyping in early readers, 'School Psychology Digest', 2, pp. 30-8.
JACKSON, P.W. (1968), 'Life in Classrooms', New York, Holt, Rinehart & Winston.
JACOBSON, E. (1953), Contribution to the meta psychology of cyclothymic depression, in 'Affective Disorders', P. Greenacre (ed.), New York, International Universities Press.
JACOBSON, E. (1957), On normal and pathological moods, 'Psychoanal. Study of the Child', 12, pp. 73-114.
JEGHELIAN, A. (1976), Surviving sexism: strategies and consequences, 'Pers. Guid. J.', 54 (6), pp. 307-11.
JOHNSON, M.W. (1965), Physicians' views on alcoholism with special reference to alcoholism and women, 'Nebraska State Med. J.', 50, pp. 378-84.
JOHNSON, M.W., DEVRIES, J.C. and HOUGHTON, M.I. (1966), The female alcoholic, 'Nurses Reg., Philadelphia', 15, pp. 343-7.

JOYCE, J. (1946), 'Finnegans Wake', London, Faber & Faber.
JUNKER, M. (1973), Recruiters Forum, 'Civil Service J.',
3-4, (US Civil Service).
KAGAN, J. and MOSS, H. (1962), 'Birth to Maturity', New
York, John Wiley.
KANTER, R.M. et al. (1975), Coupling, parenting, and the
presence of others: intimate relationships in communal
households, 'Family Coordinator', 24 October, pp. 435-52.
KARPMAN, B. (1948), 'The Alcoholic Woman', Washington DC,
Lineacre Press.
KINSEY, B.A. (1966), 'The Female Alcoholic: A Social
Psychological Study', Springfield, Ill., D.W. Thomas.
KINSEY, B.A. (1968), Psychological factors in alcoholic
women from a state hospital sample, 'Amer. J. Psychiat.',
124, pp. 1463-6.
KIRSCHNER, B.F. (1973), Introducing students to women's
place in society, 'Amer. J. Soc.', 78 (4), pp. 1051-4.
KLEMACK, D.L. and EDWARDS, J.L. (1973), Women's acquisi-
tion of stereotyped occupational aspirations, 'Sociol.
and Soc. Res.', 57 (4), pp. 510-23.
KOHLBERG, Z. (1966), A cognitive developmental analysis
of children's sex-role concepts and attitudes, in 'The
Development of Sex Differences', E.E. Maccoby (ed.),
London, Tavistock.
KNOX, W.E. and KUPFERER, H.J. (1971), A discontinuity in
the socialisation of males in the United States, 'Merrill-
Palmer Quart.', 17, pp. 251-61.
KREUZ, L.E. and ROSE, R.M. (1972), Assessment of aggres-
sive behaviour and plasma testosterone in a young criminal
population, 'Psychosom. Med.', 34, pp. 321-32.
KUHN, T.S. (1962), 'The Structure of Scientific Revolu-
tions', University of Chicago Press.
LABOUR PARTY, The (1968), 'Discrimination Against Wo-
men', London.
LABOUR PARTY, The (1969), 'Towards Equality: Women and
Social Security', London.
LABOUR PARTY, The (1972), 'Discrimination Against Women:
Report of a Labour Party Study Group', London.
LACAN, J. (1958), 'The Signification of the Phallus
Ecrits', Paris, Editions de Seuil.
LAND, H. (1975a), Social Security: a system for maintain-
ing women's dependence on men, British Association, Soc-
iology Section N, 28 August.
LAND, H. (1975b), The myth of the male breadwinner, 'New
Society', 34.
LAND, H. (1976), Women: supporters or supported, in
'Sexual Divisions and Society: Process and Change', D.
Barker and S. Allen (eds), London, Tavistock.
LAWS, J.L. (1971), A feminist review of marital-adjust-

ment literature; the rape of the Locke, 'J. Marr. and the Fam.', 33 (3), pp. 483-516.

LEIN, L. et al. (1974), 'Final Report: Work and Family Life', Nat. Inst. of Educ. Project, no. 3-3094, Cambridge, Mass., Center for the Study of Public Policy.

LE MASTERS, E.E. (1957), Parenthood as crisis, 'Marr. and Fam. Living', 19, pp. 352-5.

LE MASTERS, E.E. (1974), 'Parents in Modern America', Homewood, Ill., The Dorsey Press.

LEVINE, S.V. et al. (1974), Sexism and psychiatry, 'Amer. J. Orthopsychiat.', 44 (3), pp. 327-36.

LEVITIN, T.E. and CHANANIE, J.D. (1972), Responses of female primary school teachers to sex-typed behaviours in male and female children, 'Child Devel.', 43, pp. 1309-16.

LEWIS, M. (1972), State as an infant-environment interaction: an analysis of mother-infant behaviour as a function of sex, 'Merrill-Palmer Quart.', 18, pp. 95-121.

LINDBECK, V.L. (1972), The woman alcoholic: a review of the literature, 'Int. J. Addict.', 7, pp. 567-80.

LINTON, R. (1959), The natural history of the family, in 'The Family: Its Function and Destiny', R.N. Anshen (ed.), New York, Harper & Row.

LIPSHITZ, S. (1975), paper presented at BPS Conference in symposium on The role of psychology in the propagation of female stereotypes, Nottingham.

LIPSHITZ, S. (1976), paper to Anthropology Graduate-Faculty Seminar, University of Sussex.

LISANSKY, E. (1957), Alcoholism in women: social and psychological concomitants, I, Social history data, 'Quart. J. Studies on Alcohol', 18 (5), pp. 88-623.

LITMAN, G.K. (1971), Psychological variables affecting symptom fluctuations in chronic neurotic depressives, unpublished PhD thesis, University of London.

LITMAN, G.K. (1975a), Women and alcohol: facts and myths, 'New Behaviour', 24, pp. 126-9.

LITMAN, G.K. (1975b), A microcosm of female stereotypes: women and alcohol, paper presented at the BPS Conference, Nottingham, April.

LITMAN, G.K., STEWART, R. and POWELL, G. (1976), Evaluation of the female alcoholic: a study of person-perception, paper given at the annual conference of the BPS.

LLOYD, B.B. (1976), Social responsibility and research on sex differences, in 'Exploring Sex Differences', B.B. Lloyd and J. Archer (eds), London and New York, Academic Press.

LOBBAN, G.M. (1974), Presentation of sex-roles in British reading schemes, 'Forum', 16 (2), pp. 57-60.

LOBBAN, G.M. (1975a), Sex-roles in reading schemes, 'Educ. Rev.', 27 (3), pp. 202-10.

LOBBAN, G.M. (1975b), Sexism in British primary schools, 'Women Speaking', 4, pp. 10-13.

LOFTUS, M. (1974), Learning sexism and feminism, 'Red Rag', 7, pp. 6-11.

LOO, C. and WENAR, C. (1971), Activity level and motor inhibition: their relation to intelligence test performance in normal children, 'Child Devel.', 42, pp. 967-71.

LOPATA, H.L. (1971), 'Occupation Housewife', New York, Oxford University Press.

LORCH, B.R. (1973), Reverse discrimination in hiring in sociology departments: a preliminary report, 'Amer. Sociologist', 8 (3), pp. 116-20.

LORENZ, K. (1966), 'On Aggression', New York, Harcourt, Brace Jovanovich.

MACCOBY, E.E. (ed.) (1966), 'The Development of Sex Differences', Stanford University Press.

MACCOBY, E.E. and JACKLIN, C.N. (1974a), 'The Psychology of Sex Differences', Oxford University Press.

MACCOBY, E.E. and JACKLIN, C.N. (1974b), Sex differences: myth and reality, 'Psychology Today', December.

MACCOBY, E.E. and JACKLIN, C.N. (1975), 'The Psychology of Sex Differences', London, Oxford University Press.

MCGUINNESS, D. (1976), Sex differences in the organisation of perception and cognition, in 'Exploring Sex Differences', B.B. Lloyd and J. Archer (eds), London and New York, Academic Press.

MACK, D. (1975), Skirting the competition, 'Psychology Today', November, pp. 38-41.

MACKINTOSH, M. et al. (1974), Women's domestic labour, paper presented at CSE Conference, London.

MCNALLY, F. (1974), The little Xtra - unchanging models of female attitudes and behaviour, paper presented to the BSA Annual Conference, Aberdeen, April.

MAHONEY, J. (1975), An analysis of the axiological structures of traditional and proliberation men and women, 'J. Psychol.', 90, pp. 31-9.

MAIER, N.R.F. (1965), 'Psychology in Industry', 3rd edn, Boston, Houghton Mifflin.

MAIN, T.F. (1946), The hospital as a therapeutic institution, 'Menninger Clinic Bull.', 10 (3), pp. 66-70.

MALBIN, M.J. (1973), Employment report: proposed federal guide lines on hiring could have far-reaching impact', 'Nat. J. Reps.', 5 (39), pp. 1429-34.

MANES, A.L. and MELNYK, P. (1974), Television models of female achievement, 'J. App. Soc. Psychol.', 4, pp. 365-74.

MANPOWER AND SOCIAL AFFAIRS COMMITTEE (1975), 'The Role of Women in the Economy', OECD.

MALOS, E. (1972), Notes on the history of the women's liberation movement, 'Int. Marxist Rev.', 3, April.

MARTIN, M.K. and VOORHIES, B. (1975), 'The Female of the
Species', New York and London, Macmillan.
MARTIN, R. (1972), Student sex behaviour as determinants
of the type and frequency of teacher-student contacts,
'School Psychol.', 10 (4), pp. 339-47.
MASSOT, J., HAMEL, A. and DELIRY, R. (1956), Alcoolisme
feminin: donnees statistiques et psychoparthologiques,
'J. Med. Lyon', 37, pp. 265-9.
MEAD, M. (1935), 'Sex and Temperament in Three Primitive
Societies', New York, William Morrow (1963 edn).
MEAD, M. (1950), 'Male and Female', Harmondsworth,
Penguin Books.
MEDNICK, M.T.S. and WEISSMAN, H.J. (1975), The psychology
of women - selected topics, 'Ann. Rev. Psychol.', 26,
pp. 1-18.
MELGES, F.T. (1972), Postpartum psychiatric syndromes, in
'Readings on the Psychology of Women', J.M. Bardwick
(ed.), New York, Harper & Row.
MENDELS, J. and COCHRANE, C. (1968), The nosology of
depression: the endogenous-reactive concept, 'Am. J.
Psychiat.', 124, pp. 1-11.
MEYER, W.J. and THOMPSON, G.G. (1956), Sex differences in
the distribution of teacher approval and disapproval among
sixth-grade children, 'J. Educ. Psychol.', 47, pp. 385-96.
MILLER, K.M. (1968), 'Manual for the Rothwell-Miller
Interest Blank', Windsor, Berks., NFER Publishing.
MILLER, S.M. (1975), Effects of maternal employment on
sex-role perception, interests and self-esteem in kinder-
garten girls, 'Develop. Psychol.', 11, pp. 405-6.
MINUCHIN, P. (1964), Sex-role concepts and sex-typing in
young children as a function of school and home environ-
ments, paper presented at AOA, Chicago.
MISCHEL, H.N. (1974), Sex bias in the evaluation of pro-
fessional achievements, 'J. Educ. Psychol.', 66, pp.
157-66.
MISCHEL, W. (1967), A social learning view of sex dif-
ferences in behaviour, in 'The Development of Sex Differences', E.E. Maccoby (ed.), London, Tavistock.
MITCHELL, J. (1966), Women: the longest revolution, 'New
Left Rev.', November-December, pp. 11-37.
MITCHELL, J. (1974), 'Psychoanalysis and Feminism',
London, Allen Lane.
MOGAR, R.E., WILSON, W.M. and HELM, S.T. (1970), Person-
ality sub-types in male and female alcoholic patients,
'Int. J. Addict.', 5, pp. 99-113.
MONAHAN, L., KUHN, D. and SHAVER, P. (1974), Intrapsychic
v. cultural explanations of the 'Fear of success'
motive, 'J. Pers. Soc. Psychol.', 29, pp. 60-4.
MONEY, J. and EHRHARDT, A.A. (1972), 'Man and Woman, Boy

and Girl', Baltimore and London, Johns Hopkins University Press.
MOON, C. (1974), Sex role stereotyping in books for young children, unpublished DipEd thesis, Bristol University.
MORRIS, D. (1967), 'The Naked Ape', London, Cape.
MURDOCK, G.P. (1949), 'Social Structure', New York, Macmillan.
MYRDAL, A. and KLEIN, V. (1956), 'Women's Two Roles', London, Routledge & Kegan Paul, republished 1968.
MYRDAL, G. (1944), A parallel to the negro problem, appendix 5, 'An American Dilemma', New York, Harper. Reprinted as Women, servants, mules and other property, in 'Masculine/Feminine', B. Roszak and T. Roszak (eds), New York, Harper & Row, 1969.
NATIONAL CHILD DEVELOPMENT STUDY (1972), 'From Birth to Seven', London, National Children's Bureau.
NATIONAL AND LOCAL GOVERNMENT OFFICERS ASSOCIATION (1975), 'Equal Rights Working Party Report', London.
NEWSON, J. and NEWSON, E. (1965), 'Infant Care in an Urban Community', London, Allen & Unwin.
NEWSON, J. and NEWSON, E. (1968), 'Four Years Old in an Urban Community', London, Allen & Unwin.
NEWSON, J. and NEWSON, E. (1976), 'Seven Years Old in the Home Environment', London, Allen & Unwin.
NEWSON, J. and NEWSON, E. (1977), 'Perspectives on School at Seven Years Old', London, Allen & Unwin.
NIGHTINGALE, C. (1974), What Katy didn't do, 'Spare Rib', February.
NORTHERN WOMEN'S EDUCATION STUDY GROUP (1972), Sex role learning: a study of infant readers, in 'The Body Politic', M. Wandor (ed.), London, Stage One.
OAKLEY, A. (1974a), 'Housewife', London, Allen Lane.
OAKLEY, A. (1974b), 'The Sociology of Housework', London, Martin Robertson.
OECD,(1975), 'The Role of Women in the Economy', Paris, (available London, HMSO).
OFFICE OF HOME ECONOMICS (1971), 'Alcohol and Abuse', London.
O'LEARY, V.E. (1974), Some attitudinal barriers to occupational aspirations in women, 'Psychol. Bull.', 81, pp. 809-26.
OLIVER, L.W. (1975), Counselling implications of recent research on women, 'Pers. and Guid. J.', 53 (6), pp. 430-7.
O'MALLEY, B. (1975), Letter to Women's Liberation Campaign for Financial and Legal Independence, unpublished.
ORDEN, S.R. and BRADBURN, N.M. (1968), Working wives and marriage happiness, 'Am. J. Soc.', 74, pp. 392-407.
ORFORD, J. (1975), Self-reported coping behaviour of

wives of alcoholics and its association with drinking
outcome, 'J. Studies on Alcohol', 36, pp. 1254-67.
ORTH, C.D. and JACOBS, F. (1971), Women in management:
pattern for change, 'Harvard Business Rev.', July-August,
pp. 139-47.
PARKER, F.B. (1972), Sex role adjustment in women alco-
holics, 'Quart. J. Studies on Alcohol', 33, pp. 647-57.
PARLEE, M.B. (1972), Comments on 'Roles of activation and
inhibition in sex differences in cognitive abilities', by
D.A. Broverman, E.L. Klaiber and W. Vogel, 'Psychol.
Rev.', 77, pp. 180-4.
PARSONS, T. (1965), The normal American family, in 'Man
and Civilization: The Family's Search for Survival',
S.M. Farber, P. Mustacchi and R.H.L. Wilson (eds), New
York, McGraw Hill.
PARSONS, T. and BALES, R.F. (eds) (1955), 'Family, Socialization and Integration Process', Chicago, Free Press.
PAWLICKI, R.E. and ALMQUIST, C. (1973), Authoritarianism,
locus of control and tolerance of ambiguity as reflected
in membership and non-membership in a Women's Liberation
group, 'Psychol. Reps', 32, pp. 1331-7.
PAYNE, A.P. and SWANSON, H.H. (1972), The effect of sex
hormones on the aggressive behaviour of the female golden
hamster, 'Animal Behav.', 20, pp. 782-7.
PEMBERTON, D.A. (1967), A comparison of the outcome of
treatment in female and male alcoholics, 'Brit. J. Psychiat.', 113, pp. 367-73.
PHILLIPS, D. and SEGAL, B. (1969), Sexual status and
psychiatric symptoms, 'Amer. Sociol. Rev.', 34, pp. 58-
72.
PIACENTE, B.S., DENNER, L.A., HAWKINS, H.L. and COHEN,
S.L. (1974), Evaluation of the performance of experimen-
ters as a function of their sex and competence, 'J. App.
Soc. Psychol.', 4, pp. 321-9.
PIZZEY, E. (1974), 'Scream quietly or the neighbours will
hear', Harmondsworth, Penguin Books.
PLECK, J.H. (1975), Masculinity-femininity.   Current and
alternative paradigms, 'Sex Roles', 1, pp. 161-78.
PLECK, J.H. and SAWYER, J. (1974), 'Men and Masculinity',
Englewood Cliffs, Prentice-Hall.
PLOWDEN REPORT, THE (1967), 'Children and Their Primary
Schools', London, HMSO.
PODOLSKY, E. (1963), The woman alcoholic and pre-mens-
trual tension, 'J. Amer. Med. Wom. Ass.', 18, pp. 816-
18.
POLOMA, M.M. and GARLAND, T.N. (1972), The married pro-
fessional woman: a study in the tolerance of domesti-
cation, 'J. Marr. and the Fam.', 33, pp. 531-40.

PRATHER, J.E. (1971), When the girls move in: a sociological analysis of the feminization of the bank teller's job, 'J. Marr. and the Fam.', November, pp. 777-82.

PREDIGER, D.J. and COLE, N.S. (1975), 'Sex-role Socialization and Employment Realities: Implications for Vocational Interest Measures', Act Research Report no. 68, The Research and Development Division, The American College Testing Program, PO Box 168, Iowa City, Iowa 52240.

PRENDERGRASS, V.E. et al. (1976), Sex-discrimination Counseling, 'American Psychologist', 31, no. 1, pp. 36-46.

PYKE, S.W. and STEWART, J.C. (1974), This column is about women: women and television, 'Ontario Psychologist', 6, pp. 66-9.

RAPOPORT, R. and OAKLEY, A. (1975), Towards a review of parent-child relationships in social science, paper given at working conference, Merrill-Palmer Institute, no. 10-12.

RAPOPORT, R. and RAPOPORT, R.N. (1971a), 'Dual-Career Families', Harmondsworth, Penguin Books.

RAPOPORT, R. and RAPOPORT, R.N. (1971b), Early and later experiences as determinants of adult behaviour: married women's family and career patterns, 'Brit. J. Sociol.', 22.

RAPOPORT, R. and RAPOPORT, R.N. (1975), Men, women and equity, in 'The Second Experience: Variant Family Forms and Life Styles', M. Sussman (ed.), special edition of 'The Family Coordinator', October.

RAPOPORT, R. and RAPOPORT, R.N. (1976), 'Dual-Career Families Re-examined', New York, Harper & Row; London, Martin Robertson.

RAPOPORT, R., RAPOPORT, R.N. and STRELITZ, Z. (1977), 'Fathers, Mothers and Others', London, Routledge & Kegan Paul.

RATHOD, N.H. and THOMPSON, I.G. (1971), Women alcoholics: a clinical study, 'Quart. J. Studies on Alcohol', 32, pp. 32-45.

RED COLLECTIVE (1973), 'The politics of sexuality in capitalism I and II', Compendium Bookshop.

'Red Rag', produced by Red Rag Collective, 9 Stratford Villas, London, NW1.

REISS, E. (1934), 'Rights and Duties of Englishwomen', London, Sherratt & Hughes.

RENDEL, M. et al. (1968), 'Equality for Women', London, Fabian Research Series no. 268.

RHEINGOLD, J.C. (1964), 'The Fear of Being a Woman: A Theory of Maternal Destructiveness', New York, Grune & Stratton.

RICHARDS, M.P.M. (1974), The biological and the social,
in 'Reconstructing Social Psychology', M. Armistead (ed.),
Harmondsworth, Penguin Books.
RICKS, F.A. and PYKE, S.W. (1973), Teacher perceptions
and attitudes that foster or maintain sex-role differ-
ences, 'Interchange', 4, pp. 26-33.
RIESMAN, D. (1956), Orbits of tolerance, interviewers and
elites, 'Pub. Op. Quart.', 20, pp. 49-73.
RIMMER, J., PITTS, F.N., REICH, T. and WINOKUR, G. (1971),
Alcoholism II: sex, socio-economic status and race in
two hospitalized samples, 'Quart. J. Studies on Alcohol',
32, pp. 942-52.
RIMMER, J., REICH, T. and WINOKUR, G. (1972), Alcoholism
V: diagnoses and clinical variation among alcoholics,
'Quart. J. Studies on Alcohol', 33, pp. 658-66.
ROSALDO, M.Z. and LAMPHERE, L. (eds) (1974), 'Woman,
Culture and Society', Stanford University Press.
ROSE, S.P.R. and ROSE, H. (1973), Do not adjust your mind,
there is a fault in reality - idealogy in neural biology,
'Cognition', 2, pp. 479-502.
ROSEN, B. and JERDEE, T.H. (1974a), The influence of sex-
role stereotypes on personnel decisions, 'J. App. Psy-
chol.', 59, pp. 9-14.
ROSEN, B. and JERDEE, T.H. (1974b), Effects of applicants
sex and difficulty of job on evaluations of candidates
for managerial positions, 'J. App. Psychol.', 59, pp.
511-12.
ROSEN, B. and ROSENTHAL, R. (1975), The definition of
female sexuality and status in the two societies, paper
presented to British Anthropological Association Conference on the Body, Dublin.
ROSENKRANTZ, P., VOGEL, S., BEE, H., BROVERMAN, I. and
BROVERMAN, D.M. (1968), Sex role stereotypes and self-
concepts in college students, 'J. Consult. Clin. Psychol.', 32, pp. 287-95.
ROSENTHAL, R. and JACOBSON, L. (1968), 'Pygmalion in the
Classroom', New York, Holt, Rinehart & Winston.
ROSS, J.M., BUNTON, W.J., EVISON, P. and ROBERTSON, T.S.
(1972), 'A Critical Appraisal of Comprehensive Education',
Slough, NFER.
ROSS, J.M. and SIMPSON, H.R. (1971), The national survey
of health and development I: educational attainments,
'Brit. J. Educ. Psychol.', 41, pp. 49-61.
ROSSI, A. (1968), Transition to parenthood, in 'The Mar-
riage Game', C.S. Greenblatt et al. (eds), New York,
Random House, republished 1974.
ROSSI, A. (1974), Equality between the sexes: an immodest
proposal, 'Daedalus', 93, pp. 638-46.

ROSSI, A. and CALDERWOOD, A. (1973), 'Academic Women on the Move', New York, Russell Sage.

ROWBOTHAM, S. (1972), The beginnings of women's liberation in Britain, in 'The Body Politic', M. Wandor (ed.), London, Stage One.

ROWNTREE, S. (1922), 'Poverty, a Study of Town Life', London, Longman Green (2nd edn).

ROYAL COMMISSION ON THE INCOME TAX (1920), 'Evidence', London, HMSO.

ROYAL COMMISSION ON THE TAXATION OF INCOME AND PROFITS (1955), 'Evidence 1951-55', vols 1-4, London, HMSO.

ROYAL COMMISSION ON THE TAXATION OF INCOME AND PROFITS (1955), 'Final Report', Cmnd 9474, London, HMSO.

RUTTER, M.L. (1972), Dimensions of parenthood: some myths and some suggestions, in DHSS, 'The Family in Society: Dimensions of Parenthood', London, HMSO.

SAFILIOS-ROTHSCHILD, C. (1973), The mother's needs for child care in 'Child Care - Who cares?', P. Roby (ed.), New York, Basic Books.

SAFILIOS-ROTHSCHILD, C. (1975), Dual linkages between the occupational and family system: a macrosociological analysis, 'Signs: J. of Women in Culture and Society', December.

SAYERS, R.S. (1956), 'Financial Policy 1939-1945', London, HMSO.

SCHATTSCHNEIDER, E.E. (1960), 'The Semi-Sovereign People', New York, Holt, Rinehart & Winston.

SCHNEIDER, J.W. and HACKER, S.L. (1973), Sex role imagery and use of generic 'man' in introductory texts; a case in the sociology of sociology, 'Amer. Sociologist', 8, pp. 12-18.

SCHWENDINGER, J. and SCHWENDINGER, H. (1971), Sociology's founding fathers: sexists to a man, 'J. Marr. and the Fam.', 33, pp. 783-99.

SCLARE, A.B. (1970), The female alcoholic, 'Brit. J. Addiction', 65, pp. 99-107.

SCULLY, D. and BART, P. (1973), A funny thing happened on the way to the orifice, 'Am. J. Sociol.', 78, pp. 1045-9.

SEARS, P. and FELDMAN, D.H. (1966), Teacher interactions with boys and girls, reprinted in 'And Jill Came Tumbling After: Sexism in American Education', J. Stacey, S. Beneaud and J. Daniels (eds), New York, Dell.

SECOMBE, W. (1971), The housewife and her labour under capitalism, 'New Left Rev.', 83, pp. 3-96.

SELECT COMMITTEE ON THE ANTI-DISCRIMINATION (no. 2) Bill (1972), minutes of evidence given by Sir William Armstrong, GCB, MVO, 29 June, London, HMSO.

SELECT COMMITTEE ON TAX CREDIT (1973), 'Evidence', London, HMSO.

SELIGMAN, M.E.P. (1975), 'Helplessness: On Depression,
Development and Death', San Francisco, W.H. Freeman.
SERBIN, L.A. and O'LEARY, K.D. (1976), First lessons in
inequality, 'Psychology Today', 2, pp. 12-15.
SERBIN, L.A., O'LEARY, K.D., KENT, R.N. and TONICK, I.J.
(1973), A comparison of teacher response to the pre-
academic and problem behaviour of boys and girls, 'Child
Devel.', 44, pp. 796-804.
SETON, F. (1976), Opening myself to change, 'Spare Rib',
44, pp. 30-2.
SHEPHERD, M. et al. (1966), 'Psychiatric Illness in
General Practice', Oxford University Press.
SHERFEY, J.M. (1955), Psychopathology and character struc-
ture in chronic alcoholics, in 'Etiology of Chronic Alco-
holism', O'Diethelm (ed.), Springfield, Ill., Charles C.
Thomas.
SHERMAN, J.A. (1967), Problems of sex differences in
space perception and aspects of intellectual functioning,
'Psychol. Rev.', 74, pp. 290-9.
Shrew on Psychology (1973), produced by a group of women.
SINCLAIR, S. (1971), Women: growing force in business,
'Canadian Business', September, pp. 42-52.
SKOLNICK, A. (1973), 'The Intimate Environment', Boston,
Little Brown.
SKULTANS, V. (1975), 'Madness and Morals', London,
Routledge & Kegan Paul.
SLATER, P.E. (1970), 'Pursuit of Loneliness', Boston,
Beacon Press.
SLOCUM, S. (1975), Woman the gatherer: male bias in an-
thropology, in 'Toward an Anthropology of Women', New
York and London, Monthly Review Press.
SOLOMON, L.Z. (1975), Perception of a successful person
of the same sex and the opposite sex, 'J. Soc. Psychol.',
95, pp. 133-4.
SPAULDING, R.L. (1963), Achievement, creativity and self-
concept correlates of teacher-pupil transactions in ele-
mentary schools, cited in P. Sears and D.H. Feldman,
Teacher interactions with boys and girls.
STASSINOPOULOS, A. (1972), 'The Female Woman', London,
Davis-Poynter.
STEINMETZ, S.K. (1974), The sexual context of social re-
search, 'Amer. Sociol.', 9, pp. 111-16.
STEMPLE, D. and TYLER, J.E. (1974), Sexism in advertising,
'Am. J. Psychoanal.', 34, pp. 271-3.
STEPHENSON, H.B. (1975), De-stereotyping personnel lang-
uage, 'Personnel J.', 54, pp. 334-5.
STEWART, A.J. and WINTER, D.G. (1974), Self definition and
social definition in women, 'J. Personal.', 42, pp. 238-
59.

STOLOFF, C. (1973), Who joins women's liberation?, 'Psychiatry', 36, pp. 325-40.
STOTSKY, B.A. (1955), The authoritarian personality as a stereotype, 'J. Psychol.', 39, pp. 325-8.
STRONG, E.K. (1966), 'Strong Vocational Interest Blanks Manual' (revised by D.P. Campbell), Stanford University Press.
SULLIVAN, H.S. (1953), 'The Interpersonal Theory of Psychiatry', New York, Norton.
'Supplementary Benefits Commission Handbook' (1974), London, HMSO.
SUTER, B. and DOMINO, G. (1975), Masculinity-femininity in creative college women, 'J. Pers. Assess.', 39, pp. 414-20.
SUTHERLAND, A. and GOLDSCHMID, M.L. (1974), Negative teacher expectation and IQ change in children with superior intellectual potential, 'Child Devel.', 45, pp. 852-6.
SZASZ, T. (1961), 'The Myth of Mental Illness', New York, Harper & Row.
TAVRIS, C. and JAYARATNE, T. (1973), What 120,000 young women can tell you about sex, motherhood, menstruation, housework - and men, 'Redbook', January, Report on Women, Dept 064, Redbook, 230 Park Ave, New York, NY 10017.
TERMAN, L.M. and ODEN, M.H. (1959), 'The Gifted Group at Mid-life', Stanford University Press.
THOMAS, A.H. and STEWART, N.R. (1971), Counselor response to female clients with deviate and conforming career goals, 'J. Counsel. Psychol.', 18, pp. 352-7.
THOMAS, J.M. and BENNIS, W.G. (1972), 'Management of Change and Conflict', Harmondsworth, Penguin Books.
TIGER, L. (1969), 'Men in Groups', London, Nelson.
TIGER, L. (1970), The possible biological origins of sexual discrimination, 'Impact of Science on Society', 20, pp. 29-45.
TIGER, L. and FOX, R. (1972), 'The Imperial Animal', London, Secker & Warburg.
TIZARD, J. (1976), past President of the British Psychological Society, reported in Mind how you mind that child, L. Adamson, The 'Guardian', 29 April.
TOMLINSON, S. (1974), Commonsense and understandings about women in industrial societies, paper presented at the BSA Annual Conference, Aberdeen, April.
TOMLINSON-KEASEY, C. (1974), Role variables; their influence on female motivation constructs, 'J. Counsel. Psychol.', 21, pp. 232-7.
TORRANCE, E.P. (1963), Changing reactions of pre-adolescent girls to tasks requiring creative scientific thinking, 'J. Genet. Psychol.', 102, pp. 217-23.
TOWNSEND, R. (1970), 'Up the Organization', London, Hodder-Fawcett.

TRESEMER, D. (1974), Fear of success: popular but un-
proven, 'Psychol. Today', 7, pp. 82-5.
TURNER, C. (1969), 'Family and Kinship in Modern Britain:
An Introduction', London, Routledge & Kegan Paul.
TURNER, R. (1970), 'Family Interaction', New York, John
Wiley.
UNITED STATES CIVIL SERVICE COMMISSION (1972), 'The Fed-
eral Women's Program: A Point of View', Washington, US
Government Printing Office.
VOGEL, S.R., ROSENKRANTZ, P.S., BROVERMAN, I.K., BROVER-
MAN, D.M. and CLARKSON, F.E. (1975), Sex-role self-con-
cepts and lifestyle plans of young women, 'J. Consult.
Clin. Psychol.', 43, p. 427.
WATSON, W.B. and BARTH, E.A. (1964), Questionable assump-
tion in the theory of social stratification, 'Pac. Soc.
Rev.', 7, pp. 10-16.
WEINREICH, H.,(1975), Women's studies: or, has the female
subject a future?, paper presented at the BPS Annual Con-
ference, Nottingham, April.
WEINREICH, H. and CHETWYND, S.J. (1976), Ideology, psycho-
logy and social change: the case of sex-role stereotyp-
ing, paper presented to the 21st International Congress of
Psychology, Paris, July.
WEISSTEIN, N. (1969), Kinde, kuche, kirche as scientific
law, Psychology constructs the female, in 'Sisterhood is
Powerful', R. Morgan, Vintage Books.
WEITZMAN, L.J., EIFLER, D., HOKADA, E. and ROSS, C., Sex-
role socialization in picture books for preschool children, 'Am. J. Sociol.', 77, p. 6.
WELLS, T. and CHRISTIE, L. (1970), Living together: an
alternative to marriage, 'The Futurist - The Journal of
Forecasts, Trends and Ideas about the Future', vol, 4, no.
2, pp. 50-1.
WHITING, B. (1972), Work and the family; cross-cultural
perspectives, paper presented at International Conference
on 'Women: Resource for a Changing World', Radcliffe
Institute, Radcliffe College, to be published in the Proceedings of the Conference.
WILSNACK, S.C. (1973), Femininity by the bottle, 'Addic-
tions', 20 (2), pp. 3-19.
WIRTH, L. (1942), Urban communities, 'Am. J. Sociol.',
47, pp. 829-39.
WISENTHAL, M. (1965), Sex differences in attitudes and
attainment in junior schools, 'Brit. J. Educ. Psychol.',
35, pp. 79-85.
WITKIN, H. (1967), A cognitive-style approach to cross-
cultural research, 'Int. J. Psychol.', 2, pp. 233-50.
WITKIN, H.A., DYKE, R.B., PATERSON, H.F., GOODENOUGH,
D.R., and KARP, S.A. (1962), 'Psychological Differentiation', New York, John Wiley.

WITTENBORN, V.R. (1965), Depression, in 'Handbook of
Clinical Psychology', B.J. Wolman (ed.), New York, McGraw-
Hill.
WOLFE, J., DEFLEUR, M.L. and SLOCUM, W.L. (1973), Sex discrimination in hiring practices of graduate sociology
departments: myths and realities, 'Am. Sociol.', 8 (4),
pp. 159-65.
WOMEN'S BUREAU (1971), Employment Standards Administration, US Dept of Labour, Female workers: the myth and
reality, reprinted in 'Vocational Guidance Quarterly', 2,
20 December.
WOOD, H.P. and DUFFY, E.L. (1966), Psychological factors
in alcoholic women, 'Amer. J. Psychiat.', 123, pp. 341-5.
WOODS, M.M. (1975), What does it take for a woman to make
it in management?, 'Personnel J.', 54 (1), pp. 38-68.
WORLD HEALTH ORGANISATION (1964), 'Report on Psychosomatic Disorders', Geneva, WHO.
WORSLEY, P. (1964), The distribution of power in industrial society, in 'The Development of Industrial Societies', Keele University, Sociological Review Monograph
no. 8.
WYLIE, R.C. (1963), Children's estimates of their school-
work ability, as a function of sex, race and socioecono-
mic level, 'J. Personal.', 31, pp. 203-24.
YOUNG, M. and WILLMOTT, P. (1973), 'The Symmetrical Fam-
ily: A Study of Work and Leisure in the London Region',
London, Routledge & Kegan Paul.
ZIMMERMAN, C.C. (1947), 'The Family and Civilization',
New York, Harper & Row.
ZUCKERMAN, M. and WHEELER, L. (1975), To dispel fantasies
about the fantasy-based measure of fear and success,
'Psychol. Bull.', 87, pp. 932-46.

Index